UNDERSTANDING INDUSTRIAL RELATIONS
IN MODERN JAPAN

STUDIES IN THE MODERN JAPANESE ECONOMY

General Editors: Malcolm Falkus, *University of New England, Armidale, New South Wales*; and Kojiro Niino, *Kobe University, Japan*

An understanding of the modern Japanese economy remains both important and elusive. Its importance needs little stressing. Since the 1950s Japan's economy has grown at a rate unparalleled elsewhere and, despite predictions that such success could not last, the economy remains strong, dynamic and sustains full employment. Yet an understanding of the many unique features of Japan's economic and social life is essential if we are to appreciate the Japanese achievement, but on the other hand this very uniqueness makes communication difficult. Straightforward translations of Japanese works frequently mean little to Western readers because the underlying attitudes and assumptions are so unfamiliar.

This series has been planned in the belief that there is an urgent need for scholarly studies on the modern Japanese economy which are written by experts (both Japanese and Western) and aimed at Western readers. Accordingly, we have planned a series of books which will explore all the major areas of Japanese economic life. The books will present up-to-date material, and, where necessary, they will place Japan in its wider international context.

Published titles include:

Yujiro Hayami
JAPANESE AGRICULTURE UNDER SIEGE

Kazuo Koike
UNDERSTANDING INDUSTRIAL RELATIONS IN
  MODERN JAPAN

Ryoshin Minami
THE ECONOMIC DEVELOPMENT OF JAPAN

Mitsuaki Okabe
THE STRUCTURE OF THE JAPANESE ECONOMY

Yoshitaka Suzuki
JAPANESE MANAGEMENT STRUCTURES, 1920–80

Seiichiro Yonekura
THE JAPANESE IRON AND STEEL INDUSTRY, 1850–1990

UNDERSTANDING INDUSTRIAL RELATIONS IN MODERN JAPAN

Kazuo Koike

Professor of Economics
Kyoto Institute of Economic Research
Kyoto University, Japan

Translated by Mary Saso

MACMILLAN

First published 1988 by
THE MACMILLAN PRESS LTD
Houndmills, Basingstoke, Hampshire RG21 2XS
and London
Companies and representatives
throughout the world

ISBN 0-333-42686-X hardcover
ISBN 0-333-42687-8 paperback

A catalogue record for this book is available
from the British Library.

Printed in Great Britain by
Antony Rowe Ltd
Chippenham, Wiltshire

Reprinted 1994

Contents

List of Illustrations

List of Tables

Preface

The demystification of industrial relations and labour practices in Japan is the most important feature of this book. It serves, moreover, to demystify the role of industrial relations which scholars have emphasised as being a significant foundation for Japan's economic development. Demystification is brought about by giving close attention to technological components on the shopfloor which, in other words, are the workers' skills.

There are two factors which have made Japanese industrial relations appear to be mysterious. One factor is the supposedly singular system of permanent employment and seniority-based wages; the other is the way in which importance is attached by workers to the group. A worker's job and livelihood should be secure because of permanent employment and seniority wages. But it would be risky to presume that if workers were to have security, they work harder. As long as remuneration for a worker did not differ depending on whether one worked well or not, by far the majority of workers with a normal perspective would choose not to work hard. This approach requires, therefore, that a singular point of view be stressed: Japanese workers are thought to attach importance to the group which is their company and to cooperate in production without any promised reward. This kind of analysis, where the explanation depends wholly upon unique factors, inevitably leads to industrial relations in Japan becoming mysterious and difficult to understand.

Nonetheless if the technological aspect is given consideration by observing worker's skills, which are the software needed on the shopfloor, then the reality becomes clear. It has often been recognized that the efficiency of the Japanese economy depends greatly on the shopfloor workers' way of working. On account of completely overlooking the technological aspect, however, cultural factors have been greatly exaggerated. By closely observing work on the shopfloor, I have discovered that workers possess admirable skills, which are knowledge-intensive or intellectual skills based on their broad experience. Because they can intellectually understand the structure of the machines and products and the production process, workers are able to deal remarkably well with the unexpectedly frequent changes which occur and are able to improve efficiency. In order to build up intellectual skills long-term employment and remuneration which as an incentive steadily rises over a long period are essential. This is the foundation of the phenomena which at first sight are apparently unique to Japan. It is a significant feature of industrial relations in modern Japan that blue-collar workers' intellectual skills are partially held in common with engineers and also that their long-term employment and seniority curve for wages resemble the conditions given to white-collar workers in Western Europe. Thus what is really unique to Japan is the kind of treatment which in Western Europe is characteristic of white-collar employees extended to one section of blue-collar Japanese workers.

The attention I have given to shopfloor skills has required a methodology based on in-depth interviews carried out on the shopfloor, a distinctive feature of this book. The formation of intellectual skills depends mainly on shopfloor experience, in other words on-the-job-training, which is not simply the same as experiencing one job for a long time, but extends fairly broadly to deeply related jobs. Not to be abstract, under on-the-job-training in Japan the worker moves position not only within one workshop but also between two or three closely related workshops. Since this practice is often not recorded anywhere in writing, but is a shopfloor custom, there is no alternative but to ask the people who are really familiar with the details. Consequently actually speaking to the foremen and veteran workers next to their machines and to the shop stewards has provided results which are the main resource material in this book.

The way in which these interview results are supplemented with good data sources is another feature of this book. The number of interviews has to be limited to the extent that the deeper an interview the more it is meaningful. Even if there were a greater number of shallow interviews, they would have to be supplemented with resource material which has a wider perspective. Fortunately in the mid-seventies good statistics on wages and length of service by age in Western Europe became available for the first time. Japanese data have in any case been plentiful; statistics on wages by age have been compiled since 1927, with good annual data available since 1954. Thus I have been able to compare wage profiles by age and length of service on the basis of good statistics, rarely possible in an international comparison. The results show that the so-called seniority wages and permanent employment characteristics of blue-collar workers in large Japanese companies are similar to conditions for European white-collar workers. In fact the seniority wage curve and permanent employment should be perceived as a general characteristic of white-collar workers in Western Europe (see Chapters 1 and 2).

The above example demonstrates that an explicit comparison with Europe and North America is essential for knowing the truth about industrial relations in Japan. This point is of course particularly important concerning the central theme of this book (which is also the case in North America or Europe), the mistake of assuming, for example, that US workers only acquire skills in training courses outside the company and that the internal promotion system does not apply; consequently the greatly mistaken presumption that the internal promotion system is unique to Japan would arise.

Therefore, with the analysis of job career as the central theme, Chapter 3 is devoted to analysing workers' job careers in the USA. I cannot help but tackle this topic in order to provide an explicitly comparative structure, even though the subject of this book is Japan. On account of space only the iron and steel industry is taken up here, but I do not want there to be any misunderstanding to the effect that only the iron and steel industry was researched. In the Japanese books which I have written and on which this book is based, the results of my research in the machinery and the chemical industries' workplaces are reinforced with indirect statistics covering a range of other industries.

Not only are workers in large Japanese companies studied in this book, but also those in small and medium-sized companies (Chapter 5) and white-collar workers (Chapter 6). Many previous studies have only observed large company workers and then presumed that the results were applicable to all Japanese workers. The reality is that the small and medium-sized company workers make up the majority of Japanese workers, while the large company workers are only a minority group. Clearly demonstrating how diverse are labour conditions within Japan is one of the distinctive features of this book. In addition the legends surrounding enterprise unions, which are only relevant to the minority group of workers are tackled (Chapter 7).

Going beyond mere observation and analysis, an important objective of this book is the proposal of a theory to explain industrial relations in Japan and other countries. The theory should properly explain three aspects; first, the reasons why certain features are common to industrial relations in each country; second, why industrial relations change, which can be seen to occur in all countries depending on the stage of development; and third, why superimposed on these common features there are differences between countries. I have attempted an explanation by creating a division of the labour force into four groups according to differences in the quality of skills. By seeking a universal foundation in respect of the fact that each kind of the four labour types exists in all countries, the reasons for differences appearing in a time-series analysis can then be analyzed according to the way in which the relative weights of the four types differ depending on the stage of development. It is these differences in relative weights between countries which I have considered to be the basis of differences in industrial relations at any one point of time. For example, the internal promotion type of labour exists in all industrialized countries and everywhere is applicable to a minority of workers, but in Japan the relative weight of this type is somewhat larger than in Western Europe and the USA.

Here I would like briefly to refer to the differences between my theory and the internal labour markets theory proposed by Doeringer and Piore (1971) which has not been explicitly covered in this book. It is true that my theory does give weight to internal labour markets, and so there are many aspects which could be regarded as identical with parts of Doeringer and Piore's theory. Nonetheless my theory was something which began independently from a 1959 Japanese article (Koike, 1959) and there cannot help but be differences with the Doeringer and Piore theory.

The main difference lies in the point that, whereas Doeringer and Piore claim that internal labour markets could be completely universal, I believe that they are diffused mostly in post-1919 large companies. My exposition argues that the setting up of internal labour markets has not occurred in all, but only in two out of the four major labour types mentioned above. The reason for this distinction lies in the way of perceiving what basis is required for there to be enterprise-specific skills. Doeringer and Piore have indeed sought the general conditions required such as in workers handling individual machines and in the temperament of the group's members. Because such conditions can exist everywhere, internal labour markets may be established anywhere and at any time. In contrast, my theory demonstrates that enterprise-specific skills are mainly the outcome of the way in which careers are formed. Granted that the content of individual jobs may be similar in competitive companies, there can still be depending on each company a variety of ways of forming a job career: specifically which sort of jobs should be experienced and in what order. This is one form of specialization, which in order to be feasible requires that there are many diverse job positions in a large-scale company. Moreover, since a career should extend over a long period, internal labour markets tend to become centred in larger companies which have a longer-run perspective.

I have written this book afresh by drawing on four of my earlier books in Japanese. The centrepiece book is my comparison between Japan and the USA (Koike, 1977), for which I was fortunate enough to be able to receive two awards, the Economist Prize (Mainichi Newspaper) and the Prize for Labour Publications (Japan Institute of Labour). The other original books were *Nihon no Jukuren* (Skills in Japan) (1981), *Chushokigyo no Jukuren* (Skills in Small and Medium-Sized Companies) (1981) and *Rodosha no Keieisanka* (Labour Participation in Management) (1978). Other awards were received by the third and fourth books, respectively the Prize for Research on Small and Medium-Sized Companies and the Suntory Foundation Award. I am grateful to each of the publishers for permitting me to incorporate some of the content of each original book into this book.

For more than a quarter of a century since the late 1950s I have been visiting Japanese workplaces and observing at first hand the smallest details of employment practices. Rather than just constructing a model after reading books and carrying out calculations on a computer, my work has involved entering Japanese workplaces and actually building up a theory based on my observations and analysis of that experience. I have now summarized my work in this English publication. I have been continuing to travel along what is still of course a long road by visiting workplaces located in Southeast Asia over the past four years. I hope that this subsequent work shall continue to extend our knowledge of comparative industrial relations.

I greatly appreciate having been associated with Mary Saso, whose translation has benefited from her proficiency in both economics and Japanese. The translated draft of each chapter was scrutinised by myself and then revised again by Ms Saso.

Nonetheless to bring this book out in English has taken as long as five years with the first of the problems occurring when the booksellers who initially were handling the translation went bankrupt. Later on when Professor Masao Baba, who was one of the editors of this series, suddenly passed away, I was for ever deprived of further opportunities for receiving his sympathetic interest. May he rest in peace. Professor Malcolm Falkus, the other editor, after closely reading the manuscript has greatly improved its readability. I am indebted to the publishers' editors, beginning with Mr Tadokoro in the Tokyo office. Mrs Miyaji has willingly performed many secretarial duties beyond merely typing. To all these people I wish to convey my warm gratitude.

Apologies are above all else due to the many people whom I interviewed but am unable to name here. I wish, therefore, to dedicate this book to the workers on the shopfloor who courteously instructed me when I came as a visitor from outside. Without their cooperation the appearance of this book would have been impossible.

KAZUO KOIKE

Introduction:
Interpretations of Japanese
Industrial Relations

This book attempts to provide an explanation of Japanese industrial relations – and hence of their contribution to economic growth – through highlighting a crucial factor which has rarely been dealt with in the past: nowadays highly technical skills tend to be acquired by manual workers (in this book I will use the term 'blue-collar' workers) in large Japanese companies. In particular, the workers' wide range of workplace experience has enabled them to understand the production system. Unless this major factor of skill formation is kept in sight, significant aspects of Japanese industrial society cannot be explained.

The role of this Introduction is to justify the above assertion by looking at previous interpretations of Japan's industrial relations. Since so much has been written in Japanese on this subject, here mostly English works will be considered. At this point, part of the conclusion may usefully be anticipated: when the characteristics of skills are ignored, reality is distorted and we have the illusions of 'permanent employment' (*shūshin koyō*), 'seniority wages' (*nenkō chingin*) and 'enterprise-based labour unions' (*kigyōbetsu kumiai*). The consequent belief that these conditions are totally dissimilar to labour management practices in the West is enshrined in the culturalist thesis. This thesis in effect suggests that the Japanese mentality – and thereby its culture – is unique. The purpose of this book is, in short, to present sustainable arguments against the culturalist thesis.

HIGH WORKER MORALE

When contemporary Japan is compared with other industrialized countries, one of the most prominent features appears to be the

1

discrepancy in levels of worker morale. As an indicator of worker morale the rate of absenteeism has sometimes been used. Unfortunately, adequate and reliable statistics on absenteeism have not been compiled for any country. Nonetheless fragmentary data do reveal that Japan's rate of absenteeism is exceptionally low, whereas high rates are found in many of the industrialized countries. Yet the absenteeism rate is merely a negative yardstick of worker morale; a more positive indicator could be provided by attempting to measure the extent to which workers devise ways to improve productivity.

Indeed it is already well known that in Japan blue-collar workers contrive to better their efficiency and the production operations through engaging in QC (quality control) circle activities. Over and above the mere meaning of the words 'controlling quality', the intention of such small groups is to improve their working effectiveness. Each circle consists of about ten shopfloor workers who, with apparent enthusiasm, participate in activities geared towards raising productivity by modifying operations.

Probably the best data depicting the diffusion of QC circles in Japan can be found in the Ministry of Labour's Labour–Management Communication Survey (*Rōshi Komyunikeishon Chōsa*). 5000 private establishments, each with more than 100 employees, have been surveyed on two occasions in 1972 and 1977. Other statistical sources tend to be biased towards large companies or to be conducted on a small scale. The 1977 survey indicates that small group activities are prevalent in the largest companies of 5000 or more employees where 77 per cent of workers participate (see Table I.1). In over 80 per cent of those establishments the respondents believe that the QC circles are effective. At the same time, the smaller the company the less frequently do small group activities occur. Roughly one-third of the workers in companies employing between 100 and 299 are active in QC circles, but well below one-half of the respondents consider the circles to be successful. In other words the proportion of medium-sized companies which have fruitful small group activities may be presumed to fall below one-sixth.

In any case these figures apply only to companies with more than 100 employees, whereas more than half of Japan's employed are working in smaller companies. So, if the trends indicated by the 1977 survey were assumed to extend in the same pattern to companies with fewer than 100 employees, it would be evident that QC circles were the exception (see Table I.2). Nonetheless, while small group activities even in Japan appear to be concentrated only in large companies,

TABLE I.1   Diffusion of small group activities (percentage of employees by company size and presence of labour union)

Company size by no. of employees	Total in small groups	Unionized	Non-unionized
Over 5000	77.2	77.4	67.3
1000 to 4999	58.5	59.1	53.6
300 to 999	42.9	43.9	39.1
100 to 299	33.3	34.6	31.7

Source: Rōdōshō (Ministry of Labour), *Shōwa 52-nen Rōshi Komyunikēshon Chosa* (Labour Management Communication Survey).

TABLE I.2   Evaluation of small group activities (percentage of companies by size)

Company size of by no. of employees	Total	Rather effective	Not effective	Cannot say	No response
Over 5000	100.0	83.4	7.6	8.6	0.4
1000 to 4999	100.0	67.2	15.9	16.4	0.5
300 to 999	100.0	52.7	28.2	18.9	0.2
100 to 299	100.0	45.3	37.6	15.6	1.5

Source: See Table I.1.

they are probably far more prevalent than in the West. Although statistics cannot offer confirmation, I would suggest that the diffusion rate of QC circles in the USA would be ranked after Japan, while the rates would be much lower in Western Europe.

Certain questions need to be answered. Why should QC circles be so much more common in Japan? Will they continue to flourish in the future? What conditions would be required in other countries to encourage the diffusion of small group activities? Evidently high worker morale as demonstrated in these activities does contribute to national output and, hence, is important for economic welfare. The main attempts in the past to address these issues may now be evaluated.

CULTURALIST INTERPRETATIONS

In explaining issues such as the above, the culturalist thesis which stresses that Japanese systems are unique has tended to predominate. This interpretation has prevailed because of an undue reliance on the neoclassical theoretical framework. Under such premises a worker's enthusiasm for small group activities does appear to be really strange. The neoclassical theory of perfect market competition requires that when the company is on the downturn of a business wave either surplus labour is made redundant or wages are cut so that labour voluntarily moves away. If, on the contrary, the company's results exceed those of its competitors, because there is no theoretical rationale for raising wages beyond the ruling market rates, surplus profits naturally are paid out in dividends or invested in plant and equipment. Therefore, under neoclassical economic theory, there would be no incentive for the company's shopfloor workers to engage in activities geared towards raising productivity. When workers do display a technical aptitude for improving production methods, would they be so stupid as to be tricked by the management into engaging in such activities? Consequently this apparently odd behaviour of Japanese workers supports the culturalist thesis that Japan's culture is unique.

Even though a less superficial examination of the culturalist thesis would reveal disparities in interpretation, certain significant features are commonly agreed upon. In particular there is general agreement that there are three pillars to Japanese industrial relations – permanent employment, seniority wages and enterprise unions – which encourage high worker morale and are peculiar to Japan. The presumption is that people continue to be employed for a long time in the company they first joined, with redundancy occurring only as a last resort, that wages rise steadily along with years of employment, and that labour unions are organized within the company, to which any industrial action is confined. Furthermore the culturalist thesis views these three pillars of labour management as being largely confined to Japan. Their appearance in other developed countries would be recognized only as being the exception, whereas in Japan these systems are believed to be widespread.

In response to the query why these labour management practices should exist only in Japan, the culturalist proponent argues that the Japanese have a group-oriented mentality. People have thus traditionally directed their activities with regard to the welfare of the family (*ie*), while in modern Japan their allegiance is transferred to the company. In return, the family or company group holds itself responsible for the welfare of its members. Even though business waves bring vicissitudes to the company's profits, workers will not be made redundant when output falls. The workers' employment – and hence their welfare – is safeguarded by the group. It is further argued that the seniority wage system is designed to match changes in wages with livelihood needs, because of the company's desire to protect the welfare of its workers' families. While the group looks after its members' livelihood, the employees on their side endeavour to prevent the group from being outdone by its competitors. So they cooperate in finding ways to raise productivity. The essence of Japanese culture appears in such ways to be the kind of mentality where priority is given to the group.

Among those subscribing to the culturalist thesis different evaluations are made of the degree to which Japanese culture permits economically motivated behaviour. Up until about 1960 such behaviour was usually thought to be negligible. Since this view was supported by so many commentators, looking at just one representative book could be misleading, but the gist of their argument would be as follows. Because modern individualism had not yet been established in Japan, economic motivation was also presumed to be generally lacking. The permanent employment and seniority wage systems were thus believed to be anachronisms which should fade away as industrialization progressed.

But towards the end of the 1950s a contrary interpretation – which proposed that Japanese culture does elicit economic efficiency –

appeared in Western writings. Abegglen's first book (1958), which has frequently been commended for its understanding of Japan's labour management practices and economy, questioned whether Japan's traditional culture had in fact hindered industrialization. Insofar as the Japanese mentality was believed to be quite dissimilar to the Western norm, the feasibility of successful industrialization in Japan had been doubted. In order to examine this problem, Abegglen carried out interviews among the workers and management of large companies and the owners of smaller enterprises. His consequent portrayal of permanent employment and seniority wages simply reflected how the Japanese themselves at that time perceived them. Abegglen's insight, however, went one step further in his argument that Japan had, by utilizing its traditional culture, efficiently become industrialized by the mid-1950s. He evaluated permanent employment and seniority wages as being in their own way appropriate for industrialization. Nevertheless the efficiency of such labour management practices was considered to be lower than Western practices, even though industrialization might not be impeded. The opinion therefore was that Japanese labour management would have to be reformed as wage levels were rising closer to Western levels.

Subsequently the performance of the Japanese economy clearly improved in spite of the apparent permanent employment, seniority wages and enterprise unions systems being maintained. This phenomenon was frankly recognized by Abegglen in his later book (1973) where he modified and refined his analysis. Such changes in theoretical emphasis were not only displayed in Abegglen's interpretation of Japanese labour management and the economy. Striking lessons were also learnt from the relatively favourable response of Japan's economy to the first oil crisis. The sudden rise in oil prices led to dramatic increases in inflation and unemployment rates in all the industrialized countries. A particularly adverse impact might have been expected in Japan, where almost 100 per cent of oil requirements had to be imported. Among the factors cited for the Japanese economy's resilience were favourable industrial relations and labour morale, to which attention was drawn by an OECD's report (1977). The reasons for Japan's effective industrial relations were discerned to be as follows:

The duty of the employer to provide employment and generally to look to the well-being of employees is matched by willing acceptance by employees that their energies should be devoted to furthering the efficiency and prosperity of the enterprise.[1]

In other words, the OECD analysis was in complete accord with the culturalist thesis. At the same time, this view rejected the possibility that the efficiency of Japan's industrial relations was greater than existed in the West. The view was that while contemporary industrial relations systems in Western Europe were tending somewhat to approach Japanese methods, the latter's permanent employment, seniority wages and enterprise unions systems were also weakening to become similar to Western practices.

As time went on there began to appear another view which suggested that Japanese industrial relations are more effective than the Western kind. Western contributions on this theme are typified by Ouchi's book (1981) which attempted to discover what factors were responsible for the impressive performance of Japanese industry. Ouchi concluded that the prime factor was the high morale of workers which had been encouraged by the company's attention to both aspects of work and welfare. Such concern by the company implies a system of permanent employment. Ouchi's conclusion therefore subscribes to the group cohesion theory and thus gives a central role to the culturalist thesis. Nonetheless Ouchi also noted that similar practices were successful in some sections of American industry. In seeking the elements which are common to both Japanese and Western culture, the debate has now moved one step away towards the non-culturalist interpretation which will be examined later.

EMPIRICAL EVIDENCE INADEQUATE

Despite some disagreements among proponents of the culturalist thesis in evaluating the significance of the three pillars of permanent employment, seniority wages and enterprise unions, they unanimously believe that these are features peculiar to Japan. Yet this very unanimity may be based on nothing more than legends unsupported by empirical evidence.

Let us take the most easily understood example, seniority wages. When research is carried out into whether the seniority wage system is peculiarly Japanese, data on wages by age from other industrialized countries as well as Japan ought to be indispensable. Unfortunately, satisfactory data for industrialized countries other than Japan had to wait until the mid-1970s,[2] although some rather fragmentary statistics had been available in a few countries, such as 1940s data in the USA.[3] The USA data would appear to indicate that the seniority wage system in Japan was not unique,[4] although the quality of the statistics precludes certainty. Culturalists might reasonably have postulated seniority wages to be a special feature of Japan, but it can only be a hypothesis.

Why, then, the certainty of the culturalists without adequate comparative empirical research? The answer must be that there is a generally accepted notion that seniority wage systems are highly unlikely in the West. The assumption of market competition requires that wages are paid only in respect of work done as an incentive to work morale. This highly theoretical model has been misconceived as an accurate representation of reality in the West. So there is actually no justification for regarding evidence of an upward-sloping age–wage profile in Japan as being unique. Yet the culturalist thesis which incorporates the illusion that Western reality conforms with theoretical models received widespread acceptance despite its deficient research basis. And similar judgements may be made about the other two pillars – permanent employment and enterprise unions.

At this point, two significant lessons should be reiterated. First, one cannot dispense with explicit comparisons between actual practices in Japan and Western countries. Obviously in using the description 'Japanese approach' (*Nihonteki*), international comparisons are implied, but then the implicit standard of comparison is usually not reality in the West, but theoretical depiction.

Second, the quality of available resource material should be checked carefully so that, as far as possible, comparisons are based on reliable and appropriate data. In writing this book, I have attempted to put both these lessons into practice.

DISPARITIES WITHIN JAPAN

The culturalist position may be from another angle. Taking up once more the example of QC circles, it is indisputable that many of the suggestions made by workers depend upon technical knowledge. In other words, an understanding of the production process is essential for considering ways of improving productivity. If that technical knowledge were absent, shopfloor workers might once or twice be able to devise better production methods, but they could not continue to do so over a long period of time. Yet subscribers to the culturalist thesis argue that workers' active participation in QC circles is simply a function of their loyalty to the company. Would it be possible for a shopfloor worker without technical understanding to engage in QC activities just out of willingness? As has already indicated, and will be substantiated later, Japanese shopfloor workers' technical ability arises from having had experience in a wide range of skills.

Wide technical experience may, of course, be interpreted as being uniquely dependent upon Japanese culture. But that explanation can be rejected on two grounds. One is that only a minority of Japanese workers participate in effective QC circle activities. As was clear from Tables 1 and 2, QC circles tend to be found in large companies where their scope has to depend upon the workers' technical expertise. If the latter was embedded in Japanese culture we would expect the majority of Japanese workers to be active in QC circles. The other point is that there are workers in other industrialized countries who understand the production process and devise ways of improving productivity, the engineers and technicians. My belief is that whereas in other countries such technical skills are confined to white-collar workers, in Japan blue-collar workers may also be just as skilled. The presentation of evidence to substantiate this argument is the principal objective of this book.

NON-CULTURALIST INTERPRETATIONS

There are a number of well argued Western studies which do not adopt the culturalist view. Most persuasive is the work of Marsh and Mannari (1976), who interviewed workers and management in three companies engaged in electric machinery, shipbuilding and sake-brewing. Their research involved a questionnaire survey of 1700 employees of the companies. One of the major conclusions from this detailed study was that permanent employment is not a feature of Japanese labour management. The study supports the 'convergence thesis' of industrialized societies converging towards similar practices.

Nonetheless their research results are still rather unsatisfactory. No explicit comparison was made between Japan and other countries because only Japanese companies were studied. The extent to which employment departs from so-called 'permanent employment' in both practice and objectives has indeed been clarified through their research. That may be a valid approach, but it does not answer the contention that even though Japanese employment practices may not strictly conform with the adjective 'permanent', yet in comparison with other industrialized countries this description would be reasonable.

Also, the problem remains of explaining high worker morale in contemporary Japan. Marsh and Mannari support the convergence thesis without presenting any framework for incorporating the remaining disparities between Japan and the West. The focus was on denying the uniqueness of Japan, rather than on looking for disparities. Indeed, at the time that the survey was planned, the dissimilarities seemed of less significance, for Japan's economy had yet to surpass Western Europe, and high worker morale was not very conspicuous to observers.

Cole's first book (1973) was based on painstaking research, even though he neither carried out an international comparison nor researched extensively within Japan. Instead he worked for six months in a medium-sized Japanese factory, where his experience, supplemented with evidence from a large Japanese company, provided valuable insights. Cole's fellow workers seem to have been enlightened and independent of management, expressing their own opinions frankly and putting them into practice. These characteristics defy any explanation based on so-called Japanese traditional culture. On the other hand, Cole perceived that at the large company behaviour did appear to conform to the traditional patriarchal framework. This could easily be explained by the rapid growth of large companies resulting in a relatively large number of young workers whose subservient attitude towards management tends to be pronounced. But, needless to say, the majority of Japanese workers are employed within small and medium-sized enterprises. Detailed research like Cole's does reveal aspects of industrial relations which are common to Japan and the West. Even where procedures superficially differ, they could be considered as functionally equivalent. One of the prime concerns of Cole's book was to stress the existence of functional equivalents. In particular, his work went a long way to rectify the scarcity of thorough research on workers in small and medium-sized companies.

But even though it is reasonable to point out the features common to Japan and the West by focussing on functional equivalents, Japan's relatively high level of worker morale would remain inexplicable. An awareness of this problem is not apparent in the early stages of Cole's work (hardly surprising, since the initial research took place in the early 1960s when the view of Japan as being functionally rather similar to the West was only just beginning to emerge). At that time, few Western writers characterized Japan's economy as 'advanced', though works in Japanese along this theme had already appeared at the beginning of the 1960s.[5]

The theoretical framework developed by Cole was naturally enough carried over into his second book (1980), whose focus was QC circles. He recognized many functional equivalents with the West in the technical conditions and social system underpinning QC circles, but he did not give much attention to the disparities in acquisition of skills. Consequently he sought reasons for the high worker morale on which QC circle activities are based in the attitudes of the workers. His argument was that QC circles are a management tool which elicit workers' obedience to management demands. But if workers were merely submissive, would they be able to display technical skills to devise better ways of production?[6]

Clark's book (1970) also emanates from a participation survey in a medium-sized Japanese company, where he worked for 14 months during 1969–70. He reinforced his detailed observations with rather imperfect statistics from, secondary sources. Nonetheless, he was able successfully to challenge many commonly accepted notions. For example it has often been said that Japanese society favours a group consensus approach to decisions, whereas Western companies permit individualistic decision making. Clark showed that in Japan individuals also make decisions as they do in the West, while in the West there is sometimes consensus decision making; his compromise conclusion was that the Japanese tend to emphasize consensus decisions while in the West emphasis on individual responsibility. Again when Clark discussed permanent employment, he showed that in reality many young people transferred between companies. The motivation for staying with one company from a worker's late twenties to mid-fifties sprang nor from loyalty but because this way was judged to bring benefits to the employee. Clark's book has other examples to demonstrate that Japan's economy is not as unique as it has been supposed. Clark does point out the dissimilarities between Japan and the West, although his explanations are not convincing. For example, he discusses the speed of decision-making about job reallocation within a company. Such speed needs explanation, for it might be expected that the consensus approach delays the reaching of a decision. Clark, though, can offer only platitudes in explanation, namely that the sharp distinction in occupational categories in the West makes job reassignment awkward in contrast to the more ambiguous (and therefore more flexible) categories in Japan. Clark's suggestions are mistaken on two counts. First, close observation of workplaces in Japan, and particularly of skills, should suggest that in questions of job reallocation there are really two kinds of decisions. Decisions on work duties and reassignment which fully take into account a worker's skills are made promptly. But when the boundaries of reassignment are extended further to duties which are barely related to the worker's present skills, extra time is needed for negotiations between the union and management, so the decision is delayed. In other words, in the latter case the worker's expertise is being ignored.

The second error in Clark's interpretation is his presumption that work duties in Western European companies are in accordance with theoretical analyses. Nineteenth-century craft categories were not applicable, and the whole concept of 'crafts' is ambiguous. As on-the-job training is extended and promotion from within becomes established, this ambiguity is a natural outcome. Studies such as Clark's end up as justifying the easy accusation that European labour unions are craft-based while in Japan they are enterprise-based, but without, generally speaking, making any explicit comparison.

Rohlen's excellent research work (1974), in which he made a detailed study of the working environment of white-collar workers at a particular bank should not be overlooked. Appropriate comments on his book would, however, be more or less similar to those made on Clark's study.

DORE'S RECENT INTERPRETATION

Dore's explicit comparison (1973) of British and Japanese factories is one example of how through comparative research can yield outstanding results. He selected from each country a representative large scale electrical engineering company, where he interviewed in depth labour and management personnel. In addition an extensive questionnaire survey of engineering and steel workers, which provided some supplementary material, was carried out.

Because Dore based his analysis on a comparative framework, he could see that the significance of cultural factors was not crucial.[7]

Dore brought into sharp focus features common both to Japan and Britain (in contrast to some of the popular notions) though he did not overlook the dissimilarities. One dissimilarity noted by Dore was the relatively high level of worker morale in the Japanese factory, which he attempted to explain without resorting to cultural factors. He suggested that Japan had had the experience, after defeat in war, of undergoing 'an egalitarian revolution' in industrial society, which did not occur in Britain. The trend towards egalitarianism seems to strengthen in any country as industrialization progresses. In Japan's case, this trend was considerably advanced after 1945 when defeat in the Pacific War destroyed the power of the establishment. Also, Dore reminds us that Japan's industrialization took place after the West. He suggests that late development permits countries such as Japan to benefit from the experiences of already industrialized countries.

Dore's research breaks new ground and covers a wide range of issues. Nevertheless, problems remain. What actually are the egalitarian conditions which are supposed to give Japan an advantage in industrial progress? Earnings differentials cannot by themselves provide a sufficient explanation; there must also be egalitarianism in certain other significant areas of industrial society. I would suggest that wide ranging skills can engender egalitarianism. The acquisition of particular skills by some blue-collar workers, and the consequent narrowing of wage differentials, are tantamount to what I shall call 'white-collarization'. There are hints in Dore's work about the significance of wide ranging skills, though he did not make any explicit observations on the actual processes in their acquisition.

SUMMARY

The above comments on the results of previous research should have made evident the objectives in writing this book. The primary aim is to look for the characteristics of technical skills by observing the ways in which skills are formed. On this foundation it should be possible to explain industrial relations and hence the nature of industrial society in Japan. Secondly, subject to reliable data, explicit comparisons with the real situation in the West are considered to be imperative, so as to avoid using only a theoretical model as the standard of comparison.

What methods could be used to realize these aims? Achieving the first is no easy task. In general, statistical support is required so as to minimize errors in judgement, but often the most significant issues are not amenable to statistical analysis. Although a person's height and weight can easily be measured, measurement of ability is difficult. One of the most important themes in labour economics concerns skills, yet accurate measurement techniques have so far not been developed.[8]

In the initial stage of realizing the objectives outlined above, age – wage profiles will be compared, in order at least to begin with observations based on statistics. In the mid-1970s, the European Community (EC) brought out comprehensive age – wage related statistics while such data in Japan's case had already been available for some time. Our analysis will begin with a comparison of these statistics, so we will examine first the legend of seniority wages.

NOTES

1. OECD (1977) pp. 10–11.
2. EC (1975–6) *Structure of Earnings in Industry* (Brussels: EC) 13 vols. Extensive use of these statistics is made later in this book.
3. Vladimir S. Woytinsky, (1953) *Employment and Wages in the United States* (New York: Twentieth Century Fund). Annual income data by age for the 1930s and 1940s had been compiled in this book from the Bureau of Old Age Pensions. After 1945 the Department of Commerce, Census Bureau, gathered annual income data by age in conjunction with the census.
4. This factor had already been pointed out by Umemura in 1956: Mataji Umemura 'Nenrei to Chingin' (Age and wages), in Tōkei-Kenkyūkai (ed.) *Chingin Kōzō no Jittai Bunseki* (An Analysis of Wage Structure) (Tokyo: Tōkei-Kenkyūkai) *mimeo.*
5. Koike (1962) is probably representative. This interpretation had already been described in the 1960 article 'Chingin Rōdō Jyōken Kanri no Jittai Bunseki' (An Analysis of Wage Administration and Working Conditions) in Susuki *et al.* (eds).
6. The author's comments on Cole's second book appear in *Journal of Japanese Studies*, 6, 2, Summer 1980, pp. 407–15.
7. Although Marsh and Mannari say that Dore emphasizes cultural elements, I consider that this is a misinterpretation.
8. The so-called 'quality index' is considered to be a technique for measuring labour capabilities; but this technique makes a prior assumption (which ought to have been proved) that the labour market is close to a perfectly competitive market where wages accurately reflects skills. Since the level of expertise can either be observed directly nor measured, a set of proxy indices – years of experience, years of continuous service, qualifications –

is used. The extent to which each of these variables has influenced present wages is calculated through multiple regression techniques. One could then understand how aspects such as the length of experience and of continuous employment affect the degree of skill. Since years of experience and of continuous service for workers are observable, we could infer the level of skill, if these techniques were reliable. However the central point in the controversy about seniority wages is concerned with the possible zero correlation between the wage profile and skills. Therefore the initial stages in this technique of calculating coefficients with present wages as the dependent variable could not be considered legitimate.

Another method sometimes used in the USA to measure the degree of skills is based on comparative output levels. But this would be inappropriate for comparisons involving different kinds of work. There is another rather common method suitable for different work which is based on internal promotion, as will be discussed later. The technique adopted in this book for measuring levels of skill is discussed in Chapters 3 and 4.

REFERENCES

Abegglen, James C. (1958) *The Japanese Factory* (Glencoe, Ill.: The Free Press).

Abegglen, James C. (1973) *Management and Worker: The Japanese Solution* (Tokyo: Kōdansha International).

Clark, Rodney (1970) *The Japanese Company* (London: Yale University Press).

Cole, Robert E. (1973) *Japanese Blue Collar – The Changing Tradition* (Berkeley and Los Angeles: University of California Press).

Cole, Robert E. (1980) *Work, Mobility and Participation: A Comparative Study of American and Japanese Industry* (Berkeley: University of California Press).

Dore, Ronald P. (1973) *British Factory – Japanese Factory* (Berkeley and Los Angeles: University of California Press)

Koike, Kazuo (1962) *Nihon no Chingin Kōshō* (Collective Bargaining in Japan) (Tokyo: Tokyo University Press)

Marsh, Robert and Mannari, Hiroshi (1976) *Modernization and the Japanese Factory* (Princeton, N.J.: Princeton University Press)

OECD (1977) *The Development of Industrial Relations Systems: Some Implications of the Japanese Experience* (Paris: OECD).

Ouchi, William G. (1981) *Theory-Z: How American Business Can Meet the Japanese Challenge* (Reading, Mass.: Addison Wesley).

Rohlen, Thomas P. (1974) *For Harmony and Strength – Japanese White-Collar Organization in Anthropological Perspective* (Berkeley and Los Angeles: University of California Press).

Susuki, Shinichi *et al.* (eds) (1960) *Rōmukanri* (Personnel Management) (Tokyo: Kōbundō).

1 'Seniority Wages'?

1.1 AGE–WAGE PROFILES: AN INTERNATIONAL COMPARISON

The legend of seniority wages has two props: (a) wage increases are determined mainly by age and length of service with one company, and (b) this wage system is unique to Japan. The validity of (b) can be ascertained by comparing age-wage profiles in Japan with at least Western Europe and the USA. Yet this kind of study hardly ever seems to have been carried out by those who assert Japan's uniqueness. Indeed, most comparative work has been done by those sceptical of such an assertion. Umemura's work since 1956 could be considered as the most outstanding example of statistical studies in this field.[1] He and others provide substantial evidence which contradicts the traditional view of Japanese wage systems. Yet the traditional view still prevails, and the empirical data have been largely ignored. At the same time, satisfactory research has been hampered by the lack of appropriate data sources in the West which could be ranked in detail and scale with Japan's *Wage Structure Survey* (*Chingin Kōzō Kihon Tōkei Chōsa*).

Recently, however, comprehensive wage structure statistics have become available in Western Europe, notably those compiled by the European Community (EC). Unlike the Organization for Economic Cooperation and Development (OECD), the EC has its own parliament and – within a limited area – customs rights, which give an effective authority for the compilation of statistics. The EC has therefore been able to produce a steady stream of previously unavailable primary statistics, among which the 'Structure of Earnings in Industry' is especially valuable.[2] By contrasting the results of the EC survey with Japan's wage structure survey, this chapter aims to inquire into whether Japanese wage systems are uniquely seniority-based. A statistical analysis cannot aspire to be a study of the underlying social institutions – that aspect will be taken up later in

16

Chapter 3. So the analysis in this chapter will tend to be confined to a straightforward comparison of the two sets of statistics.

1.1.1 Two Surveys With Similar Characteristics

First of all, the characteristics of the two surveys mentioned above need to be considered. The first EC survey on the structure of earnings was in 1966. Its scope was then limited to blue-collar workers in mining and manufacturing industries and the classification categories were rather fewer than in the next survey; in particular, the age groups were quite broad. These deficiencies were rectified by the time of the second survey in 1972. The survey results were published during 1975–6 under the title *Structure of Earnings in Industry*. A standardized method was used to survey six-countries – France, West Germany, Italy, Belgium, the Netherlands and Luxembourg. For each country's results there are two large volumes of more than 1000 pages which, in addition to the explanatory volume, makes a total of 13 volumes. In 1974 there was another EC survey which, however, looked only at tertiary industry's structure of earnings; moreover, the age groups were rather broad. For the most part, therefore, only the 1972 EC survey will be used here. In Japan, rudimentary age-related wage statistics had been collected from the late 1920s. When the Wage Structure Survey began in 1954, the quality of the data greatly improved. This annual survey is carried out on a particularly detailed scale about every three years.

The 1972 European survey covered industries in mining and the secondary sector (manufacturing, construction, electricity, gas and water) for establishments with 10 or more employees irrespective of whether they were blue-collar or white-collar workers. The scope of Japan's survey is wider, covering also the tertiary service industries. For comparative purposes, it is necessary to select the appropriate sectors. The size of the establishments surveyed in Japan's case is somewhat different, because companies – rather than just workplaces – with 10 or more employees are covered. The implication is that Japan's survey could include smaller establishments, but in the case of manufacturing any disparity would not be crucial. The inclusion of white-collar workers is common to both surveys, which – as will be seen later – is valuable in shedding light on similarities and dissimilarities in occupational status between the West and Japan.

In both surveys, the methods used in collecting the data are similar. Fairly large samples as proportions of the population have been taken. In Japan the sampling rate is around one-tenth, (the proportion varies depending on the survey's scale) while the sampling rates in the 1972 European survey were for France one-tenth, for West Germany one-seventh, for Italy one-sixth, and for the smaller populations in the Netherlands and Belgium one-fifth, with Luxembourg's sample being one-half of the survey population. The method of first sampling the workplaces and then sampling workers within the selected places is common to both surveys. More significant than comparability in sampling rates is the way of obtaining the information, which in both cases was from the workplace. This point may appear trivial, but there is a crucial distinction between the two ways of obtaining data on wages. One method – as will be discussed later in relation to the US census – is initially to select a sample of individuals, who are asked directly about their wages. It is evident that the accuracy of data obtained by this method would be extremely low. Who, for instance, could correctly recall their wages before tax and their take-home pay? The alternative method – used in both the European and Japanese surveys – is to obtain the data from the workplace.

A remaining distinction is that the classification of data in Japan's survey is more detailed. While both surveys resemble each other in classifying the data by industry, sex and occupation, Japan's classification extends to company size and to length of service cross- classified with age. The European survey results do not provide a cross-classification for age and length of service, although there are independent classifications of either wages by age or wages by length of service. Similarly in the case of the European classification for establishment size, the figures are average wages for different sexes and occupations without being broken down by age. Incidentally in the European survey employees are also categorized by length of service. Indeed as probably the first substantial survey of the distribution for European workers of number of years of service, these results are extremely useful, and the figures will be used later on in this book when examining permanent employment.

The UK has also conducted an annual survey on wages by age, *The New Earnings Survey*, since 1970 with an initial survey in 1968. Since the age groups after thirty years are at ten-year intervals, the categories are broader than in the 1972 European survey. But, on the other hand, the UK survey provides figures on wages according to both age and length of service. Since the sampling of national insurance numbers for individuals makes no distinction between company size, smaller companies than in the European and Japan's surveys may be included; but the wage data are obtained in the same way from the workplace. As a part of the postwar ten-yearly census in the USA, annual income by age statistics according to occupational and educational level have been compiled.[3] The information is not obtained from the workplace, but directly from the individual, and the reliability of the data must be rather low. The system of self-declaration of income for tax purposes is, however, widespread in the USA, so the sampled individuals may have knowledge of previous earnings; the errors inherent in collecting the data on a personal basis are probably not as significant as they would be in other countries. Another problem in using the US data is that annual income is not confined to regular wage income, but may also include investment income and other 'outside' earnings. Again, during any period of unemployment there would be some reduction in income. The data characteristics are thus quite different to those of the European 1972 survey and Japan's survey on wage structure. Nonetheless a rough comparison of the gradients of the age-wage profiles should be feasible, even though there is no comparability in the absolute values.

Here the above large-scale surveys undertaken by governmental or related organizations will mostly be used. But it would be interesting to take a brief look at other data sources for wages by age. In the field of government statistics West Germany has twice carried out a survey on wage structure, but the age groups are wide and the scope does not match that of the European survey.[4] Apart from government sources, there have been a number of surveys confined to segments of the population. Blaug's work during the early 1960s included a survey on wage structure in three large companies in the London area [5]; and then there are the studies of Woytinsky and others in the USA.[6] At the time such studies appeared to be of value, but their inadequacies can no longer be concealed in comparison to the European survey results. Certainly as far as Western Europe is concerned the European survey stands alone in yielding comprehensive and reliable data, and this will probably continue to be the case for a longtime. For the USA, we have a set of very detailed statistics from a small sample collected by the Equal Employment Opportunities Commission; these statistics have already been thoroughly analyzed by Shimada (1981).

1.1.2   Seniority Wages for Blue-collar Males Only in Japan

Figure 1.1 depicts age–wage profiles for male blue-collar workers in some of the EC countries and Japan. In neither case has the simple wage rate in its classical sense been used, because the addition of bonuses and allowances makes wage earnings the more appropriate variable. The EC figures are for hourly wage earnings whereas for Japan the wage indices are derived from monthly wage earnings. As the intention is to compare the rates of change of the age–wage profiles – not absolute levels – indices have been employed with each coutry's average wage level in the early twenties age group set at 100. The vertical axis has been graded on a logarithmic scale so as to facilitate a visual comparison of rates of change. It should be remembered that the graph tells us nothing about wage levels.

The graph reveals first that the wages of male blue-collar workers in large Japanese companies do appear to rise rapidly along with age, whereas in Western Europe after the mid-twenties age group, the age–wage profile no longer rises steadily – all of which corresponds to the popular concept. In Western Europe the wage index stands at merely 110–115 for male blue-collar workers in their thirties and forties compared to 100 for workers in their early twenties; so their profile, relative to the Japanese case, may be considered flat. Since among the EC countries the age-wage profiles are strikingly similar, the figures for the Netherlands, Belgium and Luxembourg have been omitted so as to avoid presenting a confused picture on the graph (these data are all shown in Appendix Table A.1). Figure 1.1 indicates that the UK age–wage profile is also similar in shape to the other EC countries, even though, as discussed earlier (p. 8), its survey scope is rather different. It should be particularly noted that the EC profiles are less steep than the age-wage profile for blue-collar males in even the smaller Japanese companies. It seems at this point that there may thus be solid foundation for the widespread belief that Japanese wage systems are uniquely seniority based.

Yet Japan's age–wage profiles display another striking aspect, namely the steep drop in the wage index among the oldest blue-collar workers. In particular, for large companies' employees who are aged over sixty years the wage index is as low as 105 compared to the peak earnings index of 170 for middle-aged employees. In companies with between ten and 99 employees the decline in the wage index is less steep than in large Japanese companies, but it is still much more pronounced than in Western European companies. In the EC countries wages for

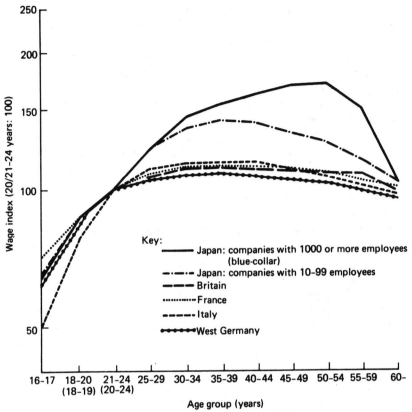

FIGURE 1.1   Age-wage profiles in Japan and the EC (male blue-collar workers)

Note: The distributions relate to male workers in manufacturing, except in the case of Britain which includes all industries.

Sources: EC, *Structure of Earnings in Industry, 1972*. Britain, Department of Employment and Productivity, *New Earnings Survey, 1975*.
Japan, Rōdōshō (Ministry of Labour) *Shōwa 51-nen Chingin Kōzō Kihon Tōkei Chōsa* (1976 Wage Structure Survey).

those in their sixties are as little as 5–10 per cent below the highest wage index. How should this drop in the wage index among older workers in Japan best be explained?

One interpretation might be that the relative steepness of Japan's age–wage profiles up to the middle-aged groups – in other words the seniority wage system – in itself is responsible for the apparent subsequent drop in the wage indices. Another explanation could be that a contra-seniority wage system operates for older workers. The former conjecture appears to be reasonable as far as can be seen from Figure 1.1. The wage index for the over sixty year old age group in Japan is close to that of the mid-twenties age group, despite the drop from the peak wage index. Similarly in the EC countries where the age–wage profiles do not display a downward slope, the wage indices for those in their sixties and those in their twenties are quite close. The major point remains that as far as male blue-collar worker's wages are concerned, Japan's age–wage profiles do have somewhat unique features compared to those in Western Europe; all of which seems to support the prevailing notion of so-called seniority wage systems in Japan. But the picture changes completely if the focus is widened to incorporate white-collar wages.

1.1.3   White-collar Age–wage Profiles in the EC

Similar methods to those for Figure 1.1 have been used for Figure 1.2, which depicts age–wage profiles for male white-collar workers in Japan and certain EC countries. The only difference is that now the EC figures are based on monthly wage earnings, whose definition is similar to Japan's for both white-collar and blue-collar wages. For comparative purposes the profile for male blue-collar workers in large Japanese companies has been carried over from Figure 1.1.

Figure 1.2 first of all suggests that the salaries of Western European white-collar male workers also conform to seniority wage, despite some superficial distinctions between the different countries' age–wage profiles. The peak wage index – with average wages in the early twenties age group set at 100 – occurs in Japan's profile among white-collar males in their early fifties. Their age–wage profile appears to have steeper gradients than in Western Europe, and the highest average wages are being earned by somewhat older employees. But close observation reveals that such disparities are not significant since Japan's peak index is close to the peak of 200 being earned in Italy (see Table A.1) and the Netherlands by employees in their fifties. Indeed only in West Germany does the peak of wage distribution occur among younger white-collar males in their early forties. Otherwise the peaks correspond to the late forties age group in France and Belgium, early fifties in the Netherlands, and among the over sixties in Italy. Even in West Germany the white-collar profile is quite different from the blue-collar wage distribution whose peak occurred in the thirties age group.

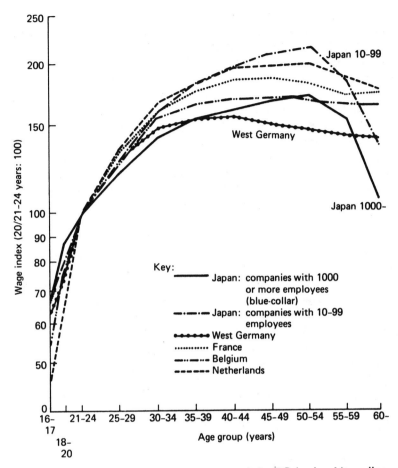

FIGURE 1.2   Age-wage profiles in Japan and the EC (male white-collar workers)

Notes: See Figure 1.1.

Sources: See Figure 1.1.

A major point to be noted is that the Western European age–wage profiles for white-collar males resemble in shape the so-called 'classical' seniority wage profile for male blue-collar workers in large Japanese companies. The European peak wage indices are close to 200 for Italy and the Netherlands, around 180 for France and 170 for Belgium and the UK, while the flattest wage distribution in West Germany peaks at less than 160. The peak index of 170 for Japan's large company blue-collar males is thus close to that of the UK and Belgium, which means that their wage distribution can be ranked somewhere just below the middle of the Western European white-collar wage distributions. This implies that large company blue-collar wage structure in Japan is very close to that of Western European white-collar workers. To put the argument another way: if male blue-collar wage systems in Japan's large companies are to be designated as being seniority based, then the same description should be applied to Western European white-collar wage systems.

In spite of this similarity in wage distributions, the second major point apparent from Figure 1.2 is that the sharp drop in the wage index for older Japanese male blue-collar workers is also applicable to the wage distribution for Japanese white-collar males. Compared to the Western European distributions, the drop in the wage index – particularly in the case of large company male workers – is all the more remarkable because of the similarity in the wage distributions up to the middle-aged groups. The wage distributions for Western European white-collar males indicate that the average salary even for those in their sixties is only 5–10 per cent lower than the highest average salary. In contrast, for both white-collar and blue-collar employees of large Japanese companies the wage distributions show that average wages among older workers are about 40 per cent below the peak age group earnings. This aspect clearly supports the latter of the two possible interpretations suggested earlier, namely a contra-seniority wage system, because the picture of seniority wages presented by the EC male white-collar age–wage profiles shows only a slight drop in the wage indices for the oldest workers. Yet up to the oldest age groups Japan's profiles are quite similar in shape to those in the EC.

To sum up, looking at the wages of blue-collar male employees of large Japanese companies, where wage systems are said to conform to the so-called classical seniority system, two significant features should be noted. One is that the worker's average wage does appear to rise steadily with age, just like EC male white-collar salaries, up until middle age, which suggests that the Japanese worker's age–wage profile has partly the same shape as white-collar profiles elsewhere. I shall term this feature the 'white-collarization' of blue-collar wage systems. The other significant feature is that Japan's age–wage profiles drop sharply for the oldest age group, unlike the EC white-collar age–wage profiles.

1.1.4 Weighting of White-collar Workers

We have seen that the chief characteristic peculiar to the wage structure of blue-collar males in large Japanese companies is white-collarization. Up until this point there has been no attempt to define the nature of white-collar status, but for further study of this issue some kind of comparison needs to be made about who actually are white-collar workers. Yet the distinction between blue-collar and white-collar workers even in the 1972 European survey varies from country to country. Indeed, a single definition is probably impracticable since each country's own historical background influences distinction in status. Instead, as a mere peg on which to hang the elusive definition, some conjectures based on the numbers of employees within certain defined groups will be made.

The 1972 European survey distinguished between white-collar and blue-collar workers in each country in accordance with the different languages' concepts, such as 'non-manual' and 'manual' in English, *'Angestellte'* and *'Arbeiter'* in German, and *'employeés'* and *'ouvriers'* in French. The survey further defined white-collar workers as being composed of the following five groups:[7]

1. Management executives with general authority and responsibility
2. Executives
3. Assistants
4. Clerks
5. Foremen.

The explanations furnished by such definitions tend to be rather abstract so that it is still hard to understand the real facts of the distinction in status. This also applies to Japan's *Wage Structure Survey*, which opts for a simpler distinction of just two named groups – 'production workers' and 'managers, clerks and engineers'. A more precise description of 'production workers' is given as 'workers who are habitually engaged in workplaces or supporting sections where the primary activity is production, or in construction work'. Nonetheless there are foremen and others working in the production department who, being primarily engaged in supervisory work, are included in the category of 'managers, clerks and engineers'. On the other hand there are no details given in the Japan survey as to the definitions of 'managers, clerks and engineers'.

Such general terms might at first sight suggest that the scope of the white-collar category is identical in both the European survey and Japan's *Wage Structure Survey*. But the status of whoever is called 'foreman', in particular, can vary from one who spends the whole day supervising without ever operating machinery to those who, though known as supervisors, are primarily engaged in machinery operation. Let us try to make a distinction by calling the latter type 'group leaders'; the real supervisors may then be known as 'foremen'. Of course, 'foremen' are included in the white-collar category in the 1972 European survey, but the classification given does not enable us to separate 'group leaders'. In Japan's *Wage Structure Survey*, both types are included in the white-collar category.

The real distinction between white-collar and blue-collar status may be approached by looking at the relative proportions of each category represented by those employed in manufacturing. Table 1.1 shows the proportion of white-collar males among total male employees. At 38.7 per cent the proportion of white-collar employees in Japan's manufacturing sector is significantly higher than in any of the EC countries. In the EC, the highest proportion is 30.1 per cent in the Netherlands; France follows at 28.8 per cent, with West Germany and the UK at 26.1 per cent, and finally Italy's and Belgium's proportions at around 20 per cent. It would appear therefore that the definition of white-collar status in Japan is wider than in the EC.

Part of the disparity may be accounted for by the way in which foremen are defined, and the second column, which shows the proportion of foremen relative to blue-collar workers *sheds light on this*. The weight of foremen to blue-collar workers in Japan is 13.5 per cent, distinctly higher than in the EC countries which are all in the 5 per cent range or below (except for 8.5 per cent in France). Such a wide range between Japan and the others may be partly due to differences in managerial organization; but probably the main discrepancy is that, whereas the Japanese definition includes 'group leaders' in the white-collar category, only real 'foremen' may have been accepted in the European survey's definition. Let us therefore subtract the proportion of foremen to total employees from column 1 in order to obtain column 4 which depicts the proportion out of all employees of white-collar workers with the exception of foremen. Japan's proportion at 30.8 per cent is still the highest, while the Netherlands stands at 26.1 per cent, followed by France and West Germany in the 22 per cent range with Belgium and Italy falling to around 17 per cent. So, although there has been some contraction in the degree of dispersion, fairly significant differences still remain.

TABLE 1.1 Proportions of white-collar males in manufacturing

Ratios	1 White-collar/ total employees	2 Foremen/ blue-collar	3 Foremen/ total employees	4 White-collar except foremen/total employees
Japan	38.7	13.5	7.9	30.8
West Germany	26.1	5.6	4.2	22.0
France	28.8	8.5	6.1	22.8
Italy	18.7	3.4	2.8	15.9
Belgium	20.6	4.0	3.2	17.4
Netherlands	30.1	5.8	4.0	26.1
Britain	26.1	–	–	–

Sources: See Figure 1.1.

What is the implication of these differences in the proportions of white-collar males for our contention about white-collarization in the wage structure for blue-collar employees of Japan's large companies? The contention receives support from the fact that in Western Europe the proportions of white-collar workers are narrower than in Japan. This comparatively narrow European white-collar category has a wage structure similar to that of Japan's blue-collar workers. To put the argument another way, suppose Japan's white-collar category was widened to include a proportion of blue-collar workers so that the relative weights became similar to Western Europe. Then there could well be a resemblance in age–wage profiles. Yet the boundaries of the categories we have make it impossible to demonstrate this. Undoubtedly the people who are doing blue-collar work in large Japanese companies do have age–wage profiles resembling those of EC white-collar workers. The underlying reasons for this need to be inpaired into later.

1.1.5 Wages by Age and Length of Service in Japan and the UK

All of the above observations were confined to the case of wages by age. The 1972 European survey does not provide statistics for wages cross-classified by age and length of service. Yet it is the interdependence between seniority wages and length of service which is emphasized in the case of wage structures in Japan. The number of wage increments does, needless to say, depend upon the length of service. So there could be a possibility that the apparent similarity in the simple age–wage profiles for Japan and Western Europe is related to length of service less than one might expect. Fortunately this issue can be resolved with the aid of the UK's *New Earnings Survey*. This provides wage data cross-classified by age and years of service, although in general the data are less detailed than in Japan's *Wage Structure Survey*. As noted earlier, the shape of the UK age–wage profiles is not significantly different to those of the other countries in the EC; the UK example should therefore also be a guide to trends in Western Europe.

In Figure 1.3 wage distributions cross-classified by age and length of service are shown for the UK and Japan. Adjustment has been made to recompute the Japanese subtotals so as to conform with those of the UK survey. Separate wage distributions for white-collar and blue-collar male workers over all company sizes for each country are depicted. In addition, the wage distribution for male blue-collar

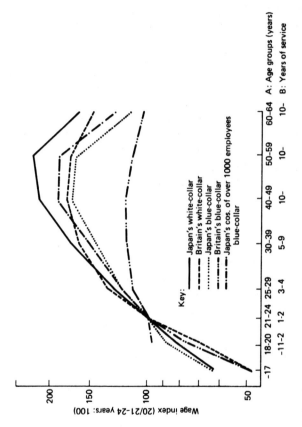

FIGURE 1.3   Wages by age and length of service in Japan and Britain (males in all company sizes)

Sources: Britain. Department of Employment and Productivity. *New Earnings*
Survey, 1975, Part F, Table 169.
Japan. See Figure 1.1.

workers in Japanese companies with more than 1000 employees has been drawn so as to link up with Figures 1.1 and 1.2.

The modified wage curve for UK blue-collar males which incorporates years of service is hardly different from the previous one in Figure 1.1. The average wage for those in their thirties and forties is no more than 20 per cent above the indexed average wage of 100 in the early twenties age group, which is tantamount to more or less equal wage levels over all the age groups. Similarly the distribution for UK white-collar males resembles that of the curve for wages related just to age, since the only changes are that the peak wage index is just a little higher and the discrepancy with the older age groups' indices is reduced. The peak wage index of 167, which is held by the forties age group in the age–wage profile, has thus become somewhat higher in this curve to reach 176. Again, in contrast to the discrepancy between the peak index and that of the fifties age group being 8 index points in the former case as the curve dropped to 159, there is now a difference of only 5 index points in the drop from 176 to 171. Therefore, in spite of the inclusion of the length of service factor, the age–wage profile should probably be viewed as changing hardly at all.

Figure 1.3 serves to confirm the earlier conclusion that the wage distribution of blue-collar males in large Japanese companies more or less resembles that of Western European white-collar workers. The wage index for blue-collar males in Japanese companies with more than 1000 employees is at its peak of 188 for workers in their fifties, which is barely higher than the peak index for UK white-collar males. Moreover, although in the UK the highest average earnings are being received by white-collar males in their forties, their wage index is only slightly above that for the fifties age group. Since there is also only a slight difference in the wage indices for blue-collar males in large Japanese companies in the forties and fifties age groups – respectively 184 and 189 – the highest average wage indices in both cases could be described as almost the same. Instead the main divergence from Figure 1.1 appears to be that the distribution of wages for Japanese blue-collar males over all company sizes has approached the seniority-style profile. In other words, in small and medium-sized Japanese companies also the wage profile appears to approach that in large companies once full account has been taken of long-serving blue-collar workers.

We may note also that even when length of service is accounted for, the observation that those in their late fifties earn, on average, less than those in their forties is confirmed as being a special feature of Japanese distributions.

The conclusions stemming from this comparison between Japan and the UK of wages by age and length of service may be extended to the other EC countries, for the similarities noted earlier in the wage distributions of European countries suggest that parallel results would be likely if other comparisons were feasible.

1.1.6 Comparing Wage Structures in Japan and the USA

Figure 1.4 depicts a comparison between age–wage profiles in Japan and the USA. We noted earlier that the data are not strictly compcomparable, so the conclusions drawn will necessarily be tentative. For male blue-collar workers, we find that whereas peak average earnings occur among those in the 45 to 54 years age group in large Japanese companies, in the USA the highest average annual income for both skilled and semi-skilled labour occurs for the 35 to 44 years old age group. Nonetheless the levels of the highest wage indices – with average wages in the 18 to 24 years age group set at 100 – are quite close, since in Japan's case the peak index is 175, while in the USA the peaks are respectively 166 for skilled labour and 168 for semi-skilled labour. Yet in small and medium-sized Japanese companies with between ten and 99 employees the peak index is at 148 in the 35 to 44 years age group – as was seen in Figure 1.1 – which is considerably below the US peak levels. Indeed in very approximate terms, if both large and small companies were integrated (as in the US data) there would be little difference between the peak levels of Japan and the USA.

How about the case of white-collar males who have graduated from secondary (high) school? A superficial reading would suggest that there is a large disparity, since the peak index in large Japanese companies is 232, while in the USA it is 194. But the US curve is only for office workers, rather than for all white-collar males who are high school graduates. Doubtless also there are some professionals and management executives whose education did not extend beyond high school, and who are not accounted for in the US distribution. The actual disparity with Japan in earnings for high school graduates in white-collar positions therefore is probably negligible.

There is less ambiguity in the case of university graduates. The highest average income age group among US professionals and engineers who have graduated from university does not differ in

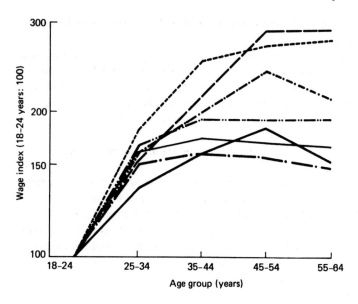

Key:

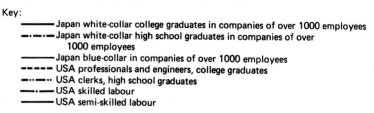

FIGURE 1.4   Age-wage profiles in Japan and the USA (males according
to occupation and educational level)

Notes: Japan, monthly salaries, manufacturing.
USA, annual income, all industries.

Sources: USA, *Census of Population, 1960*, PC(2) 7B, Table 4, Table 1.
Japan, See Figure 1.1.

either age or index level from male college graduates working in large
Japanese companies. The only significant difference between the two
distributions would appear to be that the gradient up to the 35 to 44
years age group is steeper in the case of the USA. As the figures for
Japan's distribution are confined to employees of large companies
one's initial impression might be that wages in the USA rise more
steeply with age – or at least no less steeply–than in Japan. However,
it should be noted that in the USA the youth unemployment rate is

high, and so the US figure for average annual income among the 18 to 24 years age group would incorporate for part of the sample relatively many weeks of unemployment, and hence lower income. Indeed, Shimada's 1981 research based on other more detailed data sources (whose sampling rates, however, are very low) indicates that the US wage distribution has a gentler slope than in the case of Japan.

The sum of the above observations suggests the following:[8]

(a) The shape of the US age–wage profile for male blue-collar workers is more line the profile in Japan than in the case of the EC countries. The upward sloping gradient of the US distribution is, however, rather lower than in Japan's case.

(b) Just as in the case of Western Europe, the wage distribution of white-collar males in the USA is quite similar to that of Japan. The US white-collar wage systems should thus probably be considered as being seniority-style.

(c) Because the age group categories are rather broad, there is some ambiguity in the shape of the wage distributions among older workers in the USA. Nevertheless there does seem to be a less sharp differential between the wages of middle-aged and older workers than in the case of Japan.

To summarize: since upward sloping age–wage profiles for white-collar males can also be seen to occur in the West, this feature cannot conclusively be regarded as being confined to large Japanese companies. What is peculiar to Japan is that in large companies male blue-collar age–wage profiles are similar in shape to those for white-collar males, which thereby implies white-collarization of wage structures. There is also evidence of upward sloping age-wage profiles even for blue-collar workers in the USA. Another aspect to be noted is that the age-wage profiles in Japan display a dramatic drop for the older workers, unlike in the West.

1.1.7 Age–wage Profiles and Wage Scales

Up to this point the term 'seniority wages' has been used to imply wage profiles rising more or less in correspondence with age and length of service. On this definition, seniority wages are seen as certainly not being confined to Japan. However, adherents of the seniority wage thesis often argue that a worker's wage rate is determined not by his work, but by his age and length of service. They therefore consider that this way of determining wage scales results in age–wage profiles being upward sloping. They therefore distinguish between age–wage profiles and actual wage scales. But suppose that wage scales were determined only by work (in a complete contradiction of the seniority approach), and then consider the usual practice in large US companies, where length of service is a prime factor in determining a worker's promotion to a post carrying a higher wage. In this way age–wage profiles necessarily become upward sloping, in spite of wages being nominally a function of the job. In other words upward sloping age–wage profiles and job-related wage scales are not distinct, and we should study comparative actual wage scales as well as age–wage profiles.

International comparisons of actual wage scales have been neglected for several reasons. While there are now data sources appropriate for comparing age–wage profiles internationally, comprehensive and reliable statistics on actual wage scales appear to be unavailable. We do, though, have wage agreements for the employees of the major British commercial banks. These may be taken as representative of wage scales of European white-collar workers, and are of particular interest because their age–wage profiles resemble those for blue-collar employees of large Japanese companies. In the British banks non-supervisory employees' salaries are unmistakably determined by age as well as merit. It would be rare indeed to find age explicitly incorporated to this extent in wage agreements – whether for blue collar or white-collar workers – in large companies in contemporary Japan. In this case wages are usually determined by annual increments with a merit rating for each grade of worker and grade advancement depends on work performance. Again promotion 'from within' is said to be quite customary in Britain's commercial banks.[9] It would thus appear that there is little difference between methods of determining wage scales in large Japanese companies and common practices for Western European white-collar workers. However any real judgement on this issue has to be postponed because of inadequate supporting material. Still there remains the important hypothesis that aspects of white-collarization can be recognised in the wage scales for blue-collar workers in large Japanese companies.

A much more significant reason for emphasising the age–wage profile rather than wage scales is that this profile itself is what is considered to be important. In contemporary large Japanese companies wage scales are often, apparently arbitrarily, altered. But if one looks at the way alterations are made, it becomes clear that a certain kind of age–wage profile, to which selected scales must conform, is a basic presumption, and is a presumption quite naturally rooted in an individual's customary expenditure pattern.

1.2   EGALITARIAN WAGES: DUAL STRUCTURE?

1.2.1   Blue-collar and White-collar Wage Differentials

The widely accepted concepts about seniority wages in Japan become unsustainable once satisfactory data sources have been examined. Yet statistical observation would suggest an alternative distinctive aspect of Japan's wage structures. Within a Japanese company, wage differentials appear to be relatively narrow. Let us begin by comparing wage differentials between the blue-collar and white-collar occupational groups which are distinguishable in all industrialised countries' companies. Figure 1.5 is confined to male workers, since the issue of wage differentials by sex will be dealt with later. In each age group the wage index for white-collar males relative to the average blue-collar wage set at 100 is graphed. In the case of Western Europe the hourly wage figures for blue-collar workers have been converted into monthly earnings based on the monthly working hours shown in the 1972 European survey. But the figures on weekly earnings for both blue-collar and white-collar UK workers, which have been taken from the *New Earnings Survey*, are retained.

For each country depicted on the graph the wage differentials by occupation increase with age. Yet the curves are not at all uniform even within Western Europe. In general the wage differentials are widest for Italy and France, where among workers in their late forties the white-collar wage index in 210 compared to 100 for the average blue-collar wage. Belgium and the Netherlands follow with the white-collar wage index at 150 to 160 in the same age group, and then West Germany with quite narrow differentials. The UK differentials appear to be least of all, but this judgement is subject to the qualification that the data sources are not the same. Japan's wage differential curve tends to coincide with the narrowest differentials in the UK, until the fifties are group when the differentials widen to just beyond those in West Germany. If the UK were excluded on account of its different data characteristics, Japan's occupational wage differentials would appear on the whole to be narrower than in any EC country.

The assertion needs further substantiation, however, because the

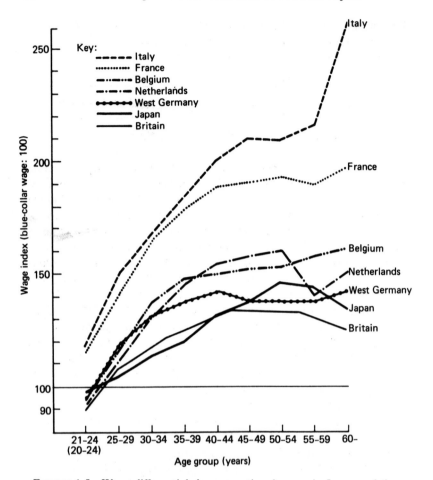

FIGURE 1.5 Wage differentials by occupational group in Japan and the
EC (male white-collar workers)

Sources: See Figure 1.1.

definitions of blue-collar and white-collar status may vary between
countries, thereby affecting the apparent differentials. As has already
been seen, the proportion of white-collar workers in Japan is relatively large. Hence the narrow wage differentials could be regarded
as the natural outcome of including lowly paid workers in the white-
collar group. It has been estimated that about half of the difference in
Japan's proportion of white-collar workers is due to the category of
foremen having a wider scope, since 'group leaders' who are not

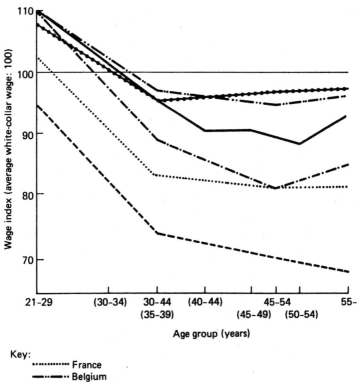

FIGURE 1.6   Foremen's wage differentials with average white-collar wage in Japan and the EC (male workers, manufacturing)

Sources: See Figure 1.1.

wholly engaged in supervisory activities are included. Figure 1.6 has been constructed to show the extent to which the different ranges in the scope of foremen influence the occupational wage differentials. The graph shows the differentials between foremen's wages and the average white-collar wage, and shows that Japanese foremen's wages relative to the average white-collar wage are not so low. Instead, extremely low relative wages for foremen are found in Italy, followed by France and Netherlands. For Japanese workers aged less than forty the differentials are comparable to those in West Germany and

Belgium, where there are the narrowest differentials. Even the widest differential in Japan is no more than 10 per cent. Therefore, even though the scope of foreman is broader, the evidence in Figure 1.6 supports the conclusion of relatively narrow occupational wage differentials.

1.2.2 Limited Differentials Between Clerical Staff and Managers

It would be useful to extend the above analysis by comparing wage differentials within the white-collar group between office staff and managers. The 1972 European survey has distinguished five groups of white-collar workers (p. 25). Japan's wage data are differentiated for companies with 100 or more employees according to department heads (*buchō*), section heads (*kachō*), subsection heads (*kakarichō*) and foremen (*shokuchō*). Would a comparison using these two sets of data be possible?

The problems in using the rather ambiguous definitions of management grades have already been discussed (p. 25), so it would be as well to check the proportions of management employees within each grade. In the 1972 European survey the highest paid grade of 'management executives with general authority and responsibility' has been further divided into two, with 1A representing the few most highly paid and 1B incorporating the rest. The number of occupants of the 1A grade have been totalled, but figures on their average income have not been provided. For the mid-forties to mid-fifties age group, in which are the majority of top management, the proportions occupying the 1A and 1B grade calculated from Table 1.2 are 9.0 per cent in Belgium, 8.8 per cent in West Germany, 8.2 per cent in France, 5.8 per cent in the Netherlands and 3.9 per cent in Italy. These proportions are all below the 14.1 per cent of white-collar personnel represented by department heads in Japan, which implies that the 1A and 1B grades correspond to somewhat more than the upper half of the department head grade. So, although the wage index for department heads is lower than that of the 1B grade in most cases, one cannot necessarily conclude that the wage differentials between top management and the average white-collar worker are narrower in Japan. Even so, in France, Italy and the Netherlands the wage indices for top management are so high as to more than compensate for any discrepancy in grade definitions, which thereby indicates wider wage differentials than in Japan. Moreover the EC

TABLE 1.2 Managerial salaries and personnel salaries in Japan and the EC (male workers, manufacturing)

Grade	Age Group (Years)	Japan 30–44	Japan 45–54	West Germany 30–44	West Germany 45–54	France 30–44	France 45–54	Italy 30–44	Italy 45–54	Belgium 30–44	Belgium 45–54	Netherlands 30–44	Netherlands 45–54
Wage index	1B /buchō	151	136	146	151	191	192	169	186	140	138	166	168
	2 /kachō	125	111	112	114	137	136	137	140	127	128	131	138
	3 /kakarichō	105	94	89	87	87	87	98	101	92	96	100	99
	4			71	68	67	61	71	76	79	78	79	74
	5	99	90	96	97	84	82	77	75	97	95	88	82
	white-collar average	100	100	100	100	100	100	100	100	100	100	100	100
Weighted average:	1B + 2 /bukachō		124		121		147		147		131		143
% of white-collar personnel	1A			1.2	2.1	0.5	1.9	0.1	0.3	1.6	2.9	0.3	1.1
	1B /buchō	1.4	14.1	6.1	6.7	3.7	6.3	2.5	3.6	8.2	6.1	3.2	4.7
	2 /kachō	11.6	14.0	31.8	27.7	25.9	25.6	24.1	20.3	18.6	15.9	21.2	21.6
	3 /kakarichō	17.8	12.3	39.2	33.7	30.6	21.7	31.0	21.4	31.1	29.5	28.8	23.7
	4			5.6	8.0	16.1	18.5	20.4	22.0	24.5	24.4	33.9	29.2
	5	21.3	32.4	16.2	21.9	23.2	26.1	21.9	32.3	16.1	19.3	12.8	19.8
	white-collar total	100	100	100	100	100	100	100	100	100	100	100	100
	1A + 1B +2/ bukachō total	13.0	28.1	39.1	36.5	30.1	33.8	26.7	24.2	28.4	26.9	24.7	27.4

Sources: See Table 1.1.

differentials would have been even wider had not the salaries of the 1A group been omitted.

Are the wage differentials wider in Western Europe when the wages of the second grade or section heads are included in the higher income group? The combined proportion of department and section heads aged 45–54 years in Japan is 28.1 per cent of all white-collar workers, but this proportion would be raised a little by the inclusion of intervening grades such as assistant department heads. The proportions of the combined 1A, 1B and 2 grades, in contrast, are 38.5 per cent in West Germany and 33.8 per cent in France. The disparity with Japan's proportion once all the intervening grades are included should thus be slight. Similarly the relevant proportions are only marginally lower in the other EC countries, which permits the weighted average wage index for the department and section head grades to be compared with that for the 1B and 2 grades in the 45–54 year age group. The former is 124, with the average white-collar wage set at 100, which is marginally more than West Germany's 121. The relevant wage indices in the other European countries, apart from Belgium's 131, tend to be much higher at 147, 147 and 143 in, respectively, France, Italy and the Netherlands. Japan does therefore appear to be one of those countries, including West Germany, with the narrowest wage differentials between office staff and managers.

1.2.3   Narrow Wage Differentials by Educational Grade

We may look also at wage differentials by the educational grade reached by workers. Level 2 of the white-collar grades is stipulated in the 1972 European survey to apply to those with status equal to university graduates, while level 3 requires at least matriculation from a secondary school or equivalent professional experience. So it would seem that just as in the case of wage differentials the distinction between office staff and managers according to their educational experience is less pronounced in Japan than in the EC. In the European survey, however, educational grade was only one factor used in stipulating the white-collar level. In any case the disparities in the university diffusion rates between each EC country, and Japan as well, are too wide to allow any comparability in the meaning held by educational qualifications.

Only in postwar Japan, USA and Korea have comprehensive wage data by educational level been compiled. The relevant US statistics come from the census referred to earlier (p. 9) and the Japanese statistics are included in the *Wage Structure Survey*.

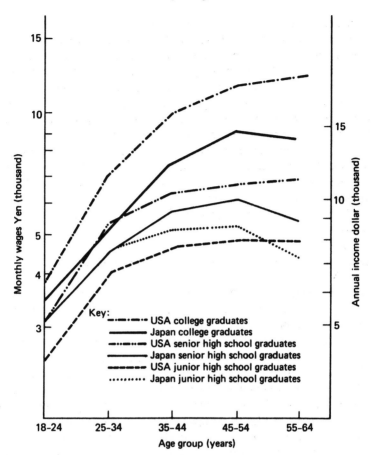

FIGURE 1.7   A comparison of Japan and the USA age-related wages by
educational level

Notes: Japan's statistics are for all industries over all companies with 10 or more
employees.
USA statistics are for all occupations in 1959.

Sources: USA, *Census of Population, 1960,* PC(2) 7b, Table 1. Japan, Rōdōshō
(Ministry of Labour) *Shōwa 46-nen Chingin Kōzō Kihon Tōkei Chōsa*
(1971 Wage Structure Survey).

Male workers' age-wage profiles for different grades of education
are graphed in Figure 1.7. Points vertically above each other indicate
the wage differentials arising from different levels of education. The
actual wages in yen and US dollars are graphed logarithmically on the
two vertical axes, but their arbitrarily adopted scales imply, of
course, that the wage levels between the two countries cannot be

compared. The slopes of the US age–wage profiles for each educational level appear initially to be somewhat steeper than Japan's. Youth unemployment and the use of annual income data in the USA tend to steepen the age–wage profile, as has been discussed earlier. Nonetheless, apart from the lower average wage among Japan's elderly workers, the age–wage profiles undeniably resemble each other, particularly in the way that the profile steepens as the educational grade is raised. At the same time there is a disparity in the degree of wage differentials by educational grade, with considerably wider differentials in the USA. In both countries the wage differentials widen the older are the workers, but the US differentials in all age groups are unmistakably wider. Nor is this distinction between the US and Japan profiles attributable to any difference in the diffusion rates of university education.

1.2.4 Comparing Differentials by Size of Company

We have seen that in Japan wage differentials within a country are among the narrowest when compared with other developed countries, it may nonetheless be argued that there must be extreme wage differentials between the employees of large companies and those of the much more numerous small and medium-sized companies. Previous comparative studies founder on data deficiencies (especially on the need to use average wages for both male and female workers).

Even the 1972 European survey has not compiled wage statistics cross-classified by size of company and age. Nevertheless the available EC data on wages cross-classified by sex and occupational group in different sized establishments can be compared reasonably accurately with Japan's data, as can be seen in Figure 1.8 and Figure 1.9. Certain differences between the categories from the 1972 European survey and from Japan's *Wage Structure Survey* should be noted. The European figures are classified by size of establishment, whereas Japan's classification is by size of company only. The resulting disparities are unlikely to be as significant in the case of manufacturing industries as in the tertiary or service industries where a single large chain store would have many small workplaces. The other discrepancy is that the intervals for establishment size are much narrower in the European survey, which may bias the results in favour of apparently smaller wage differentials in Japan.

Subject to these qualifications, Figure 1.8 shows that for blue-collar workers wage differentials by workplace size vary even within the EC, where the narrowest differentials are found in West Ger-

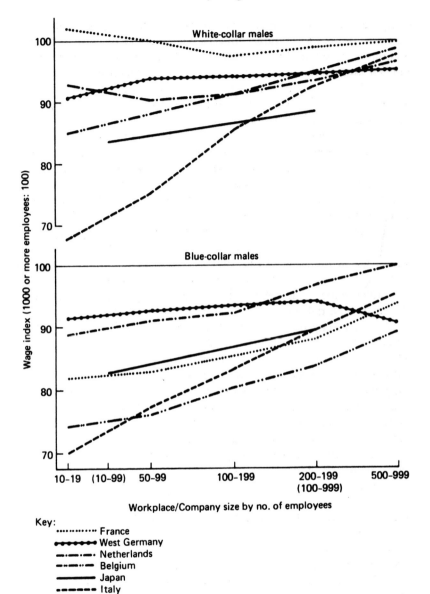

FIGURE 1.8   Wage differentials by company size in Japan and the EC
(male workers, manufacturing)

Notes: Workplace size applies to EC, company size to Japan. Parentheses indicate
company size intervals.

Sources: See Figure 1.1.

many and the Netherlands and the widest in Italy, followed by Belgium. Japan's wage differentials by company size lie close to those of France in the middle ranking area. Even if the graph depicts Japan's wage differentials below their actual value (for the reasons discussed) such discrepancies should be fairly negligible. Thus the notion that Japan's wage differentials by company size are much wider than elsewhere has to rejected.

For white-collar males, the picture changes somewhat. Japan's wage differentials by company size are clearly wider than in most of the EC countries. Only in Italy between workplaces with less than 200 employees and those with 1000 or more employees are the male white-collar wage differentials greater than those prevailing in Japan. It would appear that in this case the traditional argument is justified. Nonetheless even the widest white-collar wage differentials are just a bit narrower than in the case of the more numerous blue-collar males; the actual scale of the wage differentials is certainly far less than the 40 to 50 per cent differential commonly suggested.

Among female blue-collar workers most of the wage differentials shown in Figure 1.9 are in the 15–25 per cent range. In this case, Japan is certainly not exceptional, and its differentials lie from the middle towards the upper end of this range. In the case of female white-collar workers Japan, along with West Germany and France, has less than 10 per cent differentials, while in the Netherlands, Belgium and Italy differentials are mostly in the 10–20 per cent range.

In conclusion, Japan does not generally seem to be a country with particularly large wage differentials by company size, though the above comparison is concerned with monthly earnings. Even if we examine yearly earnings, through adding term-end bonuses to the Japanese figures. Japan's extent of wage differentials does not exceed that of Italy.

1.2.5   Wide Wage Differentials by Sex Among Workers Aged Over Thirty

The area in which Japan's wage differentials are clearly wider than those in Europe is between male and female workers over the age of 30 years. There have previously been assertions that these wage differentials are remarkably wide, but international comparisons have had to be restricted to wage differentials averaged over all age groups. The 1972 European survey now makes comparisons of wage differentials by age and by sex feasible. As is seen from Figure 1.10, all the EC countries experience wage differentials by sex, which are

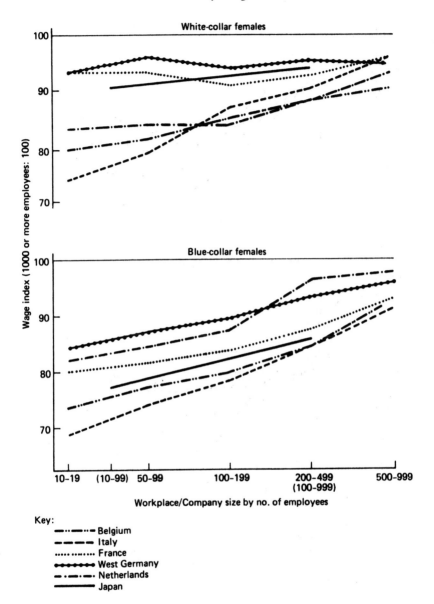

FIGURE 1.9 Wage differentials by company size in Japan and the EC
(female workers, manufacturing)

Notes: See Figure 1.8.

Sources: See Figure 1.1.

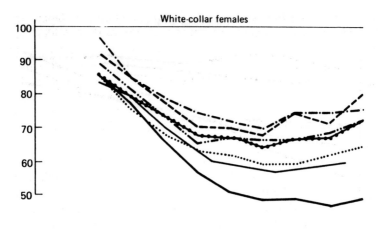

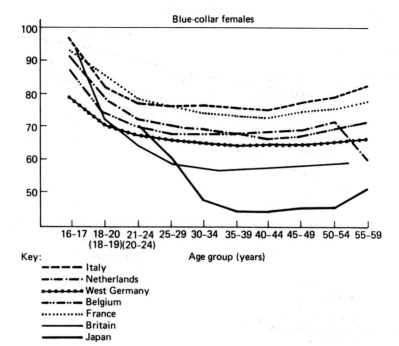

FIGURE 1.10   Age-related wage differentials by sex in Japan and the EC (male workers' wages: 100, manufacturing)

Notes: All wage figures have been converted into monthly wages.

Sources: See Figure 1.1.

narrowest among the younger age group. Similarly, in Japan, the wage differentials are not particularly significant for those under their mid-twenties. Among workers in their late-twenties Japan's wage differentials are close to those in the UK. But wage differentials between male and female workers aged over 30 years are remarkably wide. With the male blue-collar wage set at 100, the indices for EC blue-collar wages of females in their thirties and forties lie between 60 and 80, whereas in Japan the female average wage lies even below half of the corresponding male wage.

The reason is that the male blue-collar wage index rises more steeply with age than in the EC. Consequently for middle-aged workers in Japan the differential by sex becomes especially wide. In other words the white-collarisation of Japan's blue-collar male workers should be regarded as a primary factor behind the wide wage differential by sex.[10]

1.3 FRINGE BENEFITS: PATERNALISM?

It has long been thought that Japanese industrial relations are governed by a spirit of 'paternalism'. Japanese large companies are said to be diligent in taking care of their employees' welfare by providing a wide range of fringe benefits. The prevailing opinion is that employees' consequent identification with their company encourages harmonious industrial relations as well as high productivity. Dore's description of Japanese industrial relations as 'welfare corporatism'[11] is a typical example of the way in which both Western and Japanese scholars have tended to subscribe to this opinion. But, particularly in the West, there seems to have spread recently a contrary argument which insists that Western companies are obliged to spend more on workers' welfare than their Japanese counterparts. This view implies that fringe benefits are more extensive in the West, which is argued to be one of the reasons for the imbalance in international trade between the West and Japan.

1.3.1 The Sources for Studying Fringe Benefits

Any attempt at an international comparison quickly reveals that statistical sources are generally more plentiful in Japan than in the West. But the EC's *Labour Costs in Industry*, which using a standardized method and has been compiled every three years since 1966, does permit fringe benefits to be compared. The standardisation of data is especially valuable because of the diversity in fringe benefits, which reflects historical factors in the way different countries' workers have made their livelihoods.

The EC statistics were originally confined to manufacturing and mining workplaces with 50 or more employees, but in 1972 the survey was extended to workplaces with ten or more employees. This survey is carried out on a large scale with a 10 per cent sampling rate, and in a few countries complete enumeration. Because of using a standardised method, the items tend inevitably to be highly aggregated. Enterprise welfare, on the one hand, supplements the particular country's social security system, whose inherent characteristics are thereby reflected. Yet fringe benefits go beyond the field of official social security to probe into other aspects of a worker's welfare, and people's mode of living does, needless to say, differ between countries on account of historical circumstances. The resulting variety in labour costs could thus only be dealt with by establishing common broadly defined categories:[12]

1. Direct pay for time worked including overtime, bonuses and gratuities payable regularly at each pay period
2. Other bonuses and gratuities not payable regularly at each pay period
3. Payments for days not worked – e.g., paid annual holidays
4. Social security contributions and family allowances paid by the employer:

4.1 Statutory contributions
4.2 Customary, contractual or voluntary payments – e.g., insurance taken out by the firm or branch, and supplementary retirement insurance scheme

5. Benefits in kind (especially housing, heating, food and clothing)
6. Other expenditure of social nature (especially transport, cultural and medical facilities)
7. Vocational training expenditure.

Thus the figures for separate social security items, such as health and unemployment insurance, whose classification varies between countries are not obtainable. Nor can one distinguish the supplementary payments made by the employer. Similarly individual kinds of fringe benefits, such as medical expenses, housing and meal allowances, cannot be studied.

In the case of Japan, the classification systems in the *Survey of Labour Costs*, 'Rōdō Hiyō Chōsa', held since 1965, and the *Survey of Welfare Facilities for Labour*, 'Rōdōsha Fukushi Shisetu Seido Chōsa', held since 1972, are consistent with each other. In order to compare Japan and the EC we have to examine the following two ratios, because there are some subtle distinctions in the definitions of the European and Japanese survey.

A   Ratio of fringe benefits to total labour costs

This compares non-statutory welfare expenditure to total expenditure on workers. For the EC, fringe benefits consist of:

4.2 Enterprise share of customary, contractual or voluntary payments, concerned with social security

5. Benefits in kind
6. Other expenditure of a social nature.

In the case of Japan's figures, the definition of non-statutory enterprise welfare expenditure in the *Survey on Labour Costs* is much narrower, being confined to commuting expenses, luncheon vouchers and medical facilities; so retirement allowances, housing allowances, benefits in kind and family allowances are also added. Total labour costs include the company's total expenditure with respect to the workers' livelihood which, in the case of the EC, is the total of all the categories of labour costs *less* category 7 (vocational training expenditure) In Japan's case, recruitment and training expenditure are subtracted from the total labour costs.

B   Ratio of statutory enterprise social security contribution to total labour costs

This ratio is not so pertinent to the issue being examined, but has been calculated because of its close connection to the ratio concerned with non-statutory enterprise welfare expenditure.

In Figure 1.11 the vertical axis denotes ratio A, while the horizontal axis is scaled for ratio B. As well as Japan and the EC, ratios have

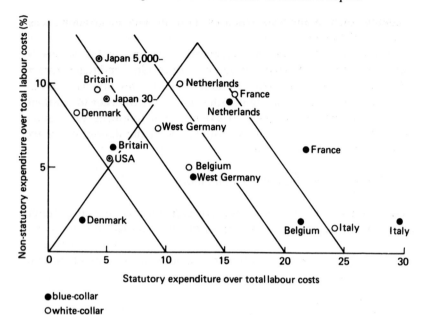

FIGURE 1.11   International comparison of enterprise welfare expenditure ratios (manufacturing and mining)

Notes: Japan's ratios apply to manufacturing only in 1968.
EC ratios are for 1969, apart from Denmark and Britain, for 1973.
US ratios are for 1968.

Sources: EC, *Labour Costs in Industry, 1972–75* and *Jahrbuch Sozialistatistik, 1974.*
USA, *Monthly Labor Review* (November 1970) p. 23.
Japan: Rōdōshō (Ministry of Labour), *Rōdō Hiyō Chōsa 1968* (Survey on Labour Costs).

been calculated for the USA on the basis of a similar survey, but with some recomposition of categories. For each EC country the relevant blue-collar and white-collar figures have been separately totalled and the resulting ratios are depicted by, respectively, dots and circles.

1.3.2   Non-statutory Fringe Benefits

When the A ratios of non-statutory welfare expenditure to total labour costs, are examined, the following interesting points emerge. The ratios in Japan are close to those for EC white-collar workers. In Japanese establishments with 30 or more employees the ratio totalled over blue and white-collar workers is approximately 9 per cent. The highest EC ratio for welfare expenditure on white-collar workers is just over 10 per cent in the Netherlands. The ratios closest to Japan's in the 9 per cent range are in the UK and France, with Denmark's ratio at 8 per cent and West Germany's not much lower at near 7.5 per cent. Exceptionally low ratios are found in Belgium with below 5 per cent, and in Italy with barely 2 per cent. In contrast, the proportion of total labour costs for blue-collar workers accounted for by non-statutory welfare expenditure are around or below 6 per cent, except in the Netherlands where the ratio at 8.5 per cent is close to Japan's overall ratio. (The US ratio is for different labour groups, and so will be ignored for the moment.)

In the EC countries the non-statutory enterprise welfare ratio A thus varies greatly between blue-collar and white-collar workers. Indeed, it is probable that in practice enterprise welfare discriminates between the occupational groups to a greater degree than indicated by the calculated ratios, since the labour costs denominator in the EC would be relatively greater for white-collar workers than in Japan. Enterprise welfare in Western Europe appears to have occurred first for white-collar workers after the First World War; a gradual extension of benefits to blue-collar workers was accelerated after the Second World War, but a discriminatory gap still remains.

An accurate comparison of fringe benefits is hindered by the fact that Japan's figures are not separately compiled for the two occupational groups. In manufacturing, however, because of the overwhelming predominance of blue-collar workers, enterprise welfare expenditure can be perceived as being comparable with that provided for EC white-collar workers according to Figure 1.11. Indeed, a Japanese company nowadays does apparently provide identical fringe benefit systems for its blue-collar and white-collar employees, so that separately compiled figures would be redundant. For example, in Japan all occupational groups right up to the factory superintendent dine together, whereas in other countries there are normally separate dining rooms or canteens. Before 1945, there was also discrimination within Japanese companies (though whether to the same extent or less than in present Western Europe is not clear), but these practices vanished with wartime defeat. Hence the provision of uniform benefits within a company is not a traditional Japanese feature, but rather reflects the white-collarization of blue-collar workers in postwar Japan.

1.3.3 Statutory Employers' Contributions

The horizontal axis of Figure 1.11 permits a comparison of the B ratio for statutory enterprise welfare contributions. As might have been expected the difference in the ratio for blue-collar and white-collar workers is significant in most countries with the relative contributions made on behalf of blue-collar workers always greater. The disparity between the relevant ratios is particularly wide in Belgium and France, followed by Italy, the Netherlands and West Germany. In contrast, the employers' contribution ratios tend to be similar for blue-collar and white-collar employees in the UK and Denmark.

But, as pointed out above, even if the statutory enterprise contributions were applied in completely uniform systems, the ratio for white-collar employees would probably turn out to be somewhat lower because of the wide occupational wage differentials in the EC. Nonetheless, apart from the UK and Denmark, the difference in the ratios appears to be greater than would result just from wage differentials. It is true that the official social security systems in many Western European countries discriminate between occupational groups, while the UK and Scandinavia have a uniform system for the whole nation. In the latter case, the social security system is primarily financed with individual contributions, so the relative smallness of the employers' contribution does not indicate inadequate social security.

Although Japan's financing of social security resembles the West German model, its ratio for the statutory enterprise contribution is close to those of the UK and Denmark. Some suggest that Japan's ratio is low because the social security system is underdeveloped. While this issue is not really relevant here, certain observations may be pertinent. Pension funds account for a sizable proportion of social security funds in all countries. But, at present, the proportion of elderly people in Japan is somewhat lower than in Western Europe, with the consequence that the relative employers' contribution becomes smaller. The accelerated ageing of the Japanese population over the next 40 years will, however, ultimately require rapid growth in the employers' contribution unless the social insurance system is reformed. In other words the ratio for 1968 indicated in Figure 1.11 will already have become much higher, and will certainly increase in the future.

The ratios for statutory enterprise contributions are high in France and Italy. Whereas elsewhere proportionate contributions to social security made by employers and individuals are approximately equal, in France and Italy the enterprise burden is about 80 per cent, while individuals contribute about 20 per cent. Moreover France provides particularly large statutory child allowances. Therefore, despite the divergencies in Figure 1.11, it is probable that the actual content of the social security system to which enterprises contribute is not more generous in France and Italy than elsewhere in Western Europe.

We may conclude therefore that Western European enterprise welfare, whether statutory or non-statutory, discriminates between occupational groups. Enterprise welfare in Japan, in contrast, tends to be close to that for European white-collar workers, which once again suggests 'white-collarization' in Japan.

1.4 CONCLUSIONS

We must reject the hypothesis that so-called seniority wages are a unique feature of Japanese wage systems. The upward slope of the age–wage profile up to the 50 year old age group is not just confined to Japan, but is common to male white-collar wages in the EC, the USA and Japan. Instead, the distinct feature of contemporary large Japanese companies is that age–wage profiles for blue-collar males are also upward sloping. This 'white-collarization' of the blue-collar wage system may also be recognised in the provision of welfare benefits to blue-collar male workers. The issue of why 'white-collarization' has occurred will be pursued throughout the rest of this book.

From Adam Smith through Marxism to the neo-classical school of economics, wages have been viewed as reflecting skills; yet a method for measuring technical ability has still to be developed and we continue to depend on the use of proxy variables. If the formation of skills were primarily a function of on-the-job training, then the number of years of experience could become a proxy variable. While there is also outside experience, on-the-job training is usually experienced within the company. Therefore this type of experience may simply be measured by the number of years of service, which can be compared between Japan and the West. Such a comparison, which is really concerned with the notion of permanent employment, could be one step – to be taken up in the next chapter – towards elucidating the nature of white-collarization.

This chapter has also brought into focus two other aspects of comparative wage systems. One was that Japan's age–wage profiles drop steeply among the oldest workers, which is in striking contrast to the usual notion of seniority wages. We saw also that Japan's wage differentials are relatively narrow when compared to those in the EC and the USA. In particular, the differentials between blue-collar and white-collar wages are narrow. This narrowness results nor from low white-collar wages, whose scale systems are not far removed from those operating in the EC, but because age–wage profiles for Japanese blue-collar males (especially employees of large companies), are upward sloping in the same way as white-collar wages. In the EC, on the other hand, the age–wage profiles for white-collar and blue-collar males are quite dissimilar, which leads to wider wage differentials than in Japan.

If a competitive economic model were to be constructed to cover this issue, the conclusion would then be that the degree of competition in Japan's labour markets has become greater than in the EC, since competition tends to equalize wage rates. The well-known legend of permanent employment, however, suggests that Japanese labour markets are non-competitive. So two particular questions must be addressed: whether permanent employment practices are really non-competitive, and whether employment in Japan is in fact more 'permanent' than in the West.

NOTES

1. Age–wage profiles for Japan and the USA were first compared and found to be similar in Umemura (1956). Umemura (1971) used Western European family expenditure surveys to demonstrate that Japanese wage systems were not a special case.
2. EC, *Structure of Earnings in Industry* for the year 1972 (Brussels: EC, 1975–6 13 vols. Volume 1 provides a detailed explanation of the survey methods.
3. Data on age–wage profiles from the 1960 census can be found in: US Department of Commerce, Bureau of Census, Census of Population *Census of Population, 1960, PC(2) 7B, Occupation by Earnings and Education* (Washington, D.C.).
4. Reference may be made to: Bundesrepublik Deutschland, *Statistiche Bundesamt, Gehalts- und Lohnstrukturerhebungen* for the year 1957, *Statistische Berichte* vi–12 (1958).
5. See Blaug (1967).
6. See Woytinsky (1953).
7. The definitions are recorded in the 1975–6 EC Survey, vol. 1, pp. 257–8.

  1. *Management executives with general authority and responsibility*
     This group includes persons to whom the employer delegates powers

of decision with regard to the general working of the undertaking, and who are in a position of authority over all or a large part of the staff. The group was further divided:

1A staff whose remuneration exceeded a certain ceiling, determined country for country, and who consequently were not included in the survey.

1B staff whose remuneration was below or equal to the above-mentioned ceiling.

2. *Executives*
This group includes members of staff who have undergone technical, administrative, legal, commercial or financial training, normally evidenced by a university degree, or acquired through personal experience and recognized as equivalent.

3. *Assistants*
This group includes staff assigned to administrative, accounting, commercial, technical or social work requiring an advanced level of secondary education or equivalent professional experience. They collaborate with the management executives and work under their responsibility and according to their instructions.

4. *Clerical staff*
This group includes employees working on precise instructions from their hierarchical superiors and their work, generally speaking, requires only a very limited amount of initiative and responsibility.

5. *Foremen*
These are workers (overseers performing supervisory duties, etc.) engaged in directing, coordinating and supervising the work of one or more groups of workers (and sometimes a certain number of technicians and foremen subordinate to them).

8. See Shimada (1981).
9. See, for example, Blackburn (1967).
10. For the details, refer to Koike (1980–1) pp. 71–2.
11. See Dore (1973).
12. EC, *Labour Costs in Industry, 1972–5* (Brussels: EC, 1975) p. 272.

REFERENCES

Blackburn, Robert M. (1967) *Union Character and Social Class* (London: Batsford).

Blaug, Mark (1967) *The Utilization of Educated Manpower* (Toronto: Toronto University Press).

Dore, Ronald P. (1973) *British Factory – Japanese Factory* (Berkeley and Los Angeles: University of California Press).

Koike, Kazuo (1980–1) 'A Japan–Europe Comparison of Female Labour-Force Participation and Male Differentials', *Japanese Economic Studies*, IX, 2, Winter, pp. 3–27.

Shimada, Haruo (1981) *Earnings Structure and Human Investment: A Comparison Between the United States and Japan* (Tokyo: Kōgakusha).

Tōkei-Kenkyūkai (ed.) *Chingin Kōzō no Jittai Bunseki* (An Analysis of Wage Structure) (Tokyo: Tōkei-Kenkyūkai, 1956) (mimeo).

Umemura, Mataji (1956) 'Nenrei to Chingin' (Age and Wages) in Tōkei-Kenkyūkai (ed.).

Umemura, Mataji (1971) '*Nenrei-shotoku Profiles no Kokusai Hikaku*' (An International Comparison of Age–Wage Profiles) *Keizai Kenkyū*, 22, 3.

Woytinsky, Vladinov S. (1953) *Employment and Wages in the United States* (New York: Twentieth Century Fund).

2 'Permanent Employment'?

2.1 LENGTH OF SERVICE: AN INTERNATIONAL COMPARISON

2.1.1 Changing Employment Rates by Age

The notion of 'permanent employment' has two distinct aspects – one, the tendency for workers to continue being employed for a long time in one company, the other to base promotion decisions largely on relative lengths of service. Since the latter tendency is hard to substantiate statistically, the main focus will be on the degree of labour immobility.

Comparative studies of labour immobility internationally have been unsatisfactory because the only data available on turnover or changing employment have been averaged over all age groups. But any consideration of economic motives would suggest that the age and the sex of the worker would greatly influence the decision on changing employment. There are thus significant disparities when 'separation rates' by age (defined as the number of leavers as a proportion of the labour force at the beginning of the period) are calculated in *Japan's Survey of Employment Mobility*. Figure 2.1 shows that Japanese labour is split into two groups depending on age, one mobile and the other largely immobile. Such divergencies make averages for all age groups quite misleading.

Figure 2.1 also throws doubt on the prevailing notion that there is permanent employment in Japan. We can see that in manufacturing companies with 1000 or more employees the annual separation rate for regular male employees is more than 20 per cent among workers under 25 years of age. This rate would tend to vary with the business cycle, becoming lower during a recession, and higher during an upswing. Lack of appropriate data makes an international comparison impossible, yet a separation rate of 20 per cent among young male workers is hardly an image of permanent employment.

57

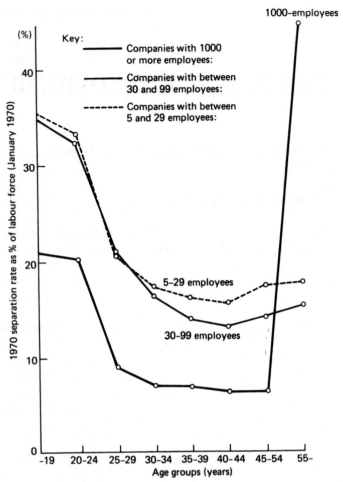

FIGURE 2.1   Separation rates by age and by size of firm (male workers in manufacturing, 1970)

Note: The figure for separation rates by age have been available since 1952; however, the figures by age and size of firm are available only for the period 1964–70. Though the graph refers to 1970, the basic pattern is common throughout the period.

Source: Japan: Rōdōshō (Ministry of Labour) *Koyō Dōkō Chōsa* (Employment Mobility Survey, 1970; 1971).

Another point revealed by Figure 2.1 is that the separation rate falls sharply once workers reach their late twenties. The annual separation rate of 6–7 per cent for large company male workers in their thirties and forties has to be the substance of the labour immobility, or 'permanent employment'.

There is, however, another aspect. For employees of large companies aged over fifty years, the separation rate suddenly jumps to over 40 per cent. The reason lies in the mandatory early retirement age, which is indeed the reverse side of the coin of so-called permanent employment.

The further point to be noted is that the separation rate also depends on company size. The curves for employees of small and medium-sized companies are the same shape as in the case of large companies, but their location on the vertical axis is higher. The annual separation rate for young workers is higher at over 30 per cent, while for middle-aged workers the rate is around 15 per cent. But, unlike the curve for large company employees, the rate does not appreciably increase for workers aged over fifty years, presumably because any mandatory retirement age system is not being implemented.

In Western Europe statistics on workers' length of service by sex and by occupational group have been compiled – apparently for the first time – in the 1972 European survey on the *Structure of Earnings in Industry*. In fact, length of service is a more direct indicator of labour mobility than the separation rate. Such statistics are also provided in Japan's *Wage Structure Survey*. Since the characteristics of these two surveys are sufficiently similar to permit reasonably accurate comparative analyses, it should be possible to ascertain whether permanent employment is a special feature of Japanese labour management.

2.1.2 Long Service Workers Also Numerous in the EC

The composition by length of service of blue-collar and white-collar male workers is shown in Table 2.1. Over all companies with 10 or more employees, Japan's proportion of blue-collar workers with less than two years' service is 12.6 per cent, whereas in all the EC countries the corresponding figure is higher. (Luxemburg is excluded from the analysis because its population is extremely small.) In Italy the relevant proportion is 18 per cent, while in the other EC countries there are much higher proportions in the 22–25 per cent range. A similar pattern holds for white-collar workers with less than two years' service; in contrast to an 8 per cent proportion in Japan, in all the EC countries the range is from 11–15 per cent. So there appears

TABLE 2.1   Composition by length of service in Japan and the EC
(Male workers in manufacturing)

		Years of service.	unit: %				
			−2	2−4	5−9	10−19	20−
Blue-collar males	*Japan*	All companies	12.6	21.6	28.1	27.0	10.9
		1000 or more employees	6.0	17.3	29.9	31.3	15.5
		100–999 employees	13.0	23.4	28.9	26.1	9.5
		10–99 employees	19.1	24.5	25.5	23.0	7.8
	EC	West Germany	22.6	23.0	17.1	24.5	12.8
		France	25.3	22.9	19.0	19.6	11.9
		Italy	17.9	28.1	22.0	21.9	8.9
		Belgium	22.8	23.6	19.6	20.1	13.9
		Netherlands	22.2	23.5	18.7	21.2	14.5
		Luxembourg	15.3	17.0	17.2	27.0	23.5
		Britain	45.0		19.8	34.8	
White-collar males	*Japan*	All companies	8.0	15.7	24.0	34.0	18.3
		1000 or more	4.0	11.6	22.0	37.7	24.7
		100–999 employees	8.7	17.3	26.0	33.9	14.1
		10–99 employees	15.3	21.6	25.1	26.8	11.3
	EC	West Germany	15.4	19.1	17.6	27.4	20.5
		France	12.7	16.8	19.0	26.7	23.1
		Italy	15.3	24.5	21.0	26.2	12.1
		Belgium	13.0	18.8	19.8	24.4	24.0
		Netherlands	11.5	19.5	18.0	27.3	23.6
		Luxembourg	11.4	17.4	21.9	27.4	21.8
		Britain	40.7		19.8	38.8	

Sources: See Figure 1.1.

to be a solid foundation for the permanent employment concept in respect of workers with very short service.

When other figures are examined, however, the picture alters. Where there is permanent employment, one would expect a high proportion of long serving workers. Yet the proportion of Japanese blue-collar males with 20 or more years of service is only 10.9 per cent, which is less than all EC countries except Italy (8.9 per cent). The relevant proportions are 11.9 per cent in France, 12.8 per cent in West Germany, 13.9 per cent in Belgium and 11.4 per cent in the

Netherlands. (The UK survey does not separately classify 20 or more years of service.) The proportion with more than 10 years' service in Japan is 37.9 per cent, which is close to West Germany's 37.3 per cent. Nor are the Netherlands at 35.7 per cent, the UK at 34.8 per cent and Belgium at 34.0 per cent far away.

Does the picture change if we look only at large companies? The European figures are not classified by company size, so we hypothesise that the composition of length of service by company size in the EC countries is not significantly different to the composition over all company sizes. This biases the comparison towards permanent employment appearing special to Japan. The 15.5 per cent of Japanese blue-collar males in companies with 1000 or more employees serving 20 or more years is, under this assumption, larger than in any of the EC countries, excluding Luxemburg. The highest proportion over all company sizes of longest serving blue-collar males in the EC is 14.5 per cent in the Netherlands. Even when the wider group of blue-collar males with 10 or more years of service is considered, the 46.8 per cent in large Japanese companies is more than 10 percentage points higher than in the EC countries, excluding Luxemburg.

Nonetheless permanent employment similar to the levels of blue-collar employees in large Japanese companies can be seen in the EC among white-collar male workers. Taking the group with 20 or more years of service first, the proportion for Japanese blue-collar males in large companies is 15.5 per cent, while in the EC the relevant proportions for white-collar males in all companies are much higher at between 20 and 25 per cent, with the single exception of Italy at 12.1 per cent. For those with 10 or more years' service, the proportion is 46.8 per cent for blue-collar male employees of large Japanese companies. The proportions for white-collar males are somewhat higher in the EC countries, apart from in Italy and the UK. (It may be recalled that the UK data characteristics are rather different, and particularly that very small companies may be surveyed.) EC white-collar workers are thus similar to Japanese blue-collar male employees of large companies in tending to stay for a long time with one company. This similarity may be due to the mandatory retirement age in Western Europe being rather later than in Japan. Nonetheless at least it can hardly be denied that labour turnover among EC white-collar males is low. If permanent employment is said to be characteristic of Japanese blue-collar male employees of large companies, then the same should be said about EC white-collar male employees. Here again can be recognized the white-collarization of blue-collar males in large Japanese companies.

2.1.3   Japan – UK Comparison of Length of Service by Age

The age composition of the labour force should influence the distribution of years of service. At present the proportion of older people in Western Europe is higher than in Japan. However statistics on length of service by age are not available in the EC's 1972 survey and can apparently be found only in the UK *New Earnings Survey*. The difficulty in making a comparison with Japan is that the UK is consistent neither in data characteristics or in its length of service pattern with the rest of the EC; and, as has been discussed earlier, the UK data are also different to Japan's *Wage Structure Survey*. Possibly the data characteristics are why the UK proportion of workers with 10 or more years of service is substantially below all the other EC countries except Italy. The relevant proportion for UK white-collar males is 38.8 per cent, in line with Italy's 38.3 per cent, whereas the other countries' figures are around 50 per cent and in the case of Japanese blue-collar males in large companies the proportion is 46.8 per cent.

While bearing in mind the above reservations, graphs on the length of service by age in Japan and the UK may be compared (see Figure 2.2). Japan's figures have been converted to conform to the UK classification of five groups for years of service: less than one year, one to two years, three to four years, five to nine years, and 10 or more years; Japan's survey applies to all companies with 10 or more employees, whereas the UK survey is over all company sizes.

The case of blue-collar male workers is examined first. Among 18 and 19 years olds (18–20 year olds in the UK classification), the weight of long serving workers is higher in the UK, but this should not be considered as significant. The diffusion rate of late secondary education in the UK is relatively low, which would certainly be reflected in earlier entry into employment by those finishing their education. Consequently the positions of the curves change for workers in their late twenties and thirties when labour mobility in the UK becomes distinctly higher than in Japan. Yet the divergence between the two countries rapidly diminishes for workers in their forties, to the extent that in the fifties age group the two curves lie more or less on top of each other. Then the positions are reversed among sixty year olds with Japan demonstrating higher labour mobility. This general pattern through the different age groups is also applicable to the case of white-collar males.

These results suggest that in the EC the tendency seen earlier towards relatively long service is not necessarily due to the different age composition. Even in the UK, where labour mobility is relatively high, workers in their forties and over are as immobile as in Japan – contrary to the pattern of younger Japanese workers being relatively more immobile than their European counterparts. Once European workers have passed through the youthful stage of frequently changing employment – to an extent greater than in Japan – they then appear to settle down in a single company for a longer period than the Japanese worker. Hence the average over all ages of these two distinct groups of mobile and immobile labour would distort reality.

2.1.4   Japan – USA Comparison of Length of Service

The above trends can be looked for in the USA also, because the Bureau of Labor Statistics has at irregular intervals since 1951 carried out the *Job Tenure Survey*.[1] Because of the way the data are compiled, a comparison of labour mobility must be based on Japan's survey on the structure of employment (which is held every three years) and the US survey on job tenure.

The US survey asks when the respondents began working at their present place of employment. This concept is the same as that used in Japan's survey, and exactly corresponds to length of service because 'unchanged employment' is defined as continuing with a single employer, even though the worker might have moved between different jobs. The self-employed are included in both surveys.[2] The figures in Table 2.2 cover as wide a range of different years as possible.[3] The results suggest some differences from the comparison between Japan and the EC (Table 2.1). In the 1960s there is a resemblance to the earlier comparison in that while the proportion of short serving workers is decisively higher in the USA, long serving workers are also relatively more than in Japan. But this pattern changed in the 1970s when the proportion of long serving workers in Japan rose, whereas the US proportion registered a slight decline. Consequently the weight of long servers in Japan overtook that in the USA, which indicates that labour must be more immobile in Japan. This conclusion contrasts with the earlier finding where the EC appeared to have more immobile labour than Japan. Also, as is shown in Figure 2.3, the composition of long serving workers by occupation in the USA is somewhat different to the EC case. It appears that in the USA white-collar workers are not always more immobile than blue-collar workers. For example, the proportion of long servers among

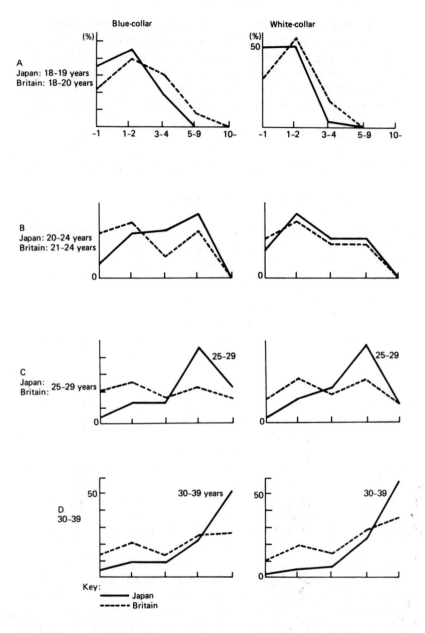

FIGURE 2.2   Length of service by age in Japan and Britain (Japan, male workers in manufacturing, 1976; Britain, all industries, 1975)

Source: See Figure 1.1.

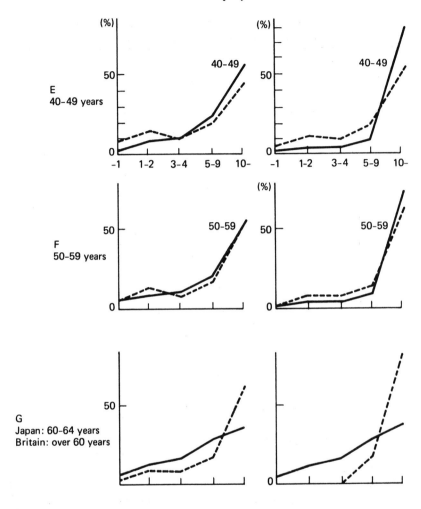

the professionals and technical workers group is equal to that of the operatives group and falls below the proportion for long serving craftsmen.

Even though in the USA, unlike in the EC, the proportion of long serving workers falls below that of Japan in the 1970s, a substantial class of immobile workers (in the 1960s comparable with Japan) can be perceived. There is also the possibility that the degree of labour immobility might be higher in large companies. But this can be ascertained only by case studies of large companies, because the data used above are not classified by company size, and this will be the main theme of Chapter 3.

TABLE 2.2   Composition by length of service in Japan and the USA
(male non-agricultural employees) (percentage)

	USA			Japan			
	1966	*1973*	*1978*	*1962*	*1974*	*1977*	*1979*
Total (years)	100	100	100	100	100	100	100
Less than 1	23.2	22.4	25.2	9.1	8.4	7.2	7.5
1	8.5	10.5	10.4	10.5	6.5	2.7	2.7
2	6.4	7.4	7.1	10.0	6.9	6.4	6.6
3–4	9.7	13.0	11.9	14.9	13.2	12.3	11.1
5–9	15.2	16.8	16.9	21.4	21.5	22.8	21.7
10–14	11.6	9.6	9.6	16.9	16.6	16.9	17.3
15 and over	22.2	20.5	19.0	17.7	26.8	31.5	33.1

Sources: 1. US Department of Labor, Bureau of Labor Statistics, *Job Tenure Survey*.
2. Japan, Rōdōshō (Ministry of Labour), *Shūgyō Kōzō Kihon Chōsa* (Survey on Employment Structure).

2.2   UNEMPLOYMENT BY AGE

2.2.1   The Relation of Employment to Output

Until this point, the degree of permanent employment has been assessed by length of service. A worker's length of service can be determined not only by a voluntary decision to leave a company, but also by involuntary redundancy. The concept of permanent employment should not imply no redundancies, which are sometimes required because of the impact of the business cycle on a company's performance.

Redundancies can hardly be avoided if some degree of economic efficiency is to be preserved. Therefore the practice of permanent employment would require instead that in a recession there is less resort to redundancies than elsewhere. An appropriate assessment cannot be made merely by comparing the relative numbers of workers made redundant, because account has to be taken of the degree to which redundancies are necessitated. The decline in output may be adopted as a proxy indicator of the necessity for redundancies. There

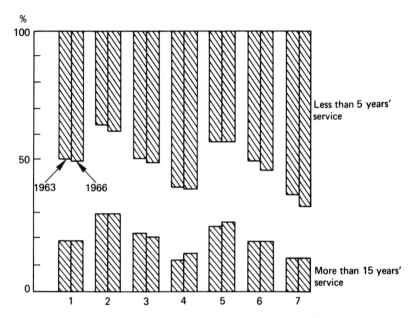

FIGURE 2.3   Length of service by occupation, USA (male workers' proportions for less than five years and more than 15 years of service)

Note: 1. Professional, technical
      2. Managers
      3. Clerical
      4. Sales
      5. Craftsmen
      6. Operatives
      7. Labourers.

Source: US Department of Labor, Bureau of Labor Statistics, *Job Tenure Survey*, *1963*; *1966*.

are data on output indices for manufacturing, but figures on the overall decline in employment have to be used instead of numbers of actual redundancies, for which statistics are generally unavailable. These two sets of data may be used to compare the elasticities of employment with respect to output, which are expressed as the proportionate change in employment divided by the proportionate change in output.

This kind of research has already been carried out by others. Shimada's main results are shown here in Table 2.3. Shinotsuka's work using production functions is more subtle and complex, but her results are not significantly different.[4] The elasticity of labour input,

TABLE 2.3 International comparison of employment elasticities
(proportionate change in employment/proportionate change in output)

	Employment index elasticity					Labour input index elasticity				
				West					West	
	Japan	USA	Britain	Germany	France	Japan	USA	Britain	Germany	France
From November 1973:										
Up to June 1974	0.09	0.43	–	–	–	0.32	3.00	–	–	–
Up to September 1974	0.13	0.26	0.04	0.19	–	0.69	1.23	0.58	0.33	–
Up to December 1974	0.19	0.79	0.16	0.32	0.07	0.59	1.14	0.46	0.52	0.60
Up to March 1975	0.25	0.87	0.34	0.36	0.18	0.85	1.14	0.81	0.91	0.64
Up to June 1975 and follows	0.38	0.85	0.43	–	0.23	0.66	1.07	0.82	–	0.66
Up to September 1975	0.49	0.97	0.58	–	–	0.86	1.20	0.91	–	–
Up to December 1975	0.51	–	–	–	–	0.89	–	–	–	–

Source: Shimada, Haruo, 'Kajō Koyō Ron o Kangaeru' (An Examination of Labour Hoarding) *Nihon Keizai Shinbun* (12 November 1976).

measured by labour hours, and the elasticity of employment with respect to output have both been calculated by Shimada. His research is concentrated on the period immediately after the 1973 oil crisis, because since the 1950s there has been no other period of dramatic general decline in output. It needs to be remarked that the elasticity of employment when output declines would be quite different to the elasticity for a rise in output.

Table 2.3 demonstrates that the USA is the exception rather than Japan, whose position corresponds to that of the Western European countries. In the USA the elasticity of employment is remarkably high, whereas there is little difference between the elasticity for Japan and that for France and West Germany. Note also that the labour input elasticity is greater than the employment elasticity in every country. In other words, before resorting to redundancies output is first regulated by reducing labour hours. In this respect also the policy in Japan of rationalizing production by regulating labour hours is hardly different to what is practised in Western Europe.

Yet the above conclusions are subject to some remaining doubts. Japanese policies of employment rationalization may indeed correspond to Western European practice over the whole economy. But the question remains whether any permanent employment practices are a feature of large companies where employment protection does predominate. This contention, however, cannot be confirmed statistically. Although there are employment indices by company size, only figures on the value of output rather than physical output indices by company size are available. This aspect will therefore instead have to be examined by observing actual practices in large companies, which is done in Chapters 3 and 4.

2.2.2 More Unemployment Among Middle-Aged and Older Japanese Workers

If an employment policy deserves the name of 'permanent employment', then at a time of unavoidable redundancies the longest serving workers should be the ones to retain their jobs. Data on redundancies by age or length of service do not exist, so we will look at unemployment rates by age in order to shed light on this issue.

The EC has carried out a standardized *Labour Force Sample Survey* every other year since 1973. This survey is consistent with the Japanese and US surveys, because households are sampled without regard as to whether the unemployed are actually registered. In the

EC countries whose population is over 50 million (West Germany, France, Italy and the UK) the number of households sampled varies between 60 000 and 100 000, while in the other countries 30 000–50 000 households are sampled. The EC sampling rates thus tend to be higher than in Japan, where out of a total population of over 110 million 33 000 households have been surveyed.

The EC defines the unemployed to be those who state themselves as unemployed and are moreover looking for work. Although this definition could be considered ambiguous, the European survey is essentially consistent with Japan's labour force survey, and a comparison of the data will yield fewer errors than using official national data (where considerable definitional problems arise).

Figure 2.4 is a comparison of unemployment rates by age for Japan, West Germany, the UK and France, based on the labour force surveys. Because the intention is to compare the concentration of unemployment among different age groups rather than the actual unemployment rates, indices have been calculated. The unemployment rates of the 30–49 years old age groups have been averaged in each country and designated as the zero base. Then each age group's unemployment rate is expressed as the percentage point difference between its actual rate and the base rate. This enables us to see in which countries unemployment is concentrated in certain age groups, without any interference from differences in unemployment rates between the countries.

The picture presented by Figure 2.4 shows that the difference between the unemployment rates among young people and the middle-aged is greatest in the UK and narrowest in Japan, with West Germany and France lying midway between the extremes. But in the case of the oldest age groups Japan's position is reversed, having the widest difference with the middle-aged in unemployment rates, followed closely by France, and with West Germany having the narrowest difference. This wide disparity between the positions of Japan and West Germany is particularly striking for the unemployed aged over 55 years; this pattern begins in the early fifties age group where the unemployment rate in both the UK and West Germany is generally below the middle-aged groups, whereas in Japan unemployment is above the base rate.

Exactly the same pattern can be seen when differences in unemployment rates are compared between Japan and the USA. This is shown in Figure 2.5, which uses the same method as Figure 2.4. Although the principles of Japan's survey were originally based on

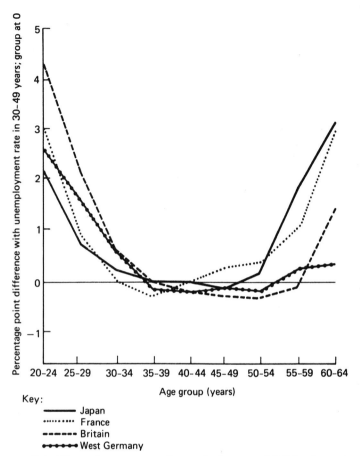

FIGURE 2.4   Unemployment rates by age in Japan and EC (male workers, 1977, percentage point differences in rates with 30–49 year age group as base)

Sources: EC, *Labour Force Sample Survey*, 1977 (Brussels).
Japan, Rōdōshō (Ministry of Labour) *Shōwa 52-nen Rōdōryoku Chōsa Nenpō* (Labour Force Annual Survey Report, 1977).

the US survey methods, certain dissimilarities in application have affected the calculated unemployment rates. Consequently, if the US stipulations were the standard, Japan's unemployment rates would be slightly underestimated – but consideration of this issue has to be left to others' research. The astonishingly high concentration of unemployment among young people in the USA is much greater than in Western Europe. On the other hand the US unemployment rate

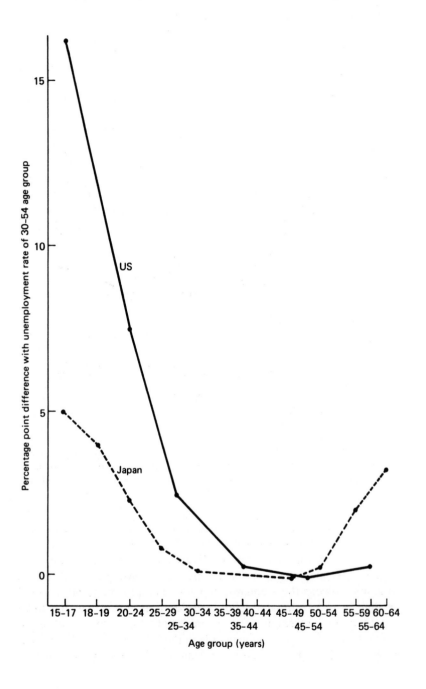

hardly rises at all for those aged over fifty. In Japan, the pattern is quite the reverse.

The above studies suggest that in Japan redundancies are more likely to be concentrated among workers aged over fifty than in the West. This can only be a suggestion rather than a conclusion because some of the unemployed have voluntarily left their jobs; but those choosing to leave a job would be relatively few among the middle-aged and older age groups. The influence of mandatory early retirement ages (*teinen*) in large companies must have affected the unemployment rate for those aged over 55 years. Yet it should be noted that this trend is becoming evident even in the early fifties age group before the customary retirement age. Statistical studies are not sufficient to understand how redundancies are determined. Therefore actual studies of the processes involved will be taken up in Chapters 3 and 4.

NOTES

1. The survey's main results are recorded in the *Monthly Labor Review*, and the detailed results are available in the *Special Labor Force Report*. The *Job Tenure Survey* stems from a supplementary question to the regular monthly 'Current Population Survey' on the labour force, which is statistically reliable because of its high sampling rate. But comparing the results with Japan's *Wage Structure Survey* would be invalid, as the US survey questions households rather than companies. The most appropriate comparison would be with Japan's monthly labour force survey which similarly questions individuals including the self-employed. But Japan's labour force survey does not compile length of service figures.
2. The US survey compiles separate figures for the total employed which includes the self-employed and for non-agricultural employees. But the category of total male employees has been adopted here since its classification of length of service is much more detailed. And the difference between these two categories is fairly negligible, because the proportion

FIGURE 2.5   Unemployment rates by age in Japan and USA (male workers, 1977)

Notes: In the USA the average unemployment rate for the 30–54 age group is 3.3 per cent, and in Japan it is 1.4 per cent.

Sources: USA, US Department of Labor, Bureau of Labor Statistics, *Bulletin 2070*, December 1980.
Japan, Rōdōshō (Ministry of Labour) *Shōwa 52-nen Rōdōryoku Chōsa Nenpo* (1977 Labour Force Survey Annual Report).

of self-employed is low. On the other hand there is a high proportion of self-employed in Japan, so the category of non-agricultural employees, whose classification for continuous years of employment is sufficiently detailed, has been used here.

3. Although the US survey was carried out in 1951, 1963, 1968, 1973 and 1978, the classification is really consistent for only the last three periods. In the case of Japan, figures on continuous years of employment were not compiled before 1959, nor in 1965 and 1968; and the figures for the non-agricultural employees category were confined to 1962 and the 1970s. In 1974, 1977 and 1979 figures were compiled only for those whose employment had not changed in the preceding year. So to estimate the number of workers with less than one year of service, the difference between total employees and those who have stayed in the same employment for more than one year has been calculated.

4. See Shinotsuka and Ishihara(1977).

REFERENCE

Shinotsuka, Eiko and Ishihara, Emiko (1977) 'Oil-shock igo no Koyō Chōsei – 4 kakoku hikaku to Nihon no kibokan hikaku', (Employment Adjustment After Oil Shock – An International Comparison Between Large Firms and Smaller Firms in Japan) *Nihon Keizai Kenkyū* 6, August, pp. 39–52.

3 Workers' Careers in the USA

3.1 INTRODUCTION

The major conclusion emanating from Chapters 1 and 2 has been that blue-collar male workers in large Japanese companies are characterised by white-collarization rather than by the practices of permanent employment (*Shushin koyō*) and seniority based wage systems (*nenkō chingin*). When wage profiles over age and over average length of service were compared in Japan and Western Europe, the closest degree of comparability was found to be between the profiles of European white-collar workers and Japanese blue-collar workers in large companies. What white-collarization really entails can be understood only through following the career path of a blue-collar worker.

Economic theorists usually acknowledge that the factor most strongly influencing wage rate differentials is skills. But, since no method for directly measuring skills has yet been developed, the character of skills can be observed only by using a proxy measure. One common way of acquiring skills is through on-the-job training. Thus one method for observing a worker's skills would be to find out in what kinds of jobs he had become proficient. On-the-job training has the important characteristic of turning a related range of jobs into a blue-collar career; and the cost of on-the-job training in a specific number of jobs can be reduced by ensuring that a worker's present job partly trains him for the jobs to which he will subsequently be assigned. A career can, therefore, be defined here as the way in which a worker progresses through a related series of jobs. This definition enables us to assess the breadth and sophistication of a worker's skills by observing his career. A blue-collar worker's career tends to evolve within a single plant, because closely related jobs within the plant permit a progression course to be structured. An invariable career structure between different companies, even within the same industry, would be highly unlikely, even though skills may not be substantially different. The disparity in career structures between companies has resulted in skills being enterprise specific. But any analysis of enterprise specific skills is hampered by the apparent impossibility of compiling statistics which account for the differences in skills.

Since there are no appropriate statistics, the analysis of workers' careers has to depend on case studies. But consideration of a necessarily limited number of cases lacks completely the comprehensiveness provided by a statistical analysis. So as to compensate for some of the bias inherent in selecting case studies, the research results will be linked with a discussion of partially relevant statistical material. In both Chapters 3 and 4 – concerning respectively the USA and Japan – the results of case study interviews covering labour unions and two dozen companies in each country follow upon an auxiliary statistical analysis. The USA has been selected for comparison because, first, the wage profiles for blue-collar workers in Japan and the USA show a closer resemblance than in the case of Japan and Western Europe. A more revealing observation of the dissimilarities and common features of workers' skills is feasible when the wage profiles bear a closer resemblance. The other justification for making a comparison with the USA is the relative plentifulness of resource material on workers' careers which has been yielded by the US Civil Rights Acts' judgements on discrimination in employment; the Federal District Judges called for meticulous research on how promotion was customarily determined in the cases being disputed.

In order to facilitate the discussion, a rather rough division into three groups of industries has been made on the basis of the kinds of technologies employed: process industries; mass production machinery industries; non-mass production machinery industries. Detailed analyses of all the case studies in these three groups can be found in the Japanese edition *Shokuba no Rōdō Kumiai to Sanka–Rōshi Kankei no Nichibei Hikaku*.[1] For this English edition case studies in the US steel industry have been chosen as an example of a process industry. Subsequently in Chapter 4, where workers' careers in Japanese companies selected from each of the three groups of industries are examined, a comparison may be made with US process industries.

3.2 RESULTS FROM SURVEY ON COLLECTIVE AGREEMENTS

Apart from the US Bureau of Labor Statistics (BLS) survey *Major Collective Bargaining Agreements*, in which workers' careers feature only indirectly, no relevant and comprehensive material is available.[2] Almost all of the collective agreements involving more than 1000 employees have been covered in the BLS survey, whose results are classified under the agreements' clauses. This survey's special value lies in the extent to which the clauses have been detailed. Earlier surveys were held on a small scale only in 1948 and 1951. The survey held in 1970–2 afforded, for the first time a classification of each type of clause, according to the number of workers covered which provides a useful start to this chapter's discussion.

3.2.1 Provisions for Promotion

Under the assumption that workers' careers are primarily furthered within a company, it is necessary to examine the procedure for promotion – namely, the movement of a worker to an assignment with a higher wage rate. The survey has calculated the number of collective agreements and number of workers involved, differentiated by industry, which fall under each of the following categories:

1. Whether the collective agreement includes provisions for promotion
2. Whether the provisions for promotion are detailed
3. Whether seniority is recorded as a factor which influences decisions on promotion
4. What weight is given to seniority in making promotion decisions
5. How the procedures for making promotion decisions have been stipulated.

The second and third categories may be used as indicators of the extent to which an internalization of workers' careers exists. When careers are internalized in the company, it would imply that emphasis is given to promotion opportunities in which seniority is an important factor. The two chosen indicators have been expressed in Figure 3.1 as the relevant proportions out of all workers. There appears to be a fair degree of correlation between the inclusion of detailed provisions

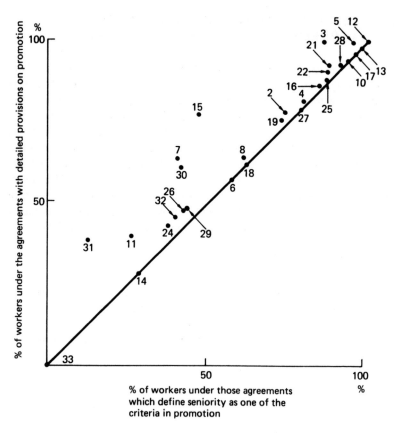

FIGURE 3.1   Detailed provisions on promotion and on seniority (by industry, manufacturing, male, 1961)

Note:

All Industries	1	Petroleum refining and related industries	13
Manufacturing	2	Rubber and miscellaneous plastics products	14
Ordnance and accessories	3	Leather and leather products	15
Food and kindred products	4	Stone, clay, and glass products	16
Tobacco manufacturers	5	Primary metal industries	17
Textile mill products	6	Fabricated metal products	18
Apparel and other finished products	7	Machinery, except electrical	19
Lumber and wood products, except furniture	8	Electrical machinery, equipment, and supplies	20
Furniture and fixtures	9	Transportation equipment	21
Paper and allied products	10	Instruments and related products	22
Printing, publishing, and allied industries	11	Miscellaneous manufacturing industries	23
Chemicals and allied products	12		

for promotion and the importance of seniority as a factor in the provisions. Figure 3.1 leads to the following conclusions concerning the internalization of careers in different industrial groups:

1. Both indicators are positive for more than 80 per cent of the total work force in most of the heavy and chemical industries and in the electricity, gas, communications and tobacco industries. In particular, more than 95 per cent of workers in the chemical, oil refining, primary metals (notably iron and steel), paper and pulp, electricity and gas industries are covered by detailed promotion provisions in which seniority is a factor. Internalized careers appear generally to prevail in the process industries, apart from the rubber industry. The low showing of the rubber industry where internal promotion is acknowledged to be well developed could merely demonstrate the fact that the clauses displayed in collective agreements do not necessarily reflect actual practices. Another exception is fabricated metal products among the heavy and chemical industries, where the presence of relatively many small and medium-sized companies might have precluded any widespread internalization of careers.
2. The industries in which about half of the workers can benefit from internalized careers are light manufacturing and the wholesale, retail and distribution enterprises.
3. Construction is the only industry in which internalization of careers does not apparently exist at all.

The indicators in Figure 3.1 showing the extent of career internalization cannot yield any information on the extent to which workers' careers are actually furthered. It does appear, however, from the discussion later in this chapter, that in the process industries, where the internalization of careers according to the indicators is most widespread, the depth of workers' careers is also considerable. Nonetheless

Non-manufacturing	24	Wholesale trade	29
		Retail trade	30
Mining, crude petroleum, and		Hotels and restaurants	31
natural gas production	25	Services	32
Transportation	26	Construction	33
Communications	27	Miscellaneous non-manufacturing	
Utilities: electric and gas	28	industries	34

Source: US Department of Labor, Bureau of Labor Statistics, *Bulletin* 1425–11.

it would not be legitimate to make any a *priori* judgement on the depth of workers' careers without close observation of their actual structure.

3.2.2 Procedures for Promotion

The extent to which seniority determines the order of promotion can be an important indicator of the degree to which labour, rather than management, has a voice in decisions on promotion. Procedures for promotion were classified under the following headings by the number of agreements and the number of workers covered:

1. 'Posting-bidding': when a position becomes vacant, it is advertized in the workplace. We cannot tell, though, if the choice among several applicants depends upon seniority (with managerial discretion at a minimum) or upon the relative merit ratings given by management.
2. 'Automatic consideration': This category seems to imply that the order of promotion is an indisputable rule which is settled in advance of any vacancy arising. Consequently the vacant post would not even be advertised in the workplace. Priority would probably be given to the worker whose position in the workshop falls immediately under the vacant position.
3. 'Employee request': The only real difference with the first category would be that the worker lodged beforehand a request with the personnel officer to move to another post. The way of choosing whom to promote among the applicants has again not been specified, as in the first category.
4. 'Company discretion'.
5. Various amalgamations centred on categories 1 and 2.

From the viewpoint of the extent to which labour could have some say in the procedures for promotion, the following three groups may be distinguished:

(a) Category 4, in which labour obviously has no say at all.
(b) Category 2 which leaves hardly any margin for managerial discretion. Thus the indisputability of 'automatic consideration' means that labour has been given some control over promotion procedures. Even in combination with categories 1 and 3, this category could still be seen as permitting labour to have a relatively large say.

(c) Categories 1 and 3, and any amalgamation of these, leave the question of the extent of labour's control completely open.

Each of the three groups' coverage of workers has been displayed in Table 3.1. Almost all of the workers surveyed fall under the ambiguous group (c). Since, however, only 1 per cent of the workers are covered by group (a) – 'company discretion' – the situation in which labour has absolutely no say in promotion procedures is exceptional. Group (b) – 'automatic consideration' and any of its combinations cover less than 9 per cent of the workers. But broken down by industry, the coverage is more than 50 per cent of the workers surveyed in the oil refining and paper and pulp industries, along with more than 20 per cent of electric and gas workers and chemical industry workers. Whereas in other industries, the proportions of workers covered by 'automatic consideration' is very low, relatively many process industry workers could be considered as having some say in promotion procedures.

In conclusion, it appears that among procedures for promotion the method of 'posting-bidding' tends to predominate according to the survey results, although 'automatic consideration' is quite prevalent in some of the process industries. But these indicators have still not provided any insight into the degree to which labour has some say in promotion. The next step, therefore, is to examine the weight given to the seniority principle in the decision on which workers to promote.

3.2.3 Seniority as a Factor in Promotion

The extent to which seniority plays a part in promotion, as recorded in the clauses of collective agreements, has been analyzed by the BLS survey in five categories:

1. The sole factor
2. The primary factor
3. A secondary factor
4. Equally important to other factors
5. Others.

The survey did not attempt to define or to explain these categories, which appear merely to have reiterated the literal expressions used in collective agreements. The most appropriate approach for assessing the degree to which labour has some say would be to concentrate on

TABLE 3.1 Procedures for promotion (USA collective agreements, 1970–1, all industries, percentage of workers covered)

	Total no. of workers surveyed	Group (c) 'posting-bidding employee request' and their combinations with other methods	Of Group (c) 'posting-bidding'	Group (b) 'automatic consideration' and its combination with other methods	Group (a) 'company discretion'
All industries	100.0	31.2	18.9	8.7	1.0
Manufacturing	100.0	42.7	23.9	11.6	0.8
Food and kindred products	100.0	66.3	62.5	7.2	–
Tobacco manufacturers	100.0	21.3	21.3	10.2	–
Textile mill products	100.0	39.8	36.5	5.5	–
Apparel and other finished products	100.0	0.6	–	–	–
Lumber and wood product, except furniture	100.0	27.9	27.9	19.1	–
Furniture and fixtures	100.0	33.1	33.1	–	–
Paper and allied products	100.0	19.0	19.0	57.4	–
Printing, publishing, and allied industries	100.0	6.5	2.1	16.4	–
Chemicals and allied products	100.0	38.6	31.1	22.4	–

Petroleum refining and related industries	100.0	24.1	6.1	55.4	–
Rubber and miscellaneous plastics products	100.0	14.6	11.8	1.0	–
Leather and leather products	100.0	26.3	26.3	–	–
Stone, clay, and glass products	100.0	54.9	53.7	1.9	–
Primary metal industries	100.0	76.4	58.5	11.9	–
Fabricated metal products	100.0	36.7	24.0	1.4	–
Machinery, except electrical	100.0	53.8	16.5	10.7	1.7
Electrical machinery, equipment, and supplies	100.0	24.8	16.8	13.2	–
Transportation equipment	100.0	44.7	5.5	13.2	3.0
Instruments and related products	100.0	32.1	22.1	15.5	–
Non-manufacturing	100.0	14.3	12.7	5.2	1.2
Mining, crude petroleum, and natural gas production	100.0	15.7	51.7	4.6	–
Transportation	100.0	31.1	30.3	2.5	–
Communications	100.0	25.7	19.7	11.9	6.0
Utilities: Electric and gas	100.0	35.5	32.5	28.5	–
Wholesale trade	100.0	17.7	17.7	–	–
Retail trade	100.0	8.4	5.9	13.0	1.7
Hotels and restaurants	100.0	–	–	1.5	–
Services	100.0	7.7	7.7	1.4	–
Construction	100.0	–	–	25.8	–

Source: See Figure 3.1.

the unambiguous definitions in categories 1 and 2 where the seniority principle prevails. Table 3.2 displays the proportions who are accounted for by categories 1 and 2 out of the total numbers of workers surveyed in each industry.

There were relatively few collective agreements in which seniority had been treated as the sole or primary factor in decisions on promotion. The only industries in which 70–90 per cent of workers were covered by categories 1 and 2 are transport equipment, tobacco, communications and petroleum. In the other manufacturing industries these factors account for less than 40 per cent of workers, apart from for the paper and applied industry workers where the seniority factor unambiguously operates for almost 50 per cent; there are few workers in the chemicals, rubber and primary metal goods industries for whom seniority appears to be the sole or primary factor in promotion. In order to judge whether the substantial differences revealed by the survey which appear even among the process industries apply merely to the collective agreements or accurately reflect disparities in the degree to which the seniority principle is important, case studies are essential.

The general conclusion from examining the results of the survey on collective agreements is that the significance of seniority in promotion is rather low, apart from a minority of industries. Apparently other factors, such as ability, are stated to be important. The clauses of collective agreements thus imply that management would inevitably have considerable discretion in decisions on promotion, even though managerial control does not extend as far as complete 'company discretion'. Alternatively, the question arises of whether or not the clauses of collective agreements do reflect actual procedures. There are substantial disagreements between the results of the few valuable research studies undertaken previously – notably the Brooks and Gamm survey (1955) in the paper and pulp industry[3] and the Shiba survey (1973) in the electric power industry.[4] Nonetheless these surveys do conclude that seniority has played a significant role in promotion to the extent that there must evidently be some disparity between reality and what is written into collective agreements.

3.2.4 Provisions for Transfers

A worker would not usually move along a straight career path on which he is successively promoted. Even for the worker staying

TABLE 3.2   Role of seniority in promotion (USA collective agreements, 1970–1, manufacturing industries, percentage of workers)

Industry	Total no. of workers surveyed	'Sole' or 'primary' factor	'Secondary factor' or 'equal with other factors'
All industries	100	14.7	33.1
Manufacturing	100	17.8	43.9
Food and kindred products	100	36.2	35.1
Tobacco manufacturers	100	72.1	18.4
Textile mill products	100	32.0	16.9
Apparel and other finished products	100	–	30.0
Lumber and wood products, except furniture	100	26.0	16.7
Furniture and fixtures	100	27.9	9.5
Paper and allied products	100	48.8	31.5
Printing, publishing, and allied industries	100	15.4	4.0
Chemicals and allied products	100	23.0	63.5
Petroleum refining and related industries	100	71.9	61.4
Rubber and miscellaneous plastics products	100	14.2	8.1
Leather and leather products	100	16.9	8.6
Stone, clay, and glass products	100	22.3	62.7
Primary metal industries	100	18.4	73.9
Fabricated metal products	100	34.2	20.1
Machinery, except electrical	100	25.4	35.2
Electrical machinery, equipment, and supplies	100	18.1	27.7
Transportation equipment	100	89.1	66.9
Instruments and related products	100	43.8	13.8

Source: See Figure 3.1.

within a single company, there are occasions when he may have to transfer to positions which are unrelated to his career. The clauses of collective agreements which are concerned with transfers should, therefore, be examined. One problem is that transfers are viewed rather differently in the USA and Japan. Both countries generally interpret a 'transfer' as the movement of a worker from one workplace to another without any accompanying change in his wage rate, and both countries distinguish between voluntary and involuntary transfers. However, there is a difference in the relative numbers of voluntary and involuntary transfers. In Japan, involuntary transfers overwhelmingly predominate, and workers accordingly view transfers as generally being disadvantageous. Among US workers – or at least their labour unions – the feeling of disadvantage seems to be much less powerful, since transfers are usually on a voluntary basis.

The adverse view of transfers in Japan also arises from the fact that the word 'transfer' includes workers having to move to another plant within the company. Such relocation is rare among blue-collar workers in the USA where a transfer usually implies only a move in the same plant to a different workshop. In fact even in Japan transfers within a plant are much more common than relocation, but workers have tended to focus on the adverse implication of having to move to another plant. Thus US and Japanese workers tend to have different views of transfers. At this point, following our analysis of the careers of US workers, we will focus on voluntary permanent transfers occurring within a single plant.

The BLS survey classified the collective agreements under three headings:

1. Whether provisions for transfers are included
2. What procedures are entailed
3. Whether seniority is a determining factor.

In the case of transfers, the survey did not provide any breakdown by industry. Table 3.3, in which the survey results are tabulated, shows first that there are fewer collective agreements with provisions for transfers than in the case of promotion. The proportion of workers covered by detailed provisions for promotion was 63 per cent, while the coverage of transfer provisions is only 51 per cent. The reason for this disparity is not apparent. One supposition might be that transfers which require workers to move between different career paths are exceptional in contrast to the normal occurrence of promotion in which the job changes within a career. The second point to be noted from Table 3.3 is that employee requests to be transferred overwhelmingly accounted for the instigation of transfer procedures. The actual procedures were similar to those for promotion. An applicant for transfer would indicate beforehand the desired position so that he could be considered for any vacancies arising there. The other

TABLE 3.3   Provisions on transfers (USA collective agreements, 1967–8, all industries, percentage of workers)

Total		100.0
With provisions on transfers		54.2
With detailed provisions on transfers		51.3
Procedures for transfers	Procedures indicated:	41.1
	Job posting and bidding	7.8
	Automatic consideration	0.5
	Employee request	34.0
	Company discretion	1.4
	Unclear	0.4
	Other	0.1
Role of seniority	Seniority as one of criteria:	38.8
	Sole factor	1.4
	Primary factor	27.1
	Secondary factor	6.2
	Equal factor	0.1
	Ambiguous	3.8
	Other	0.3

Source: See Figure 3.1.

procedural approaches are variants on the 'posting-bidding' method. But for neither of these transfer procedures did the survey indicate the extent to which labour had a say in the matter.

An alternative way of assessing labour's control is to use the yardstick of the role of seniority, which has been set out in the final section of Table 3.3. Those collective agreements in which seniority is the sole or primary factor in deciding which applicant to transfer cover 28.5 per cent of all the workers surveyed. This figure, though quite low, is higher than the 14.7 per cent of workers covered by agreements in which seniority played the major role in promotion decisions. Indeed, since only 41.1 per cent of workers are covered by any kind of procedures for transfers in collective agreements, for almost 70 per cent of those workers seniority is the sole or primary factor. In conclusion, relatively fewer workers are covered by appropriate clauses for transfers when compared to the coverage of provisions for promotion. But the proportion of appropriate provisions in which seniority plays the major role is somewhat higher in the care of transfers.

3.2.5   Provisions for Redundancies

The devastating impact on the career of a worker who has been made redundant is crucial. The three major issues to be considered when there is a threat of redundancies are:

1. How many workers should be made redundant?
2. Who should be made redundant?
3. What priority in rehiring should be given?

While the significance of 1 and 3 ought to be self-evident, some additional remarks must be made concerning the second question. There arises (in a similar way to the case of promotion and transfer procedures) the issue of managerial discretion in selecting the workers to be made redundant. If the management had complete discretion in making the selection, the labour union would be vulnerable insofar as its shop stewards could be made redundant. Shopfloor workers would, therefore, become reluctant to be shop stewards. Even though the union structure of officials and members might still be maintained, the activities of shop stewards in looking after the interests of their fellow workers, which is the basis of the union's existence, would tend to diminish.

The general impression from our research was that US labour unions permit management to make the decision on how many workers to make redundant, while maintaining close surveillance over the two remaining issues. A Japanese enterprise labour union, in contrast, does attempt to influence the decision on the number of workers to be made redundant; but its initial vigilance can ultimately be undermined, particularly during a severe recession. Consequent upon the enterprise union's defeat on this issue, managerial discretion is also conceded on the decisions about whom to make redundant and the guarantee of rehiring.

3.2.6   How Many Workers to Make Redundant

The question of whether collective agreements had made provisions for procedures to negotiate the number of redundancies was not really addressed in the BLS survey. The survey was instead apparently confined to the issue of whether there was any stipulation for prior notification of threatened redundancies. The collective agreements surveyed at the same time do contain clauses which place various restrictions on the conditions appropriate for instigating redundancies. In particular, there are provisions for reaching agreement on ways to cope with a decline in operations before effecting any reductions in the number of employees. The survey accordingly made the following classifications:

1. Whether provisions for averting redundancies are included
2. Whether those provisions entail:

(a) An equal distribution of available work
(b) Rotation of employment
(c) Reduction in the hours worked

Figure 3.2 has been constructed using the figures from categories 1, 2(a) and 2(c), because once the printing and publishing industry is excluded only a few collective agreements contained provisions for rotating employment. The following observations can be drawn from Figure 3.2.

1. Provisions for averting redundancies are not usual. Although such provisions apply to almost 50 per cent of the workers covered by collective agreements drawn up in manufacturing enterprises, the corresponding proportion in non-manufacturing enterprises falls below 20 per cent, while in the metal industries the proportion is a mere 36 per cent.
2. The majority of collective agreements making provisions for averting redundancies have adopted the measure of reducing working hours. The usual stipulation is that redundancies can be instigated when operations have fallen below a 32 hour working week.
3. The proportion of collective agreements in the light industries – apparel, textiles and leather – with provisions for staving off redundancies by dividing the available work equally is relatively high. Especially in the apparel industry collective agreements remarkably refuse to recognize any potential need for redundancies. Instead the relevant clauses state that employment can be cut only through reducing working hours.
4. In the majority of non-manufacturing industries provisions for averting redundancies are rare. In the construction industry, where skilled artisans are tantamount to being self-employed, there are no instances at all of such provisions. It may be speculated that

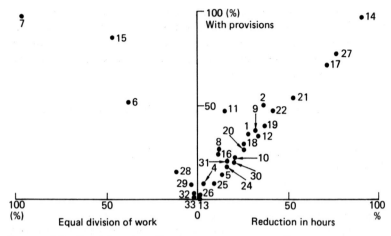

FIGURE 3.2   Provisions in collective agreements on adjustments to output decreases (USA, all industries, 1970–1, percentage of workers under such agreements)

Note: For industry notation, see Figure 3.1.

Source: US Department of Labor, Bureau of Labor Statistics, *Bulletin* 1425–13.

construction workers prefer to be responsible for regulating their own employment and can therefore dispense with appropriate collective agreements.

The overall conclusion may be that while there are few collective agreements with preconditions for instigating redundancies, in that event the most commonly prescribed measure is a reduction in labour hours. Even more striking is the paucity of clauses which lay down any conditions for negotiating the number of redundancies. This is an issue in which apparently the labour unions have barely any say.

3.2.7   Whom to Make Redundant?

The story takes on a very different appearance once the second issue of whom to make redundant is considered. Our observations indicate that the US labour unions exercise control by making a selection in advance – just as though the management's wishes play no part. Table 3.4 depicts the importance of seniority in determining whom should be made redundant. If one excludes those collective agreements in which the decision is left up to the individual plant, the proportion of workers covered solely or primarily by the principle of

TABLE 3.4   Role of seniority in lay-off (USA collective agreements, 1970–1, all industries, percentage of workers)

Total	*100.0*	
With provisions where seniority is one of the criteria	99.9	
(1) Sole factor	24.0	32.0
(2) Primary factor	34.5	46.1
(3) (1) + (2)	58.5	78.2
(4) Secondary factor	14.0	18.7
(5) Equal factor	–	–
(6) Unclear	2.1	2.8
(7) Varies with situation	0.3	0.4
(8) Total of (1) – (7)	74.8	100.0
(9) Subject to local negotiation	25.1	

Source: See Figure 3.2.

seniority in effecting redundancies is 78.2 per cent. This figure is much higher than the proportion covered by the seniority principle in the case of promotions and transfers. Even though the inclusion of all collective agreements would bring the proportion down to 58.5 per cent, the individual plants would actually have chosen often to abide by the seniority principle. It appears, therefore, that most labour unions ensure that managers will be left with very little scope should they ever try to contravene the seniority principle by making workers with longer years of service redundant.

3.2.8   Whom to Rehire

A lay-off in the USA implies an involuntary redundancy, but with some priority in rehiring once production turns upwards again. Since involuntary redundancies usually now have provisions for priority in rehiring, the terms 'lay-off' and 'redundancy' have become almost synonymous. The essential distinction as to whether priority in rehiring is given has not been overtly dealt with in the BLS survey, because in the USA the practice of rehiring before seeking new recruits is so pervasive, should employment capacity expand once more after a downturn. The survey has addressed instead the issue of whether seniority is a factor in the procedures set up for selecting whom to rehire.

It is apparent from Table 3.5 that the clauses which follow the strict seniority principle in granting priority in rehiring cover around 75 per

TABLE 3.5   Role of seniority in recall hiring (USA collective agreements, 1970–1, all industries, percentage of workers)

Total	*100.0*	
With provision where seniority is one of the criteria	97.7	
(1) Sole factor	21.3	29.4
(2) Primary factor	33.1	46.3
(3) (1) + (2)	54.1	75.7
(4) Secondary factor	13.3	18.6
(5) Equal factor	2.0	2.8
(6) Unclear	1.7	2.4
(7) Various with situation	0.3	0.5
(8) Total of (1) − (7)	71.6	100.0
(9) Subject to local negotiation	26.1	

Source: See Figure 3.2.

cent of the surveyed workers. This proportion is close to that for seniority being a major factor in selecting which workers to make redundant. The remaining 25 per cent of workers are covered by clauses which are ambiguous over the role of seniority in practice. A time limit is generally attached to the period in which there would be priority in rehiring. Usually the time limit roughly matches the worker's number of years of service with the company.

It thus appears that about three-quarters of the surveyed workers maintain control over the issues of whom to make redundant and the procedures for giving priority in rehiring. While there may have been some room for management discretion to play a part in the case of the remaining workers, the collective agreement clauses do not clarify whether the management's selection would be based on such potentially controversial factors as ability. This question has therefore to be answered through a perusal of case studies.

3.2.9 Summary

The BLS survey's classification of the clauses of collective agreements has enabled us to make a rough assessment of the industries in which careers are internalized and of the extent to which labour has some say in decisions concerning promotion, transfers and redundancies:

1. In the heavy and chemical industries careers are generally widely internalized.

2. Internalization of careers appears to be especially pervasive in the process industries.
3. Nevertheless, no assessment can yet be made of the depth to which careers have been internalized in these industries.
4. Promotion procedures are usually based on the 'posting-bidding' system in which the role of seniority is merely secondary and fairly insignificant.
5. Permanent transfers, which are mostly voluntary, give a somewhat greater role to seniority than in the case of promotion but other factors still play a considerable part.
6. The labour unions exercise hardly any influence over the decision on the number of workers to make redundant. But around 75 per cent of workers are covered by collective agreement clauses which ensure that the issues of whom to make redundant and whom to rehire are governed by seniority rights.

The criteria we have used suggest that labour has little say in the procedures for promotion and transfers. Nonetheless, a greater role for the seniority principle has been demonstrated in the few meticulous case studies which have been undertaken. This apparent disparity between the collective agreement clauses and the actual procedures practised needs to be more closely examined.

3.3 LINES OF PROGRESSION IN A STEELWORKS

3.3.1 Fair Employment Practice Cases

Internal promotion appeared from Figure 3.1 to be relatively prevalent in the heavy and chemical industries, especially the process industries among which are included iron and steel. It is fortunate, therefore, that evidence from the early 1970s concerning workers' careers in an integrated steel plant is available.

Our evidence comes from lawsuits involving US Steel's Fairfield works. Although internal promotion was known to be prevalent in US steelworks, there had been few detailed records of the actual promotion routes. Then at the beginning of the 1970s relevant material on a few cases arose from the Federal Court judgements pertaining to the Civil Rights Act Title 7. The usual procedures for the promotion of shopfloor workers had to be spelt out in order to demonstrate violations against the Act's prohibition of racial discrimination in employment. The recommendations and damages resulting from lawsuits, in which major companies' management and labour unions were the defendants, have been recorded in *Fair Employment Practice Cases*.[5]

Major companies, including the US Steel Corporation which is the industry's leader and the Bethlehem Steel Corporation, as well as their local unions, which are associated with the United Steelworkers' of America Union, were implicated in lawsuits concerning discrimination in promotion routes. But prior to 1973 the promotion routes were clearly mapped out so as to display all the judicial precedents only in the following three judgements:

(a) US Steel's Fairfield works: 42 promotion routes were graphed[6]
(b) A small integrated works centred on steel pipe manufacture: 23 promotion routes were graphed[7]
(c) An electric furnace and rolling mill work with 750 employees: 20 promotion routes were graphed.[8]

Our discussion here will concentrate on the first case judgement. Out of about 20 steelworks operated by US Steel, the Fairfield works is one of the largest, so it is an appropriate example of a giant integrated steelworks.[9] There will also be some reference to the judgement concerning another giant integrated works – the Lackwanna plant of Bethlehem steel – though a graphic representation of its promotion routes was not provided. Supplementary information is available from the records of my interviews with representatives of both management and labour at an other giant integrated steelworks and with officials of the United Steelworkers of America Union at headquarters and at district level.[10]

There were about 12 000 regular employees at the Fairfield integrated steelworks,[11] one of the largest operated by US Steel. Though this figure would initially suggest a larger scale than that of a Japanese steelworks, employees in the USA also handle most of those jobs which in Japan would be given to temporary workers and inplant subcontract workers. Thus, in terms of the total number of workers, the scale of the Fairfield works would actually be similar to a large Japanese steelworks. The hourly paid workers, who do not include foremen, amounted to 9100 production and maintenance workers distributed among more than 1000 job groups. The steel industry's system of job classification in the postwar period has been widely discussed. The system entailed dividing hourly paid workers' jobs into 33 job grades. The lowest hourly job rate at the Fairfield works in 1971 was US$4.305 for grades one and two and the highest rate was US$7.505 in grade 34, with a differential of 10 cents between each adjacent pair of the intervening grades. The differential in the job rate between the highest and the lowest grades was thus 74 per cent.[12] It needs to be emphasized that these job rates applied only to rank and file shopfloor workers, while foremen were earning different rates.

Decisions concerning the setting up of the 33 job grades and associated rates were wholly conditional upon the collective agreement between US Steel and the United Steelworkers' of America Union. The rate for each job grade was, therefore, invariable over all US Steel's plants. But the decision on which grade should be attached to which job was almost always made at the plant level. The procedure laid down in the national agreement was for the plant management to make a proposal, which would be followed by negotiations with the plant union committee on job classification. (The relevant clauses were recorded in Article 9, sections 5.1–5.4, which has been generally abbreviated in the following as 9.51–9.54.) If negotiations failed to reach a resolution, the management's proposals would be put into effect. As the same time, a procedure for appeal could lead to further negotiations between the national union and US Steel, though this was rarely adopted in such a large company. So it was at plant level that decisions affecting a worker's career were made, and it was within each plant that career formation took place.

What is significant is that the career structure itself should determine the worker's wage received over the long term, rather than focussing merely on the job rate for the job grade where he happens to be posted at the time of negotiations. Obviously the wage differentials between workers would persist indefinitely if there were no internal promotion, as the workers would remain in their originally assigned grades. But when there is an opportunity for some workers to be promoted right to the top of the job grade ladder, their long term wages do not just reflect their original assignments. The next step, then, is to examine the formation of a worker's career.

3.3.2 The Labour Pool

A production worker's career commences once he has entered employment through the 'port of entry' which is one of the lowest job grades – certainly not above grade four.[13] Subsequently the worker could take advantage of opportunities to be promoted to jobs at higher grades. Interviews with representatives of management and labour yielded the consistent reply that even those workers who had had considerable experience in similar jobs in other companies in the same industry always had to enter employment in a low job grade. The rigidity with which employment entrance conforms to this pattern may be better understood when promotion and transfers, which permit an internal labour market to function, are studied later in this chapter. The function of the external labour market, which exists across companies, is merely to provide an opportunity for employment entrance which is confined to the lowest job grades. In the US, steel industry promotion takes place within the workshop. A worker can rise up a ladder of grades known as 'lines of progression'. The lengths of different progression lines could show considerable variation, ranging from long lines extending over more than 30 grades to others not going beyond grade seven or eight. The distinction between the lines of progression and the labour pool is essential to an understanding of industrial relations in the US steel industry. The functions and the nature of the labour pool above all provide the key to any relevant analysis.

Close observation has interestingly revealed that a functional equivalent to the US labour pool does exist in a large Japanese steelworks. Identifying and comparing the functions of labour pools and their counterparts in Japan should, therefore, be of prime importance:

1. The work in the labour pool and its Japanese counterpart is unskilled – loading and unloading materials, transportation and miscellaneous jobs – and receives low pay.
2. One major difference is that the workers in a US labour pool are employees of the US Steel Corporation, while their Japanese counterparts are employees not of the large company, but of smaller companies which are subcontracted to do transporting and miscellaneous work. Since these workers are not included in the large company's employment contracts, they are known in Japan as '*shagai-kō*', of which the direct translation is 'outside workers', even though they are working every day within the large company's plant. The second major different is that these Japanese inplant subcontract workers are responsible for a greater range of work than the workers in US labour pools. From these two basic differences stem the following disparities between the functions of the two groups.

3. The labour pool is almost the only way for a blue-collar worker to enter a US steelworks. Even a worker who has had considerable experience in a similar occupation in another steelworks cannot be directly recruited into an upper grade job. Since the Japanese counterpart workers are not employed by the large company, their jobs cannot function as a port of entry.

4. When the labour market becomes slack, the labour pool has to take on the burden of redundancies. Usually there are more than ten workshops above a labour pool. The workers in a workshop with surplus labour are downgraded to the pool, from which the least senior workers are instead made redundant. The Japanese counterpart workers' similar role as a shock absorber is far less. The large company's surplus employees cannot easily be moved into the 'outside workers' jobs. Consequently the Japanese company's adjustment capability is less – or at least no larger – than of the US steelworks. In general, the larger the labour pool the better is the adjustment capability, while the more rigid is the demarcation between jobs and between employment contracts, the worse is the adjustment capability. In Japan, the functional equivalent of a labour pool is larger than in the USA, but the demarcation is more rigid. Therefore the contention that the Japanese industrial system can exploit its dual structure to permit a better adjustment capability than in the USA is highly controversial.

5. The US workers in the labour pool are members of the local union, while their Japanese counterparts are either unorganised or belong to a different union than that of the large company's employees, both of which are, however, affiliated to the same National Federation of Steelworkers' Unions. In spite of the disparities outlined above, industrial relations in both Japan and the USA depend upon there being distinct groups for the lowest paid workers, which play to differing extents the role of shock absorber.

Case studies in the USA have shown that the size and functions of labour pools have to be agreed between the labour union and the management. This is because of the need to coordinate the different union interest groups who are concerned about the response to a contraction in employment, and workers can thereby regulate matters concerning employment protection. Our description in outline has indicated that the larger is the labour pool relative to the number of shopfloor workers already on lines of progression, the greater is their employment protection. Workers on progression lines also enjoy a greater degree of employment protection, to the extent that the labour pool is more broadly based below more lines of workshops. In both cases, the corollary is that the workers in the labour pool would face a higher probability of being made redundant. The size and the breadth of the labour pool are thus of prime importance to the company's workers.

While bearing the above points in mind, the relevant clauses of the US Steel Corporation's collective agreement are given below:

(a) The labour pool's breadth 'in no event shall be less than a major operating unit such as Blast Furnace, Coke Plant, Open Hearth, etc.; however, rolling facilities need not necessarily be considered as one unit but shall nevertheless be as broad as practicable'.

(b) The labour pool's size 'shall incorporate all workers who are in the first, second and third job grades and two-thirds of those in the fourth job grade'. (13.32).

(c) The jobs done by pool workers 'shall be separately agreed between the plant management and plant union in each plant' (13.31).

Agreements made at plant level have consequently clearly indicated the breadth of each pool by their listing of all the jobs. The labour pool's structure, therefore, differs between plants as well as between companies.[14]

3.3.3 The Structure of Progression Lines

It has been observed that there are more than ten progression lines above one labour pool, and that a progression line's structure is wholly determined at the plant level. But neither the kinds of jobs incorporated in each line or their sequence were indicated in the plant agreement. The mere listing of the names of all the progression lines – though probably sufficiently informative for those working in the plant – is not clear to the outside observer. The Federal District Court's written judgement on promotion procedures in the Fairfield works, in which there is a graphic representation of the progression lines, becomes especially useful at this point. The judgement mapped out 42 of the existing progression lines which were required to be

TABLE 3.6   Job ladder in each progression line (USA steel industry)

No. of rungs in a progression line	No. of progression lines	No. of rungs in a progression line	No. of progression lines
1	–	10	2
2	6	11	1
3	4	12	1
4	8	13	1
5	7	14	
6	3	15	
7	5	16	
8	3	17	
9	–	18	1

Source: Bureau of National Affairs, *Fair Employment Practice Cases*, vol. 5, pp. 1272–96.

modified with the intention of removing discrimination against black workers. All of these 42 lines have been summarised and displayed in Tables 3.6 and 3.7. These 42 lines were less than one-fifth of all the steelworker's progression lines, which appear to have amounted to more than 200; and since it was these 42 lines which had to be modified there is the problem of it being a biased rather than a random selection. The judgement noted that white workers had generally been positioned on long progression lines, while black workers had been confined to short lines. The judgement primarily required that short progression lines should be combined with related longer lines. The 42 lines appearing in the judgement must thus have included relatively many of the short lines out of the total of more than 200. This supposition has received circumstantial evidence from the absence among the 42 lines of both the mainline progression lines in the blast furnace and open hearth and also the rolling mill's lines, which extended as far the 30th job grades. Evidently there must have been considerable disparities in the structure of different progression lines, which have not been adequately reflected in the 42 examples appearing in the Fairfield judgement.

These qualifications must be borne in mind while examining Tables 3.6 and 3.7. It is apparent from Table 3.6 that the number of grades on a progression line could vary from as few as two to more than ten. Table 3.7 has given examples of the progression lines, along with the differentials in rates over the number of grades to which the lines extended. The following four types of progression lines can be distinguished.

TABLE 3.7 Progression lines (USA steel industry)

Highest job grade in the progression line	% differential between the highest wages in the progression line and the wages for job grade 1–2	No. of progression lines	Job content of the progression line
6	9.3	2	Weighing raw materials; raw material crane operators
7	11.6	–	–
8	13.9	7	Crane operators
9	16.3	3	Crane operators; truck drivers
10	18.6	2	Rear processors, billet rolling mill
11	20.9	3	Crane operator of hot metal; boilerman, engine room
12	23.2	8	Rear processors, strip mill, rail rolling mill; maintenance, furnaces
13	25.6	3	Transportation around open hearth; power in moulding shops, maintenance of open hearth furnace
14	27.9	5	Stove operators; blast furnace transportation; reheating furnace operators, billet mill
15	30.2	–	–
16	32.5	3	Tin plate mill operators
17	34.8	–	–
18	37.2	–	–
19	39.5	1	Reheating furnace operators, slab mill
20	41.8	1	Operators, engine room
24	51.1	2	Assistant charges, open hearth; rollers billet mill
27	58.1	2	Rollers, blooming mill; rollers, rail mill

Source: Bureau of National Affairs *Fair Employment Practice Cases*, vol. 5, pp. 1274–96.

1. There was really no career structure for a worker on a short progression line, which reached up to only the eighth job grade. The job rate differential between the lowest job grade and the eighth grade was a mere 14 per cent. The kinds of jobs with short progression lines were principally related to loading, transportation and some parts of crane operations. These cranemen, who do not include those handling heated rolled steel, in Japan would usually be among the ranks of inplant subcontract workers ('outside workers').

2. Workers' careers in workshops whose progression lines reached up to grade 12 or 14 should also be considered shallow, because the associated rates rose by only 23 to 28 per cent. These jobs, such as shearing and transporting, would in Japan probably also be entrusted to inplant subcontract workers.

3. Those jobs whose job rates over the progression lines rose by more than 30 per cent would be done by regular employees in Japanese companies. Such jobs are located in the main workshops of non-mainline departments and in ancillary workshops of mainline departments, and the rates, which extended over 15 to 20 job grades, rose by between 30 and 42 per cent.

4. The four progression lines whose job rate differentials over 24 to 27 job grades was between 51 and 58 per cent appear to have been in the mainline department main workshops. But, according to the examples of job rates given in the BLS survey,[15] the highest job grade in the rolling mill is usually above grade 30. Therefore the examples of long progression lines provided by the Fairfield judgement are not wholly representative of the depth of careers in the mainline department main workshops.

The 42 examples of progression lines appearing in the Fairfield judgement do not therefore accurately reflect the total body of lines in the steelworks. Since the short lines were probably overrepresented, the relative number of progression lines in types 3 and 4 should be higher than appears from Table 3.7 (though this cannot easily be substantiated). What is obvious is that there were considerable disparities between progression lines in length and in the job rate differentials. The job rate rose by merely 15 per cent to, at the most, 30 per cent on the shallow progression lines where the jobs resemble those undertaken in Japan by 'outside workers', while on progression lines for workers whose jobs are similar to those of Japanese regular workers the differential was 30–40 per cent in non-mainline departments and 50–60 per cent in the main workshops of mainline departments.

3.3.4   The Seniority Factor in Collective Agreements and in Practice

A progression line implies a job ladder, but the procedure and the order under which workers are promoted up the ladder could not be clarified, even with reference to the collective agreements. In the national agreement between the US Steel Corporation and the United Steel Workers union, the relevant clause states:

> in all cases of promotion, the following factors as listed below shall be considered; however, only where factors 'a' and 'b' are relatively equal shall length of continuous service be the determining factor: a Ability to perform the work, b Physical fitness, c Continuous service (Art. 13.03).

A literal interpretation of this clause would suggest that the primary factors determining who should be promoted are ability and fitness. But these two factors are open to various interpretations and problems, such as whether their assessment should depend wholly on the merit rating made by supervisors. The national agreement has evaded these issues and left a wide margin to be decided by the local agreements. The Fairfield works' local agreement was not available, but in another local agreement the relevant articles are similar to those in the national agreement apart from there being more detailed provision for length of service.[16] This provision stipulates that the most senior person should be promoted among those who are occupying the position just below the vacant one, in the case of ability to perform the work and physical fitness being relatively equal. So ability and fitness remain as the primary factors without resolving the question of what are the practical procedures for their assessment.

There are few other research records of the procedures for promotion. One notable exception occurs in the Fairfield judgement among the fair employment practice cases:

> When a vacancy arises in a job in a LOP [line of progression], those persons on the immediately preceding rung of the ladder are entitled to first consideration. If one of these persons is selected, this may create a vacancy on that step of the ladder, which in turn

is filled by promotion of a person on the next preceding rung, etc. The selection of which of several employees on the same step of the LOP is to be promoted is essentially a question of which is the 'oldest' employee. Under some local plant rules the oldest employee is the one who has been on the preceding job longest [occupational seniority], while in others it is the employee with longest service in the LOP [(LOP seniority)] or in the plant [(plant seniority)].

In a footnote, it is added:

Under the contract 'age' is the determining factor only where ability to perform the work and relative fitness of the competing employees are relatively equal. In practice most vacancies are filled in accordance with the age factor.

Despite the paucity of written evidence, our interviews have made it clear that promotion is heavily dependent on strict seniority. That seniority was commonly a primary factor was openly admitted by not only officials in the local and district unions, but also by the personnel staff in other steelworks. The few exceptional cases, according to union officials, take place when the management could on rare occasions prove that the senior candidate lacked the required ability or fitness to be promoted. The practice of promotion is thus powerfully governed by a strict adherence to seniority.

The factors of ability and fitness do, however, have practical implications beyond decorating the clauses of collective agreements. These two factors could establish the constraints which would confine eligible candidates to those in the preceding positions on the same progression line. These eligible candidates would naturally be presumed to possess the required ability and fitness, because they are operating similar machines and working on closely related jobs. The importance of the factors of ability and fitness also provides some assessment of industrial democracy or the allocation of power between management and labour. A strict adherence to seniority would imply that management has been left with no discretion in deploying workers and that industrial democracy on the shopfloor has been greatly enhanced.

3.3.5   Transfers Confined to Passing Through an 'Entry Job'

Our discussion of the way promotion takes place in a US steelworks would suggest that any movement of workers between progression lines is a relatively rare occurrence. Union officials and personnel staff when interviewed were adamant that the company would always have to prove that there was no one on the progression line already with the required ability before transferring a worker from another line. In the case of a worker requesting a transfer, the national agreement has made provision for a 'posting-bidding' procedure (13.19). But no similarly appropriate clauses are included in the plant collective agreement. Evidently the promotion practices on progression lines render any voluntary transfer highly exceptional. Generally stipulation on voluntary transfers – that a worker could not carry over the years of servcice from his former workshop – has evidently existed from a time prior to the drawing up of plant collective agreements. Such a prohibitive stipulation was tantamount to voluntary transfers being forbidden. Although a worker who is involuntary transferred could carry over his years of service, such occasions are – as noted above – rare.

Serious discrimination could, therefore, arise when the differences in progression line structures caused inequality in career prospects. Progression lines in a US steelworks have been seen above to encompass those jobs which in Japan would be undertaken by inplant subcontract workers. On that account alone there were wide disparities in the prospects for wage gains and promotion depending on the progression line. Moreover for those US workers corresponding to a Japanese company's regular employees the rise in job rates over the length of each progression line ranged from around 30 per cent to up to 70 per cent. The workers would, therefore, naturally want to transfer to a progression line with better prospects, though the opportunities for involuntary and voluntary transfers were rare. The consequent dissatisfaction among shopfloor workers was severely aggravated by being interwined with racial discrimination. The method adopted in 1974 under the influence of the Fairfield judgement to alleviate this dissatisfaction was to permit voluntary transfers as long as the worker passed through the progression line's lowest rank or 'entry job'. Also a worker being promoted from the labour pool to a progression line would initially have to be assigned to an entry job.

3.3.6 Promotion from the Labour Pool to a Progression Line

The workers in the labour pool would obviously be very concerned about the opportunities for being promoted to a progression line. Yet this issue is in practice ignored in the steelworks' collective agreement, despite its overall wordiness. The furthest that any provisions go is for entering a progression line situated directly above the worker's pool.

The Fairfield judgement stated that most of the progression lines had, until the beginning of the 1960s, been clearly distinguished into those only for white workers and others for black workers. The latter group were confined to undesirable jobs, while on the progression lines for white workers the job rates were higher. Under such conditions racial discrimination had obviously taken precedence over seniority in determining which line a worker could enter from the labour pool. The principle of seniority within each racial group must costumarily have been a powerful factor in entering a progression line. But any such provision could probably not be stipulated in a collective agreement, because the racial discrimination would thereby have been overtly acknowledged. One of the most striking features of the 1973 Fairfield judgement was its prescription of a 'posting-bidding' formula for determining promotion from the labour pool to a progression line. The formula requires that any vacancy in an 'entry job' on a progression line should always be advertised in the workplace, so that workers from other lines in the section, as well as pool workers, could apply. Then the decision between applicants has to be made in accordance with years of service in the plant. A formula which is indisputably based on seniority was thus ultimately applied to resolve this issue.

A rather similar state of affairs could be observed in the other integrated steel works where union members and managerial representatives were interviewed towards the end of 1973. A worker promoted from the labour pool can benefit from length of service in the section, for according to personnel staff a pool worker can choose to refuse an offered promotion if he prefers to wait for a vacancy on one of the more desirable lines above his labour pool. Apart from this aspect, it was recognized on all sides that promotion from the pool to a line rarely ran counter to seniority.

3.3.7 Temporary Transfers

Because of strict controls in the US steelworks on permanent transfers, their occurrence has been observed above to be rare. Temporary transfers, however, would be essential during periods of fluctuating output or when workers were on prolonged sick leave. Such transfers might benefit the worker by giving him the opportunity to extend his technical skills. US steel's national agreement clearly stipulates adherence to the seniority principle and to transfers being confined as far as possible to the same progression line (13.17). But both the national and the plant collective agreement fall silent on the question of transferring a worker between two progression lines, or between the pool and a line.

According to the Fairfield judgement, temporary transfers of workers in the labour pool to a progression line directly above had been taking place at managerial discretion. The decision on whom to transfer had apparently depended on each section's own customs. Even a temporary transfer could benefit a pool worker because of the opportunity to learn technical skills. The Fairfield judgement therefore directed that the pool worker with the longest service in the plant should be given precedence in the case of a temporary transfer onto a progression line.

3.3.8 Redundancy

The earlier analysis of redundancy distinguished three major issues:

1. How many workers should be made redundant?
2. Who should be made redundant?
3. What priority in rehiring should be given?

In times of falling output, US Steel's National Agreement has made the following redundancy provisions:

(a) Before instigating any redundancies the hours worked on a progression line should be cut back to a 32 hour working week.
(b) If the production decline goes beyond that boundary, consultations should be held at plant level between management and labour on which measures to adopt. The alternative to redundancies would be to distribute the available work equally among the workers, even though the working week would then drop

below 32 hours. Unless negotiations on equally distributing the work reach a satisfactory resolution, the management could instigate redundancies (13.18) The National Agreement has no provisions, however, for calculating how many workers should be made redundant. The personnel staff at other integrated steel works, and local union officials who were interviewed on this issue replied that the negotiations were not intended to establish the number of workers to be made redundant.

As for which workers should be made redundant, the National Agreement has made similar provisions to those for promotion. Length of service is stressed in some clauses, while others focus on ability and fitness. But there is one essential dissimilarity with the provisions for promotion: workers with two or more years of service in the plant, instead of being made redundant, can displace pool workers (13.33), the displaced pool workers thus being the only ones made redundant. This provision for 'bumping' is mostly operating when seems that there would be no reemployment of laid-off workers for at least six months. In this event workers on a progression line can displace pool workers not just from the pool beneath, but from any labour pool (13.34). Other pertinent clauses provide for workers with two or more years of service who are laid off for more than 60 days to be given priority in any employment openings at other US Steel plants along with reimbursement of removal expenses (13.39 and 13.63) Considerable employment protection is thus provided for workers with two or more years of service. But the question of whom to lay off, if redundancy among these workers were ever necessary, has been left up to the individual plant collective agreements.

In the event of threatened redundancies the plant agreement begins by expressing certain principles, which appear at first sight to resemble those in the National Agreement. But the plant agreement's provisions are more practical and clearly set out. The procedure requires workers to move to positions directly below their existing grades in inverse order to their years of service on the progression line whenever a production decline leads to underemployment of the workforce. This ordered demotion of progression line workers results in the workers who are in the lowest job grades being pushed into the labour pool. The consequent surplus pool workers were the ones made redundant. It should be remembered, however, that this 'bumping' out of pool workers could be done only by workers with two or more years of service in the plant.

The plant agreement supposedly restricts 'bumping' to those workers who have the ability and physical fitness to perform the job, but this limitation does not apparently operate at all. The personnel staff who were interviewed acknowledged that the work in the labour pool did not originally demand ability and fitness and that progression line workers would have, in any case, had experience in the lower grade jobs. The sequence for priority in rehiring exactly reverses the order in which workers had been laid off. The plant collective agreement also establishes the period for retaining priority in rehiring as being generally equivalent to the number of years of service in the plant.

3.3.9 The Upper Boundary of a Worker's Career

The implication of the discussion so far is that shopfloor workers in a steelworks in the USA would stay at their place of employment and guard their seniority rights. Nor are there any provisions for mandatory retirement ages, such as are customary in Japan. Instead, under the optional retirement system, a US steel worker can receive a company pension as well as the state pension from the age of 65 years as long as he had been with the company for 15 or more years. In a large Japanese company when there was rapid growth in employment a fair proportion of shopfloor workers would have been promoted to the post of foreman prior to reaching the mandatory retirement age. A supervisory post in Japan should, therefore, be viewed as an extension of a shopfloor worker's career, especially as the lower ranking supervisors can still hold onto their union membership. In contrast, a labour union in the USA appears in its policies to draw a sharp dividing line beneath foremen, none of whom are union members. The union policy requires that a worker who is promoted to foreman should lose entirely and in perpetuity the seniority rights held while a union member. How would this union policy affect a worker's career?

Statistics which indicate the proportion of foremen and other low ranking supervisors who have been promoted from the shopfloor are not available. The analysis has to rely, therefore, wholly on our interviews held in steelworks. The response was that supervisory positions up to the post of general foreman were overwhelmingly held by former production workers, who, however, were relatively few among those in higher positions. Supervisory positions are managerial appointments. It is probably natural that the labour union would not be involved in appointing supervisors, who are not union members. Respondents argued that, nonetheless, management would have preferred to make appointments for the upper job grades from among shopfloor workers because of their experience in the jobs which had to be supervised. There is also the factor of leadership ability, which apparently justifies foreman appointments often being given to shopfloor committee members of the union. All these aspects are in general conformity with the procedures in Japanese companies.

The one prominent disparity with Japan is that there are some workers who would decline the offer of promotion to foreman. Though few in number, their significance could not be ignored by either the management or the labour representatives who were interviewed. The views of management and labour on why appointments are refused were roughly in agreement. First, the promotion might bring only a small increase in remuneration. A supervisor's pay, which is monthly, would have neither the overtime nor the piece-rate supplements earned by ordinary shopfloor workers. The second factor is the weakened authority of supervisors. Our discussion on the actual processes behind the promotion and transfer of shopfloor workers has shown that indisputable rules leave little room for managerial discretion, in spite of the supervisor's formal role in making proposals on candidates to higher management levels. Thus the respondents' comment that a supervisor's authority extends in practice only to disciplinary problems is convincing. The union respondents especially stressed the third factor, which is the loss of the union's protection in any confrontation with higher management, because union membership has been forfeited to become a supervisor. The consequent reluctance of some shopfloor workers to accept supervisory appointments has led to management partly resorting to appointing young technicians and college graduates instead.

In sum, our observations indicate that supervisory posts in a US steelworks are disconnected from the careers of union members to a greater extent than in Japan. This characteristic of workers' careers in the USA probably strengthens labour's influence in establishing the provisions affecting union members' careers. By putting supervisors well outside their sphere of interest, the union can establish rigid, indisputable rules within their own which would protect workers' careers. Conversely, if supervisors were union members whose careers were strictly protected, then the union would become involved in ensuring that seniority determined their promotion also. And if the union were to fail in this, the seniority principle would overall be weakened. Managerial resistance to such union involvement would certainly be vigorous, since supervisors have control over the workshops. Thus the US local unions have chosen to disregard foreman positions and so more effectively safeguard shopfloor workers' careers. Indisputable rules on the promotion and transfer of shopfloor workers which left no room for managerial discretion could then be established. This strengthening of labour's say in career decisions has been achieved at the cost of narrower prospects for union members' careers.

3.3.10   Summary

Our discussion of workers' careers in a US steelworkers has been supplemented with research in chemical plants and other workplaces. To a suprising extent, the careers of steelworkers and of chemical workers are generally similar. The structure of labour pools and of progression lines with varying lengths are applicable to both groups. There is, moreover, a striking resemblance in the way in which labour has a say in career decisions. Whereas the collective agreements emphasise ability, qualifications and fitness, in practice rigid, indisputable rules based on the relative years of service in the workplace have been established. The rules have been modified by racial discrimination, but observation over time would reveal that the principle has been maintained. This principle is simply that the seniority system should dominate. These features may be seen as characteristic of production workers in the process industries.

In addition to research carried out in the process industries, nine studies were made in the machinery industries. This enables us to distinguish the common features and dissimilarities with the process industries (although the number of case studies is admittedly small). The first notable dissimilarity is the absence of progression lines or labour pools in the machinery industries. Secondly, careers are shallower than in the process industries, when viewed from both the number of career steps and the wage rate profile over the worker's career. The third distinction is that the career structure in the machinery industries does not necessarily embrace experience in all of the workshop's jobs. In many cases more than one job is included in each of the three or four steps which divide up the workshop's jobs. The apparent tendency is that a worker does not become experienced in all the jobs within each step. It is possible for a machinery industry worker to move widely between jobs, but in practice fewer jobs are experienced than in the process industries. In other words, the careers of machinery industry workers are not consistently structured on the basis of progression lines in every workshop. There are two common characteristics of workers' careers in the process and machinery industries. First, the internalization of careers prevails, although in a minority of engineering occupations the acquisition of technical skills inevitably has to take place outside the company. But engineering workers' techniques are mostly acquired through on-the-job-training. Secondly, the seniority rule is powerful throughout both industrial groups. Even though collective agreement clauses state only that if ability and qualifications are equal, precedence should be given to seniority, the seniority principle has actually been established as paramount. This characteristic becomes all the more striking in comparison with what is actually practised in a Japanese company.

NOTES

1. For a detailed analysis of all the case studies in these groups, see Koike (1977).
2. US Department of Labor, Bureau of Labor Statistics, *Major Collective Bargaining Agreements*, Bulletin, 1425–11, 1425–14 (Washington DC, 1970–2).
3. Brooks and Gamm (1955). This meticulous research is one of the earliest studies of promotion practices in the USA.
4. Shiba (1973). 34 large electric power plants in various countries (India, Pakistan, Malaysia and Singapore were included as well as the USA, Canada and Japan) were the object of case studies on the deployment, transfer and promotion of personnel. Subsequent to its appearance in Japanese, an English edition of this impressively through research was published.
5. Bureau of National Affairs, *Fair Employment Practice Cases* (hereafter FEPC) yearly (Washington D.C.: Bureau of National Affairs, 1969–80).
6. FEPC, vol. 5, pp. 1253ff; vol. 7, pp. 322ff.
7. FEPC, vol. 7, pp. 1279ff.
8. FEPC, vol. 7, pp. 1029ff.
9. As well as steelworks, US Steel operates many other plants, whose total number at that time amounted to about forty.
10. Other indispensable references were made to Livernash (1961) and various surveys carried out by the US Bureau of Labor Statistics. The course of wage negotiations at US Steel over the past 30 years has been recorded in the Wage Chronology Series, Bulletin 1603 (1968). The object is the iron and steel industry in the Industry Wage Survey Series, Bulletins 1358 (1963) and 1602 (1968), but this series was not especially

useful for our research. One famous feature of the US steel industry is its implementation of a job classification plan after 1945. The basic text on this topic is Stieber (1959), although this makes hardly any reference to workers' careers.

11. The Fairfield judgement estimated that 12 000 employees would have been working on days when operations were relatively active (FEPC, vol. 7, p. 324).

Those jobs which in Japan would be entrusted to temporary and inplant subcontract workers are done in the US by regular steelworkers, as long as the work is on the plant's premises in ordinary working hours. Consequently a business fluctuation requires alterations in shifts and in working hours: some workshops may be on a three shift, seven day working week, while others can operate only a five day working week with no shifts.

12. The number of job grades was 33. The rates quoted here, which were applicable from 1 August 1974 to 31 July 1975, were the hourly standard wage rate where payment by results was not applied (The wage rates would be lower where there was payment by results). Although payment by results is customary in the steel industry, data on hourly wage earnings in each company was not available. The quoted rates (which can be found in US Steel's national collective agreement) for each job grade were identical throughout all the company's plants. Until 1971, the wage differential between the highest and the lowest job grades was 91 per cent.

13. The only exception are the skilled workers in the maintenance departments who have completed their apprenticeships; they may be directly assigned to their own occupational positions without going through the labour pool. The apprenticeship system in large steelworks has superficially remained unchanged since the last century insofar as there is a four or five year period of training both in the classroom and on the shopfloor. In practice, however, the system has largely been internalized; most of a steelworks' apprentices have previously been working in other departments of the same works, and on completing their apprenticeships they usually stay rather than find jobs in other plants.

14. This is a plant agreement for another US Steelworks, nor Fairfield.

15. US Department of Labor, Bureau of Labor Statistics, *Wage Chronology, US Steel Corporation, Bulletin 1603*, (Washington DC, 1968).

16. FEPC, vol. 7, p. 25.

REFERENCES

Brooks, George W. and Gamm, Sara (1955) 'The Practice of Seniority in Southern Pulp Mills', *Monthly Labor Review*, 78.7. July, pp. 757–65.

Koike, Kazuo (1977) *Shokuba no Rōdō Kumiai to Sanka – Rōshi Kankei no Nichibei Hikaku* (A Comparative Study of Industrial Relations on the Shop Floor in the United States and Japan)(Tokyo: Tōyōkeizai Shinpōsha).

Livernash, Edward Robert (1961) *Collective Bargaining in the Basic Steel Industry* (Washington, D.C.: US Department of Labor).

Shiba, Shōji (1973) *A Cross-National Comparison of Labor Management – with Reference to Technology Transfer*, IDE. occasional papers series 11 (Tokyo: Institute of Developing Economies).

Stieber, Jack (1959) *The Steel Industry Wage Structure* (Cambridge, Mass.: Harvard University Press).

4 Workers' Careers in Large Japanese Companies

4.1 SCOPE OF THE INTERNAL PROMOTION SYSTEM

The US and Japanese analyses of labour markets generally differ in the emphasis placed by Japanese scholars on the existence of internalized careers. The descriptive words may vary in speaking of an 'internal labour market' in Japan, and the Japanese 'seniority system', but there is general agreement that these features are applicable to male white-collar employees and regular employees of large companies. Yet this common perception of internalized careers has rarely been proved on the basis of comprehensive statistical data. Statistics are also necessary to carry out a time-series analysis, so as to deal with issue of whether internalization of careers has tended to disappear under the impact of economic and technological development. The usual view of Japanese-style industrial relations suggests that the internalization of careers is an anachronism in Japan's industrial society.

Chapter 3 approached the issue of whether there were in the USA detailed promotion rules which mention seniority by examining the clauses of collective agreements. This approach is inappropriate in Japan's case despite there being Labour Ministry and Central Labour Relations Commission surveys on collective agreements.[1] One problem lies in the Japanese company practice of recording insufficient detail in the printed record of a collective agreement – only the bare essentials of the agreements, or in an approximate form. The details are recorded more precisely in additional papers which are not, however, the object of surveys on collective agreements.

A more fundamental problem lies in the interpretation of the

114

Japanese word for 'promotion'. Chapter 3 showed that in the USA 'promotion' is interpreted as moving into a different job with a higher wage rate attached, which includes the movement of rank and file workers between jobs. In the case of regular employees of large Japanese companies, however, their jobs and wage rates are not directly connected. The rather exceptional situation in the major Japanese steel works, where part of the wage is job related, is tending to disappear. There would be a connection between the job and the wage rate in the long term because a merit rating is carried out every year or half-year, but in the short term this connection is not apparent. On that account there is rarely the notion of moving only to a better paid job. In Japanese workplaces the interpretation of promotion is confined to moving into a supervisory position, so that the conception of promotion among rank and file positions is quite vague. Therefore a different approach to Chapter 3, and material other than collective agreements, have to be used.

4.1.1 Comparing Years of Service and Years of Experience

Once again, the *Wage Structure Survey* is chosen as the most appropriate and detailed source for data on workers by industry and by company size. Annual data on workers' average years of experience and average years of service by occupation, by industry and by company size can be found, though there are a few gaps in coverage. Firstly it is assumed that when an internal promotion system exists:

1. The average length of service and the average length of experience in each occupation are both relatively long
2. The lengths of these two averages tend to be almost equal.

The internal promotion system permits workers to make progress within the company through having experience in a series of related jobs which are generally all within one workshop. The workshops – or in some cases a rather wider boundary – roughly correspond to the occupational categories designated in the *Wage Structure Survey*. The internal promotion system encourages workers to remain for a long time in one company, with the result that the average length of service becomes relatively long. And since the worker tends to gain experience in a given occupation within the company, the average length of experience would lengthen and closely approach the average length of service.

The two assumptions have been given more concrete expression as follows. Both the average years of service and the average years of experience should be more than five years to satisfy the existence of internal promotion. The second assumption has been expressed alternatively as a strict and as a relaxed condition. The strict condition requires that the average length of service should equal or surpass the average length of experience. The length of service would be longer for a worker who is transferred to a different workshop within the company. The relaxed condition permits the average years of service to be less than the average years of experience, but by no more than one year's difference.

The *Wage Structure Survey* supplies comprehensive data (annual since 1954,) but our objectives cannot be served for each year. The periods with appropriate data for 1955–61 (average years of service and average years of experience by company size and by occupation) and 1964–69 (average years of service classified by years of experience, by company size, and by occupation). The survey has been held on a major scale every three years, with a particularly large scale survey in 1961. Therefore the cross-sectional analysis will focus on 1961 to find out in which industries and for which company sizes internal promotion existed. The time-series analysis of the trends in the internal promotion system will then be carried out by comparing the figures for the two periods of 1955–61 and 1964–9. Additional constraints to be noted are that the analyses will be limited to male workers who are in manufacturing industries, because in other sectors the occupational categories which the survey covers are too few.

4.1.2 Internal Promotion Extensive in Large Companies

The proportion of occupations in which the internal promotion system operated during 1961 is displayed in Figure 4.1. Under the specific conditions established above, the shaded bar indicates satisfaction of the strict condition, with the unshaded bar for the relaxed condition. Figure 4.1 suggests that in all industries, the larger the company the higher the proportion of occupations benefitting from internal promotion, though there are distinct differences depending on the industry. The internal promotion system is most extensive in the chemical industries where, under even the strict condition, it covers more than 80 per cent of occupations in companies with 1000 or more employees. Even in medium-sized companies in the chemical industries internal promotion operates in more than half of the occupations under the relaxed condition. In the primary metals industries also, the internal promotion system in companies with 1000 or more employees is as extensive as in the chemical industries. On the other hand in the machinery industries the extent of internal promotion is considerably lower, while the light industries occupy an intermediate position.

It is significant that even in the machinery industries, where the internal promotion system is least extensive, the proportion of occupations satisfying the relaxed condition in companies with 1000 or more employees generally surpasses 50 per cent. The single exception is transportation equipment, but in this case the result has been distorted by a high concentration of occupational categories surveyed being in the shipbuilding industry. Since this is one of the most traditional industries in Japan, the average length of service is usually over 12 years in each occupation, which is longer than in other industries. On that account the average years of service, though long, often end up as being more than one year less than the average years of experience. Thus the mechanical application of the conditions which we established above have rendered transportation equipment exceptional, whereas a more relaxed condition, such as within two or three years' difference or not more than 20 per cent, would have shown that the internal promotion system did operate.

An aspect which is especially significant when compared with the US pattern is that even in the case of light industries internal promotion prevails in large Japanese companies. In contrast, the internal promotion system appears to be rather rare in US light industries. Internal promotion in Japan's light industries covers over 80 per cent of occupations, under the relaxed condition, in companies with 1000 or more employees. Particularly in the classical light industrial sphere, such as textiles and apparel, the proportion is close to 100 per cent even under the strict condition. It is this aspect which seems to reflect the most extreme divergence between Japan and the USA in the extent of career internalization: whatever the industry the internal promotion system seems to be widely diffused throughout large Japanese companies.

4.1.3 Diffusion of Internal Promotion Over Time

Reference has already been made to the necessity of dividing the time-series analysis into two periods of 1955–61 and 1964–9. For the first period figures on the average length of service and of experience

118

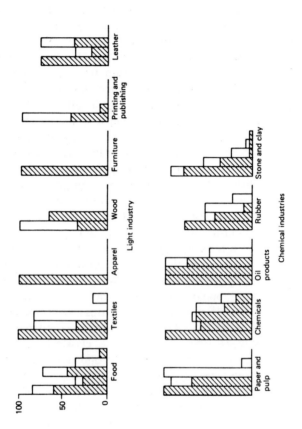

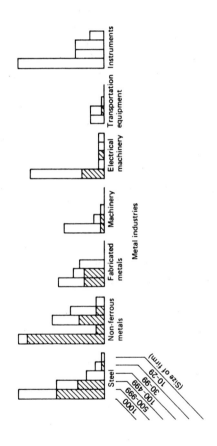

FIGURE 4.1   Percentage of occupations under internal promotion (by industry and by size of company, manufacturing, male, 1961)

Source: Rōdōshō (Ministry of Labour) *Shōwa 36-nen Chingin Kōzō Kihon Tōkei Chōsa* (Wage Structure Survey).

are available, and the number of occupations surveyed was increased from 63 in 1955 to 246 in 1961. Since the number is too few to examine the separate occupations within each industry, only the three overall groups of chemical, machinery and light industries are depicted in Figure 4.2. The strict condition that the average length of service equals or surpasses the average length of experience has been applied in determining the existence of internal promotion. Figure 4.2 demonstrates that in the three industrial groups the internal promotion system became more diffuse between 1955 and 1961 whatever the company size, though especially in large companies.

After a gap in 1962–3 with no appropriate classifications, in the 1964–9 period the survey has provided figures on the average length of service classified by length of experience and by occupation. The four groups classified for years of experience are: (i) less than one year; (ii) one – four years; (iii) five – nine years; (iv) ten or more years. The fourth class cannot be used because it is open-ended. Therefore, in conjunction with the third class of five – nine years of experience, the condition for an occupation having internal promotion has been relaxed to an average of seven or more years of service, which results in this period not being directly comparable to the 1955–61 series. The time-series analysis under the above conditions, shown in Figure 4.2, permits the following conclusions for the 1964–9 period. In companies with 1000 or more employees, the internal promotion system became more widespread. The rate of diffusion was highest in the machinery industries, followed by the light industries, with only a low growth rate in the chemical industries. The reason for this divergence in rates is simply that in 1964 the extent of internal promotion was almost 100 per cent in the chemical industries, while the greatest room for growth was in the machinery industries. The second significant conclusion is that the internal promotion system's coverage in the smaller companies tended to contract between 1964 and 1969.

Figure 4.1 and Figure 4.2 together clearly demonstrate that from the mid-1950s to the late 1960s the internal promotion system, far from breaking down, became more widely diffused through large companies in all industrial groups. During this same period there were considerable technological and economic advances in Japanese industrial society. The common notion of internal promotion as being anachronistic in modern industrial society therefore becomes highly dubious in the light of the above analysis of the data. The next stage in our analysis requires case studies so as to understand the nature of internalized careers.

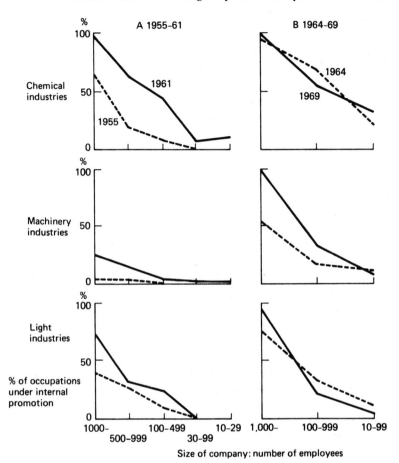

FIGURE 4.2   Changes in the extent of internal promotion (chemical, machinery and light industries, male, 1955; 1961; 1964; 1969)

Source: Rōdōshō (Ministry of Labour) *Chingin Kōzō Kihon Tōkei Chōsa* (Wage Structure Survey)

4.1.4   The 1959 Survey: Enterprise Unions Do Voice Their Opinions

To what extent do the workers have a say in decisions affecting their careers? Often it is supposed that Japanese workers are ineffectual in voicing their demands because of enterprise unions. The theory presumes that an industrial union of workers covering more than one enterprise is necessary to ensure that it can establish the rules of labour supply, and so gain bargaining power. Conversely, an enterprise union is thought to be unable adequately to safeguard its members' interests, which implies that its power is confined to negotiating average wages with absolutely no say in procedures for promotions and transfers. This theory has barely received any substantiation from hard facts.

Probably the only case study on this topic, made in the late 1950s, contradicted the usual notions on the basis of its research into seven Japanese plant and company unions.[2] Yet after the results were published in 1959 this contradiction received little attention – perhaps because the authors themselves did not attach sufficient emphasis to the implications of their study – so their findings must now be thoroughly discussed here. This 1959 survey, which was primarily based on interviews, looked into the organization and functions of two unions each in the steel industry, the machinery industries and private railways, and one union in the coal industry. In choosing the unions to be studied the authors aimed at including five unions which at that time appeared to be functioning effectively, as well as two relatively inactive unions. When the research results are read again today all the unions seem to have had a considerable say in various work-related issues, in addition to negotiating wages.

The unions' influence in decisions on transfers appears to have been widespread, and their voices were by no means confined to those transfers which seemed particularly disadvantageous to workers – such as to plants within the company but located far away. Even the apparently inactive unions had a say in the case of less controversial transfers to other workshops within the plant. The unions' influence in this matter covered temporary transfers and transfers of even just one worker.[3] The more active unions were, of course, even more influential. But in the case of movements within the workshop, which were often tantamount to promotion, even the active unions appear to have had no influence. It might be argued that this was natural, since promotional matters are always thought to rest wholly in the hands of management. Yet other kinds of transfers which also affect the workers' careers are subject to some interference from the union.

Before examining this contradiction, two exceptions to the above comments ought to be considered. One is that there were some labour unions which did participate in negotiations on workers' movements within the workshop. Both of the major and local private railway unions included in the 1959 survey had an effective voice in negotiations on postings, and hence on movements within the workshop.[4] This characteristic was not confined to the private railway unions as the Japan National Railway Workers union had a similar bargaining power.[5] So as to ensure the railway workers' agreement with the requirements of the timetable, whose strict maintenance is crucial to the railway company's effective performance, the corresponding assignments of who should drive what train from where to where are in effect subject to negotiation with the union.

The other exception, concerning one of the steel industry unions, is quite remarkable. The 1959 survey reported that the union had a say in promotion to foreman. This steel works' usual management practice was to inform the union in advance of the candidate for foreman. The union would then find out whether the candidate was acceptable to the shopfloor workers.[6] This union's role is in striking contrast to the role of US local unions. The latter have established fixed rules for promoting rank and file workers between non-supervisory posts, but the unions have no say at all in the case of promotion to foreman. The Derber and Chalmers survey (1965) which covered 40 local unions at two different points of time, found out that not one of the unions had a say in promotion to foreman, despite usually having considerable influence on promotions between rank and file positions.[7] Foremen in the USA are not union members, whereas in Japan union members and even shop stewards may be foremen. Japanese unions do sometimes have a say in promotion decisions – though in the 1959 survey it was only one union. But on the other hand for promotions between rank and file positions the unions, apart from the railway workers, are silent.

4.1.5 The Workshop as a Semi-autonomous Group

What does this union silence imply? The prevailing notion is that promotions are, therefore, unilaterally decided by management because of the weakness of enterprise unions. But this line of reasoning is obstructed by the recorded fact that the unions do have a considerable say in transfer decisions, which also impinge on output levels and the levels of personnel thus required. The meaning of 'transfers' and of 'promotion' has to be considered in more depth in order to answer the question of why Japanese unions have a voice in the former, but not in the matter of promotions.

There must be some real distinction between transfers and promotion, despite both involving movements of labour within the company. When a blue-collar worker is promoted he moves to another position within the workshop, but when he is transferred he moves to another workshop. A promotion thus represents progress in a worker's career, whereas a transfer implies moving onto another career track. Since unions are influential in the case of transfer decisions, their bargaining power covers the issue of the coverage of a worker's career. Over the long term all the workers in one workshop group are following the same career, which means that they hold interests in common. The union's silence on promotion decisions reflects the fact that the union does not intervene in matters occurring within the workshop group, only in what concerns the group as a whole and in what extends beyond the group.

Do the members of the workshop, therefore, in some way separate from the union, have a say in matters internal to the group? The 1959 survey has indicated that the way in which movements within the workshop to different assignments take place depends on each workshop's own customs.[8] So it is neither the management nor the union but the workers' group in the workshop which would be participating in the decision, insofar as their customs are followed. Although the foreman was reported as being the main arbiter in all the case studies, he was a union member – as is often the case in West Germany. The foreman, almost without exception, has been promoted from within the workshop and so his career route corresponds to that of rank and file union members. These are sufficient grounds for arguing that his workshop's customs influence the foreman's promotion decisions. Further evidence will be considered below, since the discussion so far has centred only on seven case studies made over 20 years ago. It would have been preferable to supplement the studies with comprehensive statistics, but available figures which probe the influence of labour unions on promotion and other career-related decisions are much too meagre. It is therefore necessary to rely on the evidence from detailed case studies.

4.2   BROAD CAREERS IN AN INTEGRATED STEEL MILL

A large integrated steelworks belonging to a major Japanese steel firm, which can be contrasted with the US case study in Chapter 3, was chosen from among the process industries. The tapping shop was adopted as the object of this case study. The plant union, which is affiliated with the company union and the Japanese Federation of

Iron and Steel Workers Union, was made up of about 8000 regular employees. At this point, the example of the workers responsible for tapping in the blast furnace will be considered. In each of the mill's three blast furnaces there was a small workgroup for tapping operations. Since four groups operated over the three shifts, the three furnaces required a total of 12 workgroups.

The group, which was composed of one subforeman and about ten rank and file workers, was divided into four kinds of work assignments, according to the job classification plan. There was one tapping leadman, four men in the first tapping group, three men in the second tapping group, and two men for flushing. More detailed observation would reveal that there were really ten separate assignments, because each worker's job differed. The nature of these jobs may be better understood by looking at the job rates which the major Japanese steel works adopted in 1962. The job rate was only about one-third of the worker's standard wage, but each job had been formally evaluated in order to set the rate for this wage element. In 1971 the job rates in the tapping shop had been set as follows:

Assignment	Job grade	Job rate/month (yen)	Differential (base=100)
Subforeman	19	25 017	137
First blast furnacemen (tapping leadmen)	16	21 486	118
Second blast furnacemen (tapping)	15	19 385	106
Second blast furnacemen (flushing)	15	19 385	106
Third blast furnacemen (tapping assistant)	14	18 261	100

Between the rank and file workers in the group the differential in the job rate was as little as 18 per cent. Even with the inclusion of the subforeman the differential was only 37 per cent. This evidence alone shows lower wage differentials than in the US steelworks, but rates in other workshops and mills where assignments and their evaluation differ from the above ought to be examined. Nor must the basic wage element (which accounts for two-thirds of the standard wage) be overlooked.

4.2.1   Job Rates in Major Steel Firms

From 1962 all the major Japanese steel works had operated a system of job-related wages. But when Nippon Steel Corporation was established after a 1971 merger, job rates were standardized among the merging companies, which somewhat weakened the linkage between the job and the wage rate. It is of interest to note that even among other major steelmakers there was a tendency, discussed later, to relax the linkage. Our main purpose now is to examine the wage profile over a steelworker's career using relatively detailed data supplied by the Nippon Steel Corporation labour union.[9]

Table 4.1 shows the job rates before standardization for workers in the blast furnace and the hot finishing strip mill of each plant. The differentials between the Yawata group of plants (marked with an asterisk) and the Fuji group were wider than the differentials between plants within each group, though there were evident differentials within the Fuji group. The lowest job rates paid in the hot finishing strip mills vary considerably, between 18 261 yen at Hirohata, 14 047 yet at Nagoya and 16 014 yen at Muroran, though all three were in the Fuji group. The more striking disparity between the mills lies in the number of job grades. Whereas in the Yawata and Sakai mills there were respectively seven and six different grades, in the newly built Kimitsu mill there were merely two. Therefore the 1971 standardization of job rates over the different plants somewhat inevitably had to be divorced from the actual jobs. The standardization has established 13 job grades from grade 10 to 22, which are far fewer than the 33 job grades in the US Steel Corporation. Nippon Steel, however, adopted the range rate system where each job grade has been allotted three job rates. The first rate applies during the worker's first six months on the job and the second rate for the next two years. After two and a half years a worker reaches the top rate in his job grade, though the difference between the three rates is as little as 8–10 per cent.

It is hard to say whether the differentials under the standardized system of job rates are wider than in the US Steel Corporation. Two months after a recruit has entered Nippon Steel he is assigned to a workshop in the lowest job grade. Table 4.2 shows what job grades are attached to each workshop. The main workshops in the mainline departments, such as tapping in the blast furnace, are given a range of job rates which permit a 56 per cent rise from job grade 18 up to 22. However this differential cannot be directly compared with cor-

TABLE 4.1 Job rates in each plant before merger (large Japanese steel company, monthly yen payments, 1971)

	Plant	Monthly job rate (yen)		$\frac{A}{B} \times 100$	Differential
		Lowest A	Highest B		No. of job grades
	Yawata*	16,110	25,820	160	4
	Hirohata	18,261	25,017	137	3
Blast	Sakai*	16,110	25,820	160	3
furnace	Nagoya	18,261	25,017	137	5
	Kimitsu*	16,110	25,820	160	3
	Kamaishi	18,261	25,017	137	3
	Muroran	18,261	25,017	137	3
	Yawata*	14,030	25,820	184	7
	Hirohata	18,261	23,840	131	2
Hot	Sakai*	14,030	25,820	184	6
finishing	Nagoya	14,047	23,840	170	5
strip mill	Kimitsu*	16,110	25,820	160	2
	Muroran	16,014	28,840	149	4

Source: Shinnittetsu Rōdōkumiai (Nippon Steel Confederation of Trade Unions), *Chōsa Jihō* (Bulletin) August 1971.

responding differentials in a US steelworks because of two special factors. One is that subforemen are included in the job grades shown here. If only the rank and file workers in grades 18–19 were considered, the job rate differential would be as little as 20 per cent. The second factor is the way in which promotion in the US Steel Corporation begins from the fourth or fifth job grade in the progression lines, which should therefore be the base in calculating the differential. Although these two factors make a direct comparison impossible, it superficially appears that the job rate differential in the main workshops in the mainline departments is steeper in US Steel at 40–50 per cent than in Nippon Steel at around 40 per cent.

On the other hand, when areas other than the main workshops in the mainline departments are considered, the job rate differential is probably wider in Nippon Steel than in the US Steel Corporation. Table 4.2 demonstrates that in ancillary workshops in the mainline departments (grades 17–21) and workshops in the maintenance departments (grades 16–21), and in the non-mainline departments (grades 16–21) both the highest and the lowest job rates are somewhat lower than in the main workshops in the mainline departments,

TABLE 4.2   Job rates in each occupation after merger (larger Japanese steel company)

Job grade range	Wage differential $\frac{Highest}{Lowest} \times 100$	Workshop
18–22	156	Blast furnace, converter, steel pourer, hot finishing strip mill, cold strip mill, seamless pipes, rolling mill
17–22	171	Galvanized sheets
16–22	188	Plate rolling mill, hot rolling mill, pipes
15–22	209	Coke oven
17–21	158	Reheating furnace, hot rolling mill, blast furnace operation, sintering
16–21	165	Machinery maintenance, Machine shop
16–20	159	Coke gas, roller grinding, cranes shearing, pipes, power house, mechanical testing
15–20	176	Buying
10–11		Miscellaneous works

Source: See Table 4.1.

but the percentage differentials are similar or higher. In contrast, the wage differentials in these ancillary workshops in the US Steel Corporation are much narrower than in the main workshops in the mainline departments.

It should be recalled, however, that the above picture relates only to the job rate, which accounts for about one-third of the standard wage in Nippon Steel. The problem in trying to examine the worker's basic wage is its composition of accumulated increments and the merit supplement which is determined annually. As an unavoidably rough expedient the average figures on wages in the 'steel industry – F311 blast furnace' category in the *Wage Structure Survey* may be used to compare standard wage differentials. In 1970 the differential between 50–59 year-old and 18–19 year-old production and mainten-ance blue-collar workers was 113 per cent, which is steeper than in the longest progression line in the US Steel Corporation.

Because of inadequacies in the data used above, conclusions have to be rather tentative. The wage profiles over the careers of regular workers in large Japanese steelmakers appear to be quite steep relative to those for US steel workers. This disparity in differentials seems to be rather less in main workshops in the mainline departments, but the wage differential over the careers of workers in other workshops appears to be much wider in Japan than in the USA. The reason is that there is a minimal difference between workshops in the slopes of wage profiles for regular Japanese steel workers whereas, depending on whether or not US steel workers are in main workshops in the mainline departments, there is a large difference in wage profiles.

Examining wages in the above way could encourage the common perception that assignments in Japan are given as promotion in accordance with seniority. Nevertheless the actual situation is significantly at variance with this.

4.2.2 Egalitarian Assignments

Interviews with the officials of a steelworks union indicated that movements of workers in the blast furnace were wide-ranging and the ten workers in the group moved between the group's ten assignments every half-day in an 'egalitarian' way. The subforeman oversaw the whole rotation, which he sometimes entered in order to substitute for an absent worker.

This egalitarianism is not the outcome of negotiations between the steelworks union and management. Since the union rarely has a say in assignments within the workshop, it would hardly be in a position to participate in negotiations and agreements on such rotations. Nor was there any evidence that the rotation stemmed from a unilateral managerial decision. If we wanted to pinpoint who made any decision on the matter, the response would have to be the subforeman or his senior. Yet in practice he could not exert his own will to any extent, because the rotation applies to all in a systematic fashion.

The other reported feature of this rotation was that the mobility of workers extended over a wide range of jobs. The three blast furnaces in this steelworks are not identical, with the largest one, in particular, being more automated. Still, every year one or two workers from each workgroup move to work in another blast furnace shop. And there are also movements of workers from the group to the furnace-operating shop. Although a procedure for whom to move and over what time period has never been established as a custom, all of the group's workers would generally have had, over a ten year period, experience in many of the positions in the three blast furnaces and in the operation shop. This undoubtedly wide mobility of workers between assignments is not the result of any agreement between the steelworks union and management, but instead depends on the decisions of the department chief and the subforemen, who ensure that the workers have a common experience in almost all of the jobs in these four closely related workshops.

Doubts will inevitably be raised about the feasibility of this kind of approach to a wide range of assignments. Each of the ten positions in the blast furnace work group and each of the operation jobs require a different level of skill, and the extent of each worker's experience differ. These differences could indeed have been a severe impediment to achieving such an egalitarian rotation. Yet, if not, the question becomes whether that blast furnace work might perhaps have special circumstances.

The widest difference in the degree of difficulty between the work group's jobs could be estimated from the job evaluation plan at around 20 per cent, when the sub foreman's position is excepted. Even the easiest job, however, can be done only by a worker who has passed through the initial two month training period after entering the company. But then the worker immediately participates in the work group's rotation of assignments. In practice, the differences in levels of experience are offset by a careful arrangement of assignments. A recent entrant to the rotation is closely supervised by the subforeman. And until he becomes experienced he is always assigned to a position next to an experienced worker who supervises his work in various ways. The senior workers are in effect responsible not only for their own assignments, but also for training the inexperienced workers whose positions are adjacent to their own. Thus within the formally egalitarian structure the jobs are shared out in a way which reflects different levels of experience.

Despite this modification, the rotation remains amazingly egalitrian in comparison to the situation in a US steelworks. The question might then arise whether this rotation is feasible only because the blast furnace operations are automated and on a large scale. Nevertheless the various positions in the blast furnace do require different kinds of work. So the question remains whether there are exceptional circumstances in the blast furnace which permit workers to be posted to a variety of assignments without any distinction based on seniority.

4.2.3 The Diffusion of Job Rotation Systems

The Nippon Steel labour union's 1971 report on job rates made a detailed coverage of the characteristics of the jobs in 79 workshops.

In 63 of these workshops there appears from the report – though the amount of detail given is uneven – to have been rotation of jobs, whose extent can be distinguished into one of the following four categories: (i) regular job rotation to all positions in the workshop; (ii) rotation to all positions (though not in a regular fashion); (iii) partial rotation; (iv) no rotation. These categories are used in Table 4.3 to show the extent of mobility in each workshop of Nippon Steel's plants. In the case of the blast furnace shop the union report covered seven workshops, in five of which there was rotation to all positions, including three shops with regular rotation. Mobility among workers in the blast furnace described above was thus not at all exceptional. Out of all of the 79 workshops, rotation to all positions occurred in 31 and partial rotation in 26 shops. So there was some degree of mobility in 72 per cent of the workshops covered by the report, and in 36 per cent there was rotation to all positions, which suggests that complete mobility was certainly not exceptional, though occurring in less than half of the workshops.

Table 4.3 indicates that the differences in mobility depended to some degree on whether the steelworks formerly belonged to the Yawata group or the Fuji group. Whereas in the latter case 78 per cent of the workshops had some degree of mobility, the corresponding proportion was only 59 per cent in the former Yawata group plants. Furthermore there was rotation to all positions in 69 per cent of the workshops in the former Fuji mills, but in only 18 per cent of the former Yawata workshops. These discrepancies could reflect differences which were present in the two companies' managerial policies. At the same time, the degree of mobility tends to have been greater in the more recently established steelworks, whichever company was the owner. For example the Kimitsu and Sakai steelworks display a greater extent of job rotation than in the workshops of the Yawata steelworks. And out of the plants in the Fuji lineage, the degree of mobility was highest in Nagoya. But there are still inconsistencies in this pattern, insofar as some workshops in plants other than Nagoya had adopted complete rotation, whereas in the same Nagoya workshops the rotation was only partial. The stove operation shops in the Kamaishi and Muroran works had regular rotation to all positions, and in the Hirohata shop all jobs were rotated, but in the Nagoya shop the rotation was only partial. Similarly in the Nagoya steelworks the reheating furnace shop and the hot strip finishing shop practised only partial rotation, whereas in the same workshops in the Muroran works there was rotation to all positions, which was regular in the hot strip finishing shop; and in the Hirohata hot strip finishing

TABLE 4.3 Mobility within a workshop (large Japanese steel company)

	Yawata	Hikari	Hirohata	Sakai	Nagoya	Kimitsu	Kamaishi	Muroran
Blast furnace charging	−				⊙	★	⊙	⊙
Stove operation	+		★	−	□	★	⊙	⊙
Coke oven operation	+	★	★	−	⊙			⊙
Steel converter operation	□		□	□	⊙	−	□	□
Steel pouring	□		⊙	□	⊙	−	★	★
Reheating furnace operation, hot strip mill					□	□	+	
Hot strip finishing mill operation	□		★	□	□	★		⊙
Plate finishing mill operation			★		⊙			
Crane operation			−	⊙	□	−	⊙	−
Cold strip mill operation	+		+		□	□		
Pipe mill operation		□	□		□			
Gilding	+				□			
Boilers engine room	□	□	★	□	⊙	□	−	−
Analysis		□		−	⊙	□	−	−
DL driving	★		★		⊙		★	−

Note: ⊙ Regular rotation to all positions in the workshop
      ★ Rotation to all positions, not regularly
      □ Partial rotation
      + No rotation
      − No reference to rotation.

Source: Shinnittetsu Rōdōkumiai (Nippon Steel Confederation of *Trade Unions*) *Chōsa Jihō* (Bulletin) August 1971.

shop also there was complete job rotation. The customs of the individual steelworks and workshops thus appear to have taken precedence over such factors as the mill lineage and when it had been established.

4.2.4 Extent of Job Rotation in the 1950s

The next step required after this cross-sectional study of Nippon Steel plants should be a time-series analysis. The main question now to be asked is whether the 'egalitarian' rotation of jobs is a recent phenomenon. Since no appropriate statistics are available, the analysis will have to depend on studying the reports of four case studies which took place in the late 1950s.[10]

Case studies at the Yawata steelworks, in which job rotation was least practised according to Table 4.3, include the Tsuda survey (1959) and the Totsuka and Takahashi survey (1961). The former reported that partial job rotation was evident in the newly equipped workshops, whereas there was no mobility in the workshops with old equipment. Three years later when Totsuka and Takahashi studied five workshops in the rolling mills, they noted that the system of deciding assignments on the basis of seniority was being replaced by some kind of job rotation. Although actual examples were not provided, a partial rotation can be surmised, since Table 4.3 shows that by 1971 partial job rotation was being practised in the Yawata rolling mills.

The two other relevant surveys were the Takanashi report (1967) and the Kōshirō report (1959). Their studies of integrated steel mills in the Keihin industrial areas have demonstrated that job rotation was quite prevalent. The Kōshirō survey reported that there was substitution between two to three assignments in the small shape rolling mills, while in the blooming mills jobs were evenly rotated every two hours. The Takanashi survey noted partial job rotation in the plate rolling mills.

It thus appears from these four surveys that partial job rotation was quite widespread in the late 1950s, and even cases of regular rotation to all positions could be found. Since that time the rotation of jobs has, therefore, gradually become more widespread.

4.2.5 Separation of the Job and the Wage Rate

When the presence of 'egalitarian rotation' over a wide range of jobs is placed alongside the fact that two-thirds of the standard wage is not job-related, two issues need to be resolved. Why is there such a tenuous relationship between the job and the wage rate? And why are wage profiles apparently on a seniority basis, despite the assignments and the mobility between jobs being egalitarian?

The first question is well answered by the case study above of the ten workers in the blast furnace workgroup changing their positions every half-day so that over five days each job was repeated. In such a situation the job rate becomes more or less meaningless. Therefore instead of applying rates for each job a 'pool' system of rates was established for this workgroup, and redistributed to each member according to their basic rate. The remaining two-thirds of the worker's standard wage had anyway originally been determined without any reference to his job. The point may be argued in reverse that egalitarian mobility over a wide range of assignments is feasible because of the job and the wage rate being unrelated.

The second question can be answered by remembering that the egalitarianism of the job rotation is qualified by positioning inexperienced workers next to senior workers. Indeed to permit any kind of egalitarian mobility such a measure is essential. The seniority system of wage rises can consequently be viewed as compensation for the more experienced workers. Since the amount of time and effort the senior workers spend in training the inexperienced is continually fluctuating, establishing wage rates for each job would hardly be possible. And as the compensation given to senior workers in return for training others cannot be set at a fixed amount or rate, the rather ambiguous seniority rise is instead considered appropriate.

Moreover, the seniority-based wage profile in itself reflects mobility over a wide range of jobs, because the longer is the worker's employment the greater is the number of jobs he will have experienced. The senior worker can thus be substituted in a range of other jobs whenever there are minor changes in the composition of output. Also his flexibility in moving between assignments, including those in the operation shop, gives the senior worker a better understanding of the machinery and other equipment. The overall conclusion may be that it is no longer necessary for a worker's wage to correspond with his job in the short term when his career is internalized on the basis of his long-term employment in the company. Instead his wage profile is compatible with his long-term career.[11]

4.2.6 Little Competition With Inplant Subcontract Workers

Workers in the Fairfield plant of US Steel were seen in Chapter 3 rarely to transfer between workshops. When the demand for labour in one workshop increases, workers are brought in from the pool of unskilled labour and if labour demand falls the pool soaks up under-employed workers. First appearances in Japan suggest that the prevalence of inplant subcontract workers – often almost one-half of the employees in a newly built plant[12] – constitute a similar pool of unskilled labour, which proportionately would account for a higher proportion of workers than the labour pool in US Steel.[13] Inplant subcontract workers have been seen as a safety value for regulating employment, whose effectiveness increases the higher is their proportion relative to total employment. But this view cannot be sustained in the face of the real situation which is examined here.

In this case study, the required numbers of personnel for each assignment had been listed in *ad hoc* collective agreements. Although the management reserved the right to make changes in the listing, the customary practice was to obtain the prior approval of the steelworks union. The list of assignments was wholly confined to jobs for regular employees, and there were no stipulations allowing for subcontracting workers. There are thus clear limits on the jobs for which subcontract workers could be hired, with the regular workers' positions being effectively protected. The distinct boundary between jobs for regular employees and those for subcontract workers could be modified at times, but any modifications would be quite difficult to achieve in view of the custom of obtaining the union's approval. Consequently a reduction in labour demand would rarely lead to regular employees moving into the positions of subcontract workers who would then be made redundant. In fact the inplant subcontract workers associated with each steel works have formed their own unions, which are affiliated with the Japanese Federation of Iron and Steel Workers Unions. Except in the long term, regular and subcontract workers represent non-competing groups.

4.2.7 The Procedures for Transfers

Even in the process industries – especially the steel rolling mills which bear a close resemblance to a machinery industry – fluctuations in the demand for labour do occur. But the change in labour demand is usually specific to a certain product in the case of a company manufacturing a range of items. Employment can therefore be regulated by transfers, in addition to the usual approach of adjusting recruitment levels. One special feature observed in the course of this case study in a steelworks was the rarity of temporary transfers, to the extent that they were not even recognized under the plant union's policy. In any case labour demand in the steel industry appears to be quite stable for minor fluctuations in output levels relative to the pattern, discussed later, which is found in the machinery industries. Vacancies which arose because of workers retiring were filled by the recruitment of new personnel and any temporary gaps were covered by overtime work. But long term or large fluctuations in output inevitably required changes in workers' assignments. In particular, there were sometimes changes in shifts – for example, from one daytime to two daytime shifts, or the converse. Consequently changes in the number of workers in the department and corresponding transfers are required. All these issues are subject to negotiation between the plant management and the union. The established custom in this case is for the management side to make detailed proposals, explaining the reasons and changes required, in order to obtain the union's consent. Obviously personnel changes in one department requiring transfers would influence assignments in other department. The question of which other departments should be involved was made by the personnel manager with the assent of the plant union.

The major problem then remaining is to select the personnel to be transferred. In this case, rules such as the 'posting-bidding' system or the right of seniority, which were observed in US steelmakers, did not appear to be recognized. Instead the three relevant supervisors – department head, foremen and subforeman – hold discussions to decide on which workers should be transferred. When the transfer is to a workshop requiring completely different technical skills, the worker would once again have to learn specific skills which are not necessarily dependent on his already acquired ability. But a transfer to a workshop requiring similar technical skills would, in contrast, give the worker an opportunity for extending his ability; so consideration has to be given to not only the negative aspects of a transfer, but also its potential benefit to a worker. Giving significant consideration to factors such as improving promotion prospects by transferring to a workshop whose personnel have a different age composition has also been observed in the chemical industries.

In the case of this steelworks the custom is for the three supervisors concerned to convey their intentions about whom to transfer to the relevant senior shop steward, who would then confirm that the candidate agreed to the transfer. It would be up to the senior shop steward's judgement in the case of an unwilling candidate whether to exert persuasion or to discuss with the department head the possibility of withdrawing his name from the transfer list. Nearly a half of the senior shop stewards were themselves subforemen, but their way of dealing with the issue of an unwilling candidate did vary. On occasion the senior shop steward himself tried to persuade the candidate to participate in the transfer. On other occasions, the senior shop steward chose to ask the department head to revoke an unwilling candidate's name as the latter's feelings were given due weight. There were even times when the unresolved issue was taken up to plant union level, whereupon negotiations with the plant management led to the proposed transfer of a worker being rescinded. In conclusion, it did appear that the agreement of the concerned worker to a proposed transfer was customarily confirmed by the union. But it is significant that no fixed rules exist on how to select the workers to be transferred.

4.2.8 Workers' Careers in a Process Industry

As well as the above case study in a steelworks, four cases in the chemical industry were observed, which led to the following general conclusions:

1. Mobility within the workshop, which occurs fairly often, appears to be conducted on egalitarian principles. And each worker would thereby have experience in almost all of the positions in his workshop.
2. In addition, workers are often moved between workshops which perform similar operations. The workers' careers are consequently extended to incorporate the skills required in related workshops.
3. This mobility within the worker's career is subject to neither the management's nor the labour union's involvement in negotiations. Instead, each workshop appears to follow its own customs without any management directives.
4. Transfers of workers to unrelated workshops do also occur, though infrequently. In such cases the plant union plays a greater part, because such permanent transfers are potentially more disadvantageous for union members.
5. The main way of protecting employment in the case of output

fluctuations is to transfer regular workers between workshops, without necessarily changing the number of inplant subcontract workers. What contradicts the usual view of the role of subcontract workers is the clear distinction between their job content and that of the regular workers. There is therefore little scope for the union to utilize inplant subcontract workers as a safety value for changes in employment levels.

These five conclusions refer to workshops of process industries. But in a machinery industry, where fluctuations in output have a much greater impact on the level of employment, one would suspect that the plant union must have struggled to achieve any kind of career structure for its members.

4.3   RELIEF TRANSFERS AND EMPLOYMENT PROTECTION IN MACHINERY WORKS

The author was able to observe about 20 different workshops in seven machinery works. 'About 20' relates is the fact that the depth of the interviews varied considerably, so that the information obtained from quite a few of the workshops was insufficiently detailed. And, indeed, such inadequacies are inevitable because – in just the same way as in the process industries – written rules concerning mobility of workers within the workshop are non-existent. Nor are the workshop's own customs when postings are formally egalitarian easily recognized, unlike in the workshops of the process industries. The mobility of workers within machinery industry workshops is therefore subject to some ambiguity.

The technological factor ought to be the first to be analyzed out of the various factors which may affect a worker's career. There are distinct technological differences between the following four kinds of workshops:

1. Non-mass production machinery workshop
2. Non-mass production assembly workshop
3. Mass production machinery workshop
4. Mass production assembly workshop.

When each of these four groups is closely observed in a large industrial machinery works, the technological factor can be deduced as being significant in affecting the shape of a worker's career, because other variables stemming from the economic and social environment as well as tradition can be taken as constant. These initial observations will then be supplemented with information from other cases. The large industrial machinery works with about 4000 employees (Which was the prime example among the case studies) will here be called plant A.[14]

4.3.1 Mass Production Workshops

A mass production machinery workshop in plant A consisted of one foreman and 24 men, who were divided into three workgroups. Each group was responsible for the machine manufacture of one out of somewhat different products in a single manufacturing process. Both situations of one man being responsible for one machine and of another operating two or three machines could be observed. The new employees who were high school leavers were initially trained by spending about one month each in seven different workshops under the same department. They were then posted to the work group's easiest jobs within their assigned workshops, and they would subsequently move to other jobs while acquiring experience. One workgroup's manufacturing process is not always confined to exactly the same product specifications. So once the new employee has acquired the ability to cope with slight alterations in the product specifications, he could enter the rotation of jobs handled by the workgroup. The group's members, who numbered around eight, would rotate their jobs about once a week, and there was also some shifting of workers between the workgroups at certain times. Thus, after about five to six years the workers should finally have had some experience in all of the workshop's positions.

In a workshop for assembly mass production at the same plant A there were 20 men under a foreman. It should be remarked that the work bore little resemblance to the mass production of an automated assembly line, since in one month the workshop produced only about 800 pieces of a single product type. The newly assigned workers began by undertaking the easier jobs, such as fastening bolts. Then their jobs would be changed until finally over some period of time they had experienced all the workshop's positions, though the order of postings and the time spent in each were not fixed. The job changes are decided by the foreman who takes into account the operational and personnel conditions at the time. Nevertheless workers can either directly tell the foreman, or communicate through the shopfloor committee, about their desired postings.

In the mass production workshop it appeared that a worker's career was formed through his experience in all the workshop's postings, though the customs of the individual workshops differed as to whether the rotation of jobs was made at fixed intervals. The decisions on mobility within the workshop are made neither by the plant union on its own or in negotiations with the management. Certainly the union has no say in the matter, but neither does the practice of job rotation depend wholly on managerial initiatives. The foreman has planned that in the long run most workers should have had experience in all the workshop's postings, even when the jobs are rotated at arbitrary intervals. So even though the foreman makes the relevant decisions, the room for his own discretion is very limited, particularly when the rotation is at fixed intervals. These characteristics of mobility in the workshops of plant *A* were also observed in the mass production workshops of three other machinery works. In two of the factories the custom is for the workers to have had experience in all the positions, although the order of movement and the time intervals are not definitely established. In the remaining factory mobility was evident in only a few of the workshops, although in other respects the factory's operations resembled the earlier examples.

4.3.2   On the Auto Assembly Line

The classic kind of mass production shop is often cited to be the auto assembly line. Interviews were, therefore, carried out in two different companies' auto assembly plants. In one of the plants a work group was comprised of 10–15 positions on the assembly line, between which the regular worker would move at indefinite intervals so as to have experience in all the different positions. At one point in time the regular and the seasonal worker resemble each other in that both are doing simple, repetitive operations; but in the long run only the regular workers, who become experienced in most of the group's positions, could be substituted easily into any job. Their ability contributes greatly to the efficiency of auto production. Daily changes occur very frequently in an assembly line workshop. Along the same line are assembled cars with various specifications, such as with two or four doors or with an air conditioner. Although these changes are of a minor nature, they require adjustments in the deployment of the workforce in order to maintain a high speed of production. A certain job, which has been done by a less experienced worker when two-door vehicles predominate, may be more efficiently carried out by an experienced worker when the output of more four-door vehicles are required. Similar changes may happen in the composition of the work force; at times relatively many of the workers may be inexperienced because of there being more new recruits, while the converse holds at other times. And inevitably an absentee worker's position has to be covered by someone. To cope with such changes in conditions a flexible workforce who can work anywhere on the line is needed. The foreman was observed in the case study to make the decisions on when to move workers and to which positions. But the custom is to ensure that the regular workers are proficient in almost all of the positions in their workgroup, so that the subforeman can be appointed from among those with experience in all the group's assignments.

In another automobile plant where workers, mobility was much more deliberately practised, the 20–30 assignments in one workshop were rotated about every three months. A chart, which was hung in the workshop area, showed which positions had been held by each worker. It was thus apparent that the number of jobs experienced by a worker was directly related to his length of service; nevertheless, it appeared that there was no difference with other mass production workshops in that over time workers customarily had experience in all the positions. And the way in which the plant union's influence in practice was almost nonexistent is also similar to the situation in other mass production workshops.

4.3.3 Non-mass Production Assembly Workshop

The pattern of mobility observed in these workshops resembled that in the mass production shops. In a non-mass production workshop at plant *A*, 15 workers were divided into three–five small work groups, each of which consisted of both experienced and inexperienced workers who were responsible for assembling one large industrial assembly machine. Even one small group has to handle the assembly of many types of goods, whose differences are highly detailed. The inexperienced workers could thereby become proficient in assembling a variety of goods while working within the small group. In addition workers were shifted between the groups so that in the long run they would have participated in assembling all the goods handled by their workshop, even though the workers' mobility between the groups was irregular.

This aspect was more apparent in the case of another plant's non-mass production assembly workshop, where there were 30–40 workers assembling one type of heavy electrical good. One of the observed workshops was responsible for assembling switchboards, which could be divided into seven types according to their detailed specifications and size. Each type had been assigned to one small workgroup, which consisted of about five workers. About once a year the small groups rearranged themselves when they would move on to assemble another type of switchboard. There was also mobility between this and two other workshops which were handling similar goods of different sizes, with the result that the shopfloor workers could become proficient in assembling all the goods handled by these three closely related workshops. The overt decisions on these movements among workers are taken neither by the management or the plant union, but by the foreman in exactly the same way as in the other cases studied.

4.3.4   Non-mass Production Machinery Workshops

The conditions in a non-mass production engineering shop are quite different to assembly work. In one of these workshops in plant *A* 20 workers, who are operating various types of multipurpose machine tools including lathes, turret lathes and fraises, would carry out more than 100 diverse kinds of operations in one month. Since the number in a lot never goes beyond 25 units, the epithet 'non-mass production' is certainly appropriate. A high school leaver on entering the company spends six months moving round the plant's non-mass production machinery shops so as to have had a short experience in using each kind of machine tool. He then would be assigned to a workshop where at first he would be allotted either a lathe or a fraise to operate. Usually he would operate the most common six foot lathe rather than the four foot or eight foot lathe. After a few years he would also be given experience in operating the two other types of lathe, but not often would he be allotted a machine other than a lathe. Although the management had recommended that the workers should have had experience in operating each kind of machine tool so as to become more versatile, the shopfloor workers – especially the older men – were unwilling to be assigned to other machine tools. Since any mobility which did occur was indeterminate as to the order or time interval of assignments, the workers over a long period of service would have handled at most only two kinds of machine tool. The non-mass production machinery shop does not, therefore, display the trends evident in the mass production and non-mass production assembly workshops where workers enjoy mobility between all the workshop's positions.

The conclusion that mobility is limited does not, however, imply that the content of each job is static. Since each machine tool has many functions in machining various products, the worker has to be experienced in performing diverse operations. When the foreman is taking decisions on how to allocate the various jobs, he has to take into account each worker's level of ability, whose measure is clearly perceptible within the workshop. Even so, there are times when relatively many jobs require a high level of ability which could not be matched by the workshop having a good balance of proficient workers. Such variable conditions mean that jobs would have to be allocated flexibly, with inexperienced workers not necessarily being given only easy tasks. The worker's career could, therefore, be furthered by the instruction he has to be given in work methods. The way in which the foreman and experienced workers assist in training others varies from detailed direction and continuous supervision to just giving instructions and then leaving the job up to the inexperienced worker. In such ways, workers are able to experience a variety of jobs over a long period of employment.

Similar patterns can be found in the non-mass production machinery shops in the other plants. In one plant, it was more evident that a worker was normally required to have had experience in operating at least two kinds of machine tool during his career, though he would hardly ever have been responsible for more than two. As is common to all the non-mass production engineering shops, the plant labour union plays no part at all in decisions concerning the allocation of jobs within the workshop.

4.3.5   A Theory of Semi-autonomous Work Groups

The above general observations stemming from case studies of mobility within different kinds of workshop lead to the following propositions:

1. Apart from the case of non-mass production machinery shops, a common aspect in all the machinery industry companies is mobility

among workers, who thereby experience all the positions in the workshop. The scope of a worker's career thus at least encompasses all the operations in his workshop, in which respect his career resembles that of a worker in the process industries. Even in the non-mass production engineering workshops where the worker rarely changes his posting, the content of his work does vary so that his career in effect resembles that of other workers, comprising diverse jobs.

2. It appears that the scope of US workers careers is narrower than in Japan (although this conclusion must be qualified because of the limited interviews carried out in US machinery industries). There are few job grades and many jobs are incorporated within one job grade in the US workshop. Consequently, even though the US worker can pass through all the job grades over a period of years in accordance with seniority rights, he does not necessarily experience all the positions in his workshop. The implication is that when a simple comparison of mobility in the workshop is made, the Japanese regular worker's career does appear to be somewhat broader because of his experience in all the workshop's operations. This feature is strikingly exemplified by the case of the automobile assembly line. Many US workers – apart from the reliefmen – hardly ever move to other positions on the assembly line. And though the US reliefmen have had wide experience, their proportion relative to the total labour force in a US company must inevitably be much lower than that of Japanese regular workers. This distinction in the breadth of workers' careers between the Japanese and the US machinery industries becomes more marked when mobility beyond the workshop is examined later on.

3. Mobility in the Japanese machinery industry workshop does not depend on established rules about whom to move, to where and for what period of time. While a systematic egalitarian rotation of jobs can often be observed in the process industry workshops, in the case of the machinery industries this kind of formal rotation is not apparent, except in some of the mass production workshops. The movement of workers to other workshops occurs irregularly in response to conditions at a given time.

4. The common feature in all the workshops observed concerned who should be the arbiter of mobility within the workshop. Any kind of agreement resulting from negotiations between the plant management and union had never been adopted. Nor had the

management – whether in the guise of the personnel section or the production management section – given any directives on moving workers between the workshop's positions. Indeed the pattern of mobility varies even within the same plant because, in every workshop, it is the foreman who is the arbiter.

That statement is not intended to imply that the foreman has complete autonomy in taking decisions on mobility in his workshop. Especially in some of the mass production workshops (where egalitarian rotation as in the process industries exists), the foreman had little room for using his own discretion. Even though such an egalitarian rotation does not exist in most of the workshops, limits to the foreman's discretion are imposed by the custom of ensuring that each worker should have had experience in almost all of the workshop's positions after a certain period of time. These limits are a function of the foreman's role as representative of the group of workers in his workshop, among whom he has previously worked himself. He is not merely the tip of the management's administration, which task is indeed not so significant for him because of the improbability of further promotion. But because the workshop scale is relatively small in the process industries, and because in the past era of high economic growth there had been a rapid increase in the machinery industries' labour force, the prospect of being promoted to foreman was quite high. So the career of a foreman is comparable to that of the shopfloor workers, among whom he can really be perceived as just the most senior within the group, even though the majority of the workers would never themselves become foremen. It is therefore quite natural that, as in West Germany, foremen continue to be union members.

The foreman's margin for his own discretion in making decisions on mobility is therefore primarily governed by the need to allocate jobs flexibly in response to changing conditions in the amount and content of the work, in the quality of the labour force and in the installation of improved machinery and equipment. A highly flexible allocation of jobs is the most effective way of coping with such incessant changes in working conditions. The placement of jobs can be shifted to correspond to the expanding skills of each worker in the group. And measures such as positioning proficient workers next to the inexperienced can greatly lower the cost of adapting to changing conditions. The mangement thus find it expedient to recognize tacitly the autonomous function of the workshop group, with the foreman as leader, in following its own customs in mobility. Indeed this autonomous group of workers who themselves decide on their work methods and assignments is sometimes considered as representing a highly sophisticated form of participation by shopfloor workers in management.

4.3.6   'Familiar' and 'Remote' Workshops

The existence of the semi-autonomous workshop group does not preclude any movement of its workers to other workshops within the company. The amount of completed work which the management calls for has to be altered in response to fluctuations in the business cycle, shifts in demand and changes in the company's market share. The main way to implement adjustments in the output of different departments was observed in all the case studies to be transferring workers to other workshops. Movements between workshops can be divided into normal or permanent transfers and those which are temporary. In the latter case the worker returns to his original workshop after a period of one, three or six months, whereas a normal transfer would be considered to be more permanent. In many Japanese workplaces a temporary transfer is known as *ōen*, which may be translated as 'relief'.

One characteristic observed in the machinery industries was that mobility between workshops was more prevalent than in the process industries. Though statistical corroboration is unavailable, interviews have shown a distinct difference in the extent of such movements, which probably arises because output fluctuations in the machinery industries require a speedy response in employment levels. But the relationship between output and employment in the process industries is much less direct. The second observed characteristic of mobility between workshops in the machinery industries was the overwhelming predominance of relief transfers, which appeared to occur frequently as opposed to permanent transfers to other workshops.

Relief transfers consequently have a major impact on the career of a worker in a machinery industry. The most obvious inference is that employment security is thereby enhanced. A relatively large machinery industry works, which has a labour union, usually manufactures a range of products, which differ also in size and other specifications. Trends in demand are generally not consistent across all the products manufactured by one factory. Employment security can therefore be heightened by transferring workers from a workshop whose product faces a fall in demand to one where demand is expanding. Yet in the US industries which were discussed in Chapter 3, relief transfers are not apparently practised. Instead surplus workers in one workshop would be temporarily laid off, while new employees are being accepted in the workshop whose product is enjoying gains in demand. There was some limited evidence from the case studies that when the US company gave precedence to seniority rights, senior workers might be transferred while the younger ones would be made redundant. In Japanese machinery industries, in contrast, relief transfers are much wider in scope, which thereby enhances employment security by averting redundancy.

There is, however, a trade-off to some extent with relief transfers' second function which affects workers' careers – namely the impact on the quality of employment. What is really important for workers who have certain skills is the protection of appropriate employment utilizing their own skills. Ensuring the quality of employment will here be called job protection. There are usually two distinct alternatives when a worker is temporarily transferred to another workshop. One is that his new assignment does not involve any extension or utilization of his already acquired skills. Consequently his career is adversely affected by the transfer, which implies a lack of job protection. The other possibility is that the worker gains the opportunity of extending his acquired skills because of their resemblance to the techniques required by the workshop to which he transfers. This distinction between these alternative kinds of transfer is crucial to the potential for a worker's skills and career. Therefore, in analyzing the incidence of relief transfers, a transfer which furthers a worker's career will be denoted as occurring between 'familiar' workshops, while the alternative kind of transfer takes place between 'remote' workshops. The most crucial issue in relief transfers is, therefore, whether they are to familiar workshops or remote ones. The definition of which workshops are familiar is, though not explicitly written in any rules, quite clearly understood by the shopfloor workers. In most cases, familiar workshops comprise the primary administrative grouping of workshops, such as the subsection or section. The union's regulation of relief transfers must vary, depending on whether or not the transfer is to take place between familiar workshops.

4.3.7 Relief Transfers Between Familiar Workshops

The adjustment needed in personnel to cope with imbalances in the workshops' labour force is initially conducted at the subsection or section level. In three out of the seven case studies in machinery industries on the incidence of relief transfers the levels of required personnel could be confirmed overall at the section level where there were consultation facilities, while in the other four cases discussions between the foremen of the concerned workshops and the section chiefs could establish whether there was a need for personnel adjustments. Relief transfers which took place within the subsection or section in practice barely affected the plant union. The only union regulation which was observed in five out of the seven cases was the maximum period allowed for temporary transfers – namely one – three months or, at the most, six months. Other relevant issues were settled within the section or subsection without any interference from the plant union or plant management.

The settling of decisions relating to temporary transfers within the section is not necessarily because of negligence on the part of the plant union, which will be seen, in contrast, to have a reasonable influence on transfers between remote workshops. Since relief transfers within the section were usually between familiar workshops – for example, between the large scale switchboard assembly shop and the workshop for small scale switchboards – workers could extend their own technical skills. The view that workers transferred relatively willingly was therefore substantiated by the general response to interviews of individual shopfloor committee members in 15 workshops. The respondents also indicated that transfers between familiar workshops occurred rather frequently, except in the case of the non-mass production machinery workshops. In the latter case the multipurpose machine tools being used in familiar workshops were similar, so that job assignments rather than workers could be transferred between these non-mass production workshops.

The unavailability of data which would directly show the incidence of transfers between familiar workshops has been partially remedied by the opportunity of making an indirect estimate in the case of plant *A*, where there was a record of movements between remote workshops over a two year period. In both years five–six per cent of union members were transferred to remote workshops, though the true figure could be higher because of omissions in the data. All the shopfloor committee members interviewed were in agreement that the incidence of transfers between familiar workshops involved many more workers than transfers between remote workshops. Supposing, therefore, that 10 per cent or more of the workers were transferred to familiar workshops each year, the clear inference is that such transfers, which can extend even insubstantial careers, were certainly not exceptional. This aspect is worth noting, particularly in comparison to US machinery industry plants.

But the problem of choosing which workers to transfer still remains. Although the worker's skills may be extended by a transfer between familiar workshops, he has to cope with somewhat different jobs. What was stressed as a depressing factor by the shopfloor committee members was the awkwardness of entering into new relationships with other workers. Thus most workers were aware that there were some disadvantages in being selected for a transfer. Despite the selection always being made by the foreman, his approach was apparently affected by the workshop's own customs. Relatively inexperienced workers would be selected for transfer in many of the workshops, while in other workshops the more experienced would be transferred with the intention of extending their skills. There were few examples of any prior consultation on selection with the shop steward, doubtless because of the absence of fixed procedural rules. In three cases out of twenty the rotation system evidently played a part with egalitarianism in determining who should be transferred. It would seem, therefore, that – just as in the egalitarian rotation of jobs in the process industries – the functioning of Japanese workplaces is influenced to a surprising extent by egalitarian principles.

4.3.8 Relief Transfers to Remote Workshops

Our report on the case studies will concentrate on examples from plant *A*, where the information obtained was most plentiful. When imbalances in the workshops' labour force cannot be rectified within the section, recourse has to be made to relief transfers beyond the section. The custom was observed in which the plant management would inform the union – in principle one week beforehand – so as to obtain its consent to the proposed transfer. The plant union would be provided with a detailed plan showing the reasons for transferring which personnel to which workshop, and when. Before giving its consent, the plant union would confirm that the proposed workers were agreeable to the relief transfer. Such formalities seem to suggest that the union has some control over all aspects of transfers, including consequent changes in working conditions. Indeed, the union set the time period for relief transfers at less than three months, with the result that, if the transfer period had to be extended, the union's consent would have had to be obtained once more.

Despite such practices, the problem of how to select the workers had not been wholly resolved. It was earlier remarked (p. 37) that the senior shop steward would make sure that the workers chosen after discussions between himself and the foreman were agreeable to the transfer. Responses to the interviews indicated that the foreman's unofficial request was rarely refused by the workers concerned. There were also just a few workshops where – as in the case of transfers between familiar workshops – the shop steward would be consulted, and others where a rotation system had been adopted. Since the plant union, however, does play a part in confirming that the workers selected by the foreman for transfers between remote workshops are willing, this is an essential difference to the procedure for transfers between familiar workshops.

4.3.9   The Labour Union's Involvement in Permanent Transfers

There is a certain amount of government data available on the extent to which labour unions have a say in permanent transfers.[15] In roughly one-third of the instances surveyed the union negotiates, in another one-third it is merely notified, and in the remaining one-third it is not involved at all. Such overall figures, however, do not throw any light on the actual nature of the union's intervention, which would differ depending on the kind of transfer being undertaken.

For convenience, voluntary transfers will not be considered because they are a minority. Involuntary transfers may be generally divided into those which occur between workshops in a single plant and those which take place between plants. In the latter case, there is the additional cost of removal expenses. When the issue of job protection is considered, transfers between plants can be further distinguished by whether or not the worker is transferred to a similar workshop. The establishment of a new plant could, for example, enhance job protection for workers transferring into workshops which require extended utilization of their acquired skills. In particular the disadvantage of moving residence could be outweighed if there were more opportunities for promotion to supervisory posts. There are occasions, nevertheless, when transfers to other plants imply less job protection, because at the same time a plant is closed or employment in the company is being cut back. As such occasions are highly disadvantageous to the labour force, the union's intervention is much more evident than in the case of other kinds of transfers. Among the case studies, in all but one the labour union negotiated in detail the number of workers to be transferred, and the conditions for transfers. One example was the length of the period during which the merit rating in the former workshop had to be maintained. When a worker was transferred to an unfamiliar job in a remote workshop, he would naturally be assessed at a lower rating than in his previous position. Because this disadvantage was so apparent, the plant union regulated the minimum period – say, to three years – in which his former rating should be maintained, even though his achievement level in the new workshop might actually be lower. The selection of the workers to be transferred, however, remained as an area in which the union had little say. Where many workers were to be transferred, the approach in principle would be to invite volunteers through bidding and applications, though actual examples did not appear within the scope of our case studies. In the case of just a few workers being transferred, discussions with the union would concern matters such as maintaining wage levels, rather than the selection of workers to be transferred. Generally, this issue remains as the foreman's prerogative, with the shopfloor committee being consulted in only a relatively few workshops. But the union would still have the right to confirm that the proposed workers were willing to transfer to other plants. And it is common that the workers, having been unofficially informed of the transfer by the foreman, would consult the shopfloor committee. There were some examples where the workers would not accept the transfer without submission to plant level negotiations. In the case of permanent transfers between a single plant's workshops, most of the above comments are still relevant, though the union's involvement falls to four cases out of seven. Still it does appear from the case studies that the union's intervention or voice in permanent transfer is relatively effective.

4.4 FOUNDATIONS OF QUALITY CONTROL CIRCLES

The premise of a wide range of skills being held by individual workers helps to clear away the fog from many enigmas. One of the questions which can now be unravelled is that of high labour morale in Japan. The Introduction suggested that high labour morale may be most positively expressed in QC (quality control) circle activities geared towards raising productivity. Explanations of why QC circles have become widespread generally ignore the technical background and the importance of wide-ranging skills.

4.4.1   Common Explanations of QC Circles

A common explanation of QC circles is that of group loyalty. But this fails to account for the uneven incidence of QC circles, which in Japan are mainly confined to large companies (Table 1 in the Introduction).

Another explanation stems from the assumption that Japanese labour unions are weak, and that workers meekly follow managerial directives. It is indeed true that QC circle activities are under managerial initiative. Yet the assumption of labour unions having no power – or at the most being weak – would suggest that QC circles should proliferate where there were no labour unions and consequently more powerful management leadership. However, QC circles tend to be more prevalent where there are labour unions whatever the company size (see Table 1).

A closer look at QC circles reveals that most are actually dealing with technological aspects requiring sophisticated technical know-how. If workers' attitudes were merely governed by loyalty to the company and obedience to the management, how could they think of technical improvements? One necessary condition for QC circles should thus be that workers have acquired some technical capabilities. Second, unless there is the opportunity for workers to demonstrate their technical capability, through the right to try out ways of raising productivity, any flow of suggested improvements will be curtailed. The third condition requires some kind of incentive so that it is in the interest of workers to improve their productive efficiency. The fourth requirement is that there should be a framework for guaranteeing workers a share in the productivity gains to which they have contributed. Let us now examine our proposed conditions in order.

4.4.2   Understanding the Production Process

Since QC circles activities are geared towards devising different work methods, three intellectual attributes are usually indispensable:

(a) Workers should be able to utilize problem solving techniques such as Pareto analyses, checksheets, cause and effect diagrams, etc. The acquisition of such knowledge is widely encouraged by QC circles in both Japan and the USA.
(b) For workers to have the aptitude to acquire such knowledge a

certain intellectual standard is necessary. A reasonable proxy would be the level of school education attained. This proxy is fairly invariable among the industrialized countries at least. Thus neither of the above attributes can be considered to be especially advantageous in Japan's case.

(c) The workers should have a good understanding of the production process itself (this attribute is the one which will be analyzed here). Let us take the example of a large and complex machine being operated by the workers apparently simply pushing buttons and pulling levers. Yet the workers have to understand the machine's operations in order to be able to improve their productivity. Another more specific example of a QC circle's success took place in an automated workshop for wrapping sausages. The workers had been aware that the defect rate for imperfectly wrapped sausages consistently remained above zero. The QC circle found that imperfect wrapping resulted from the sausages bending on account of heat. Corrective measures required, therefore, that the heating treatment of the sausages should be adjusted not only in this QC circles's workshop but also at the earlier processing stages. Thus to be able to engage in effective QC circle activities workers have to understand the production process in a wider sphere even than their own workshop.

Such detailed technological knowledge can hardly have been learned in the worker's schooldays or in general training centres, and must have been acquired while working on different assignments. In other words the significant factor, as was examined in Sections 4.2 and 4.3 above, is the wide ranging skills of the workers and their consequent ability to understand the production process.

The importance of understanding the production process has given this factor first place among the basic conditions outlined above for QC circles to function, and such technical knowledge is one aspect of the way blue-collar workers in large Japanese companies have achieved white-collarization.

4.4.3 Industrial Democracy on the Shopfloor

Even though workers may thus have the ability to devise ways to improve productivity, their ideas will not be realized unless they are given the right to try out different work methods. If workers constantly have to seek the approval of production management to try out their ideas, their enthusiasm would quickly diminish. This right to experiment has, therefore, been designated as the second condition for QC circles.

One of the major findings in Chapter 3 and Chapter 4 has been that the movement of workers in large Japanese companies to different positions within the same workshop mostly depends on each workshop's own customs. As has been demonstrated, the principal route for skill formation stems from the worker's wide experience in holding various positions within the workshop. Such movements between different jobs is not a subject of negotiation with the labour union. Nor is the decision made by the personnel department or any other managerial section. Instead the individual foreman decides, while giving due consideration to the customs of his workshop. Thus the ways in which such movements between jobs occur vary even within the same plant of one company.

In the US, by contrast, the work manual, compiled by the industrial engineering department, precisely determines the approach and the routine for carrying out each job; work methods are thus determined at the plant level. In Japan, work manuals are produced by the production management and other departments and standard work routines are recorded, but once the shopfloor workers have demonstrated a creative aptitude for improving work methods, the manual is disregarded. Work manuals are not held sacrosant in Japan and their compilation is not taken very seriously.

The general conclusion is that the actual authority in large Japanese companies to decide on aspects such as the shopfloor workers' assignments, their movements on the shopfloor and work routines mostly appears to be held at the shopfloor level. The consequent right to try out devices in the workshop for improving productivity must therefore also usually exist on the shopfloor.

Whitehill and Takezawa's study (1968) is one of the few surveys which presented identical questions to Japanese and US blue-collar workers in the same industries' large companies.[16] One question, shown in Table 4.4, asked to what extent the supervisor should consult lower ranking workers before making any change in their work methods. The response rates were only minimally different between Japan and the USA, with the overwhelming majority believing that the workers should be consulted beforehand. For the further questions, though, there was a clear distinction between Japan and the USA. Table 4.5 shows the response to the question of how

TABLE 4.4   Consultative versus unilateral supervision (worker's attitudes in large companies in the USA and Japan, percentage distribution of answers to opinion survey)

When changes in work methods must be made, I think a supervisor should:	All Respondents	
	USA (%)	Japan (%)
Allow workers to decide for themselves what changes should be made and how to make them	3	2
First ask workers for their suggestions regarding proposed changes, and then decide what to do	66	73
First decide on the changes, and then ask for the cooperation of the workers	22	21
Decide himself what the changes shall be and put them into effect, since he is in charge of the work	9	4

Source: Whitehill and Takezawa (1968).

TABLE 4.5   Unjustified changes in work routines (worker's attitudes in large companies the USA and Japan, percentage distribution of answers to opinion survey)

If I am unable to convince my supervisor that a change which seems unjustified to me should not be made in my work methods or assignment, I would:	All Respondents	
	USA (%)	Japan (%)
Resist his orders and refer the disagreement to the union	39	34
Resist his orders unless convinced by my co-workers that I am wrong	7	25
Obey his orders to avoid any unfavourable consequences	4	15
Obey his orders since, as supervisor, he must have the authority to give orders	50	26

Source: See Table 4.4.

the worker would react when his supervisor was making an apparently unjustifiable change in his work methods or assignment. Half the US workers surveyed would have obeyed the supervisor's orders because of his greater authority; but only a quarter of the Japanese workers felt the same way. The responses from shopfloor workers to the question concerning consultation over promotion decisions are shown in Table 4.6. Two-thirds of US respondents thought that management should use its own judgement, whereas the corresponding rate for Japanese workers was only a little over one-third, results may be interpreted as demonstrating that the right of Japanese shopfloor workers to voice their opinions is relatively high, although an alternative interpretation might suggest that the response rates indicate only desires rather than the realization of workers' rights. Nevertheless, case studies have shown that the trends in Table 4.6 do correspond to reality. The Derber and Chalmers survey, which investigated 40 US cases on three occasions in the late 1950s, found that not one of the local unions had a say in the appointment of supervisors,[17] yet a case study of plant unions in large Japanese companies during the same period revealed that shopfloor workers' opinions were sounded out on the appointment of foremen.[18] This practice of eliciting workers' opinions produces an environment conducive to the activities of QC circles. At the same time, it does not necessarily follow that industrial democracy on all levels functions well in Japan. In particular, the right of labour unions to influence the company's overall practices may be greater in the USA than in Japan. So our observations here are confined to the conclusion that Japanese shopfloor workers have rather more discretionary rights than their US counterparts.

4.4.4   Career Progression Inside the Company

Even with the capability and the right to engage in productivity improving experiments, little would be achieved unless workers were given appropriate incentives. In general economics terminology, such incentives stem from 'internal labour markets'; the allocation as well as pricing of the labour force are conducted and determined within the company by the functioning of the internal labour market. The internal labour market serves to benefit workers staying in the company because of promotion and wage increments, while those who leave suffer a corresponding loss.

If the employee of a certain company would suffer a considerable

TABLE 4.6 Consultation before promotion (workers' attitudes in large companies in the USA and Japan, percentage distribution of answers to opinion survey)

In deciding upon promotion to various supervisory levels, higher management should:	All respondents	
	USA	Japan
Secure agreement from subordinates who will be affected	6	38
Secure agreement from the labour union on all such decisions	6	14
Consult the labour union before making such decisions	20	10
Make such decisions carefully on the basis of its own judgement	68	37

Source: See Table 4.4.

loss on moving elsewhere, it can be presumed that the vicissitudes of this company greatly influence its employees' prospects. When the company expands, their promotion occurs more rapidly. And if the company's sales contract, then not only is promotion delayed, but also there may be a real fear of redundancy. The costs associated with redundancy are more severe where an internal labour market is functioning. Even though employment may be found in another company, the original promotion prospects disappear. Therefore the employees have to support the growth of their company so as to avoid any substantial loss in promotion prospects. The employees realize the necessity of devising measures to raise productivity in order to make their company more competitive.

The above analysis is evidently applicable to both Japan and the USA. There is little difference in the degrees of internalization of labour markets for blue-collar male employees of large companies and the consequent incentive for them to improve productivity. In Western Europe as well it appears (from the limited interviews I have made) that blue-collar employees of large companies acknowledge the existence of internal labour markets, though the degree of inter-nalization is much shallower than in Japan and the USA, and the corresponding incentive to productivity improvements is probably somewhat lower. Still the European environment could be appropri-ate for QC circles as long as other conditions were fulfilled.

4.4.5   Unions and the Distribution of Gains

Unless there is an agreed formula for redistributing the gains from productivity improvements devised by the workers, their willingness to participate in QC circles will soon disappear. A suitable framework would first of all require that there should be regular discussions between employees' representatives and the management. Western European companies are known to have set up more extensive frameworks than elsewhere for employee consultations, to the extent that representatives attend executive meetings. While such attendance does not yet exist formally in Japan, the practice of consultations between the enterprise union leaders and the management is widespread. Despite there being a lack of agreement on the real significance of these consultations, some case studies – as discussed in Chapter 7 – suggest a fairly strong influence on managerial policy.

Employee contracts should clearly show how the workers would benefit from contributing to productivity gains. Much of this comes within the workers' traditional sphere of interest, and recent case study research[19] has demonstrated that enterprise unions do engage in vigorous negotiations on issues affecting shopfloor workers. A comparison between different countries of labour unions' negotiating strength will be undertaken in Chapter 7.

We should note the Japanese labour unions are in principle reluctant to take the path of positive cooperation intended to improve productivity. But, since the union members are aware that productivity gains are necessary, cooperation has had to be tacitly approved. Explicit negotiations on the conditions for participating in QC circles tend to be rare.

4.5   SKILLS TO DEAL WITH UNUSUAL OPERATIONS

4.5.1   'Unusual Operations'

The contribution to efficiency from workers having a wide range of skills is much broader and deeper than the contribution made by QC circle activities. In order to disclose fully how wide skills contribute, the content of work itself should first be considered. A close examination of work on the shopfloor suggests a division into two major components: (a) usual operations, and (b) unusual operations to deal with problems or changes. In the mass production machinery industry or the processing industry, 'usual operations' are supposedly repetitive and monotonous, and people are apt to conclude that hardly any skills are necessary. But, in any mass production workshop, although the work seems to be extremely repetitive, changes occur more frequently than is generally believed; the ratio of inferior products to the total, the type of defect in goods and the grade of defects can vary, along with minor changes in products, in product mix, and in the method of production.

Dealing with such changes falls under the (b) heading of 'unusual operations'. Machine operators in a typical workshop in Japan are required to locate the most minor problem or product defect as soon as possible, to identify the cause and to devise a way to eliminate the problem. Ideally, the workers are expected to be able to read the smallest indication and to forestall any problems, so that there is no actual damage. The importance of unusual operations is heightened in mass production processes where the production speed is great; the longer it takes to identify and eliminate any problems, the longer is the production line stopped, and hence the greater becomes the cost. Quick responses are of prime importance; ideally, any problems should be solved while the production line remains in motion.

It might be argued that a careful study of unusual problems would reveal patterns, which could be dealt with by standard ways as described in a manual, so that neither much skill nor much time would be required for their solution. According to experienced workers in mass production workshops, however, potential problems are so varied that standardization in the form of a manual is impracticable. And even if it were possible to compile a manual analyzing problems in terms of many standard patterns, the number of patterns to be consulted would be too large to permit a quick response.

A more significant argument is that standardization might conceivably reduce efficiency. An example would be illustrative. In a biochemical plant, since the volume of oxygen is of crucial importance, its minute adjustment is vital to the process. This minute adjustment could not be formalized by any practical standardization, which at best would simply set the upper and lower limits requiring adjustments of the oxygen volume when exceeded. Highly skilled workers, on the other hand, could adjust the oxygen volume even between the two simple limits.

An important feature which emerged in our observations on the shopfloor is that workers engaged in usual operations are also responsible for the component (b), unusual operations. There appears to be no reason why there should not be some kind of separated system with two different groups of workers responsible for different operations so that only the more highly skilled technicians undertake unusual operations. The Japanese system, however, is integrated since the same workers are responsible for both the components of usual and unusual operations. Provided that the workers are capable of dealing with unusual operations, an integrated system appears to be generally more efficient than a separated one. No more explanation would be necessary, once two contrasting scenes are compared: in one the shopfloor worker under a separated system has to call for a technician whenever he feels that some kind of adjustment is required, and in the other scene of an integrated system the worker himself deals with the problem. A proviso must made here: this analysis is not intended to imply that Japanese shopfloor workers handle almost all the unusual operations required to deal with problems. Naturally there are many production problems with which they cannot cope.

Another facet of the component (b), unusual operations, arises when the problem requires mending machinery. Although overall maintenance is obviously not within the shopfloor workers' job span, they are expected to handle minor maintenance tasks. In one Japanese biochemical plant, for example, the workers who are responsible for one section are usually divided on a rotation basis into five teams, each of which consists of two men. Four of the teams are engaged in shift work comprising the component (a), usual operations, and the non-maintenance part of component (b). The four teams, one of which is resting, cover three shifts of eight hours each. The fifth team works in the daytime only, mostly on maintenance by searching for pinholes in the pipes, of which they try to mend as many as possible by themselves, only contacting the maintenance men for the more difficult repairs.

It is important to realize that when capital equipment is comparable, differences in productive efficiency depend primarily upon the way in which 'unusual' operations are tackled. According to case studies, efficiency in dealing with usual operations is largely dependent on the workers' physical capability, insofar as the machinery is the same. In contrast, the conduct of unusual operations can show a large variance in efficiency.

What kind of skills are necessary for operators to be capable of undertaking the 'unusual' component of work? A series of skill requirements are involved. First, the worker needs to have accumulated experience on unusual patterns, which could otherwise not be understood by their very nature of being exceptional. But experience alone is not sufficient since the causes of problems lie in the product structure or in the machinery mechanisms; the worker must have some knowledge of those structures and of the functions and mechanisms of the machinery. These skills of the shopfloor workers are shared with the technicians, whose formal role requires them to know (and improve) the production processes. Thus it again emerges that operators in Japan share this knowledge, which is a crucial element of skills, with white-collar technicians.

4.5.2 Short, In-service Off-the-job Training

The main way for shopfloor workers to acquire intellectual skills is, as has been described earlier, through broad on-the-job-training to experience a wider range of production, which affords a better understanding of the production process as well as of the machinery. But such training alone cannot engender intellectual skills unless it is supplemented with short in-service off-the-job-training. It should not be thought that off-the-job-training is confined to the initial training course of about two weeks, which is too short a time for acquiring 'intellectual' skills; our concern here is with another type of training which serves the extremely useful purpose of providing a theoretical background to the workers' wide ranging experience. In order to understand this purpose, a specific case study would be more appropriate than a general exposition.

In a large plant producing electrical industrial machinery there are a variety of short training courses, which cater for blue-collar workers, about every five years. The way in which the courses are set is connected to the ranking system, which is of a type common in a contemporary large Japanese company. The blue-collar workers, including group leaders as well as foremen, are divided into five ranks: master, first, second, third and fourth class. Upgrading through these ranks partly depends on achievement in the training courses, which have the following features.

First, their duration is short. The course lasts 32 hours for the fourth class, 44 hours for the third class, and 16 hours for the first, amounting to less than 100 hours in aggregate. Some other voluntary courses in preparation for national skill tests which correspond to the second class, which will be explained later, may be added, but even then the total barely exceeds 120 hours. The effectiveness of the courses, though, lies in the way they reinforce and supplement the workers' long experience. It may incidentally be noted that there are lengthier in-service courses, which are, however, designed only for the small minority of supervisors.

Secondly, the course topics do not always seem to be very relevant to the work on the shopfloor. Even in the course for the fourth class who have had only a little work experience, a lecture on sales is included, although other topics are more reasonable: lectures on materials used and on safety, and a group discussion on how to promote work efficiency and on problems on the shopfloor. Still, an important fact remains: there is little in the course directly aimed at teaching skills necessary for conducting daily work. The same applies to the next course for the third class; the 44 hours consist of 4 hours of lectures on plant management policy by the plant manager, 20 hours of lectures on quality control, cost control, and improvement of work methods, with another 20 hours for learning theory related to the workers' own field, such as basic machining theory. It is only the last which is directed towards blue-collar workers; all of the other topics appear to be more suitable for white-collar workers. Similarly, the course for the first class is composed of a series of lectures on the demand situation, concerning which types of products sales are growing or declining, and the production situation concerning equipment development plans, and a group discussion on the role of workers holding the first class title. Thus in all of the in-service training it is difficult to find a course which is specifically designed for imparting the skills required for handling unusual operations. Instead there is a wide coverage of topics concerned with management problems which appear to be beyond the workers' sphere of interest; or, in other words, the blue-collar workers are learning much of what concerns white-collar workers.

A part of the in-service training does cover theoretical aspects of the workers' own field of work. In the third class 20 hours are allotted, as mentioned above, to learning such theory as machining. Subsequently the screening procedure for the second class comprises two parts: achievement in work performance so far and a paper test on the worker's own field, such as electrical machine assembly. The latter is functionally equivalent to the national skill test which under the Vocational Training Act consists of both a written and a practical test. Those with national skill certification of the second class are exempted from taking the paper test in the upgrading screening.

Since the national skill test, which is designed for 119 occupations, covers only a fraction of all occupations on the shopfloor, it can assess only general skills rather than the many specific shopfloor skills which are now required in large companies in industrialized countries.

It is particularly true of mass production companies that many jobs require a specific skill; for example, an estimation by managerial staff in a large mass production company has suggested that the national skill test is appropriate for testing the skills of only 20 per cent of the workers. Even in the non-mass production electrical industrial machinery plant described above, not all the workers can be covered by the national skill test, which is the main reason why a test apart from the national one has been prepared. The company encourages those workers for whom the national skill test is suitable to sit it by preparing lecture series and by making plant facilities freely available for the practical test.

Although theory designed for specific occupations does provide information on structural and functional aspects of production and machinery, it must be remarked that a theoretical course, which has been seen to be characteristic of off-the-job training is too general to teach workers the structure and functions of each machine which they operate daily. Nor could a training course ever impart the knowledge accumulated through experiencing a range of problems. Therefore off-the-job training is basically a supplement to what is the core task of acquiring skills.

Our conclusion has been based on just one case study, but the major features observed above of short in-service training courses have been corroborated by two recent statistical surveys on vocational training in Japan[20]. The data demonstrate that, as well as courses in preparation for the national skill test, off-the-job training is widely diffused. The case described above may, therefore, be inferred to be unexceptional for large Japanese companies.

4.6 REDUNDANCIES IN LARGE JAPANESE COMPANIES

4.6.1 The Cost of Redundancy

There is a popular impression that redundancies are exceptional in large Japanese companies where permanent employment (*shushin koyō*) is assumed to prevail. But in a competitive market redundancies can hardly, in practice, be avoided. The hypothesis that Japan has a dual economy suggests that an uncompetitive large company which refrains from making its regular workers redundant has to shift the burden of employment adjustment onto its subcontract workers and associated smaller companies. This theory, however, obscures the fact that in all economies there is a tendency for the burden of adjustment to business fluctuations to be borne by the weakest groups. The case study reports in Chapter 3 and in Sections 4.2 and 4.3 above have indicated that, in fact, large Japanese companies are less prone than their US counterparts, such as the steelmakers, to shift the required employment adjustments onto lower ranking workers (who would be made redundant), while the senior workers enjoy employment protection. From the viewpoint of the kind of work undertaken, the lower ranking workers in the USA are equivalent to Japanese subcontract workers. The boundary line between the jobs done by Japanese regular workers and those done by subcontract workers in the short term is not easily shifted. There is little scope, therefore, for an employment protection policy in which regular workers are moved into jobs vacated by redundancies among subcontract workers. The question must then arise of how the employment of regular workers in large companies can be regulated.

When the procedures for employment regulation and redundancies are being observed, on what aspects should our attention be focussed? In a situation where the internal promotion system and its associated enterprise specific skills prevail, a considerable loss has to be borne by those workers who are made redundant. The first obvious measure to minimize the scale of that loss would be to bring the number of workers made redundant to a minimum. For a given decline in output, actual redundancies can be minimized by reducing the labour hours worked and by transferring workers to different workshops within the company. In a large company it is quite probable that a need for employment cut backs in one area is accompanied by employment expansion in other departments. The scope for regulating employment by effecting transfers within the company is greater to the extent that the workers possess wide ranging skills which can be utilized in different jobs.

The second measure for minimizing the cost of redundancies for both the individual worker and the national economy depends on the degree to which those made redundant suffer losses stemming from the partly unrealized investment in acquiring skills. One of the losses suffered by the individual worker is that while he is unemployed he cannot use his skills. The higher the level of his skills and the longer is the duration of his unemployment, the greater is the worker's loss. This loss becomes greater still the more specific are the worker's skills, which may moreover exacerbate the possibility of finding new employment. The next loss arises if the only employment which the worker can find does not utilize his already acquired skills. This second loss also becomes greater the more specific and the more sophisticated are the worker's original skills. Under the assumption that internal promotion exists, these variables may be measured by the proxy variables of the worker's length of service and age. The question can then become whether large Japanese companies are making redundant those workers for whom there is a relatively high loss.

4.6.2 Employment Adjustment Procedures

In the Ministry of Labour's survey on trends in the labour market (*Rōdō Keizai Dōkō Chōsa*) there are statistics relevant to employment adjustment aggregated by company size. The statistics begin from 1966, but methods of employment adjustment became a prime subject in the survey only after the first 1973–4 oil crisis.The survey has been carried out four times a year by sending a questionnaire to 3400 manufacturing and distributing establishments with 30 or more employees. (The number of establishments surveyed was 4000 until 1978.) And the response rate is around two-thirds. The resulting statistics from the survey held in the last quarter of 1977 have been used in Figure 4.3 to show what kinds of employment adjustment were favoured after the oil crisis. Two particular aspects should be remarked upon. One is that the most common methods of employment adjustment in large companies were cutting overtime and transfers. Although the highest proportion shown is for cutting back on recruitment, this moderate measure barely merits the description of 'employment adjustment'. Neither reduction of labour hours by cutting overtime nor transfers of workers within the company stand out among the measures adopted by small companies. Therefore it does appear that in favouring these methods of adjusting employment the large companies, who have adopted the internal promotion system, are endeavouring to keep the number of workers made redundant as low as possible.

The second aspect of Figure 4.3 to be noted is that redundancies could not be avoided altogether. Over 2 per cent of large companies implemented the measure of 'voluntary redundancy' which is equivalent to redundancy. The practice of enlisting volunteers for redundancy by boosting the retirement allowance is quite prevalent also in

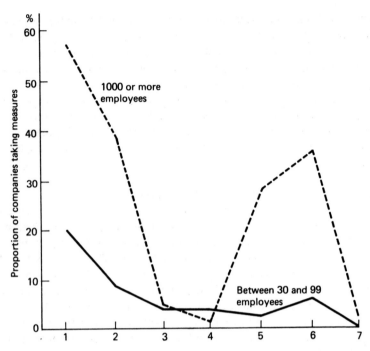

FIGURE 4.3   Measures for employment adjustment by company size
(manufacturing and distribution, November 1977)

Note: 1. Employment adjustment measures taken, total
        2. Cutbacks in recruitment
        3. Temporary workers made redundant
        4. Regular workers made redundant
        5. Transfers
        6. Overtime cutbacks
        7. Temporary lay-offs.

Source: Rōdōshō (Ministry of Labour) *Rōdō Keizai Dōkō Chōsa* (Labour Market
        Survey).

some West German industries. But is it really true that large Japanese companies resort to the emergency measure of voluntary redundancy only in a crisis when large income losses have been registered over a long period? As there is no statistical material directly relevant to this issue, case studies will have to assist in providing the answer. The Ministry of Labour publishes annually a bulky collection of Documents on History in the Labour Movement (*Shiryō Rōdō Undō-Shi*). This case study material is confined to the main industrial federations of unions, because redundancies affecting their members are considered important to developments in industrial relations.

Thus the reports on redundancies tend to be concentrated on those occurring in large companies, whose annual financial statements on corporate performance can also be easily obtained elsewhere.

In examining the relationship between redundancies and corporate performance, the cement industry has been chosen as the first example because there is an industrial federation covering the major cement company unions and there were redundancies during the 1970s. This example is followed by a tabulation of figures from the electrical machinery companies so as to make a comparison with a high growth industry. The net profit per employee in seven major cement companies in each year since 1973 has been plotted in Figure 4.4. The years in which the company has instigated redundancies have been indicated with a superimposed circle. Corporate deficits were registered in some years by four companies, out of which three companies had recourse to redundancies. The one exception was a company which merely registered a small deficit in just one year with clear surpluses in the surrounding years. In contrast, the companies effecting redundancies either suffered deficits for two consecutive years or registered a very large loss per employee. On the other hand, the remaining three companies where redundancies did not occur continually registered net profits on their income accounts. There does thus appear to be an unambiguous relationship between a company's recourse to redundancies and the registering of deficits for two consecutive years. This result implies that only two years of registered deficits are enough to justify redundancies by large Japanese companies, even though the financial situation has not reached a crisis.

Table 4.7 shows figures for the occurrence of redundancies accompanied by corporate losses in electrical machinery companies classified by size. Evidently there is some correlation between corporate deficits and a recourse to redundancies. But even when a deficit is registered for two consecutive periods, redundancy measures cannot be considered to be either a common or an exceptional option. What may instead be tentatively concluded is that a large company which registers a deficit might make regular workers redundant, even when the company's existence is not precarious.

4.6.3 Which Workers are Made Redundant?

The next issue to be investigated concerns whether those workers whose loss through unemployment is high are made redundant. It

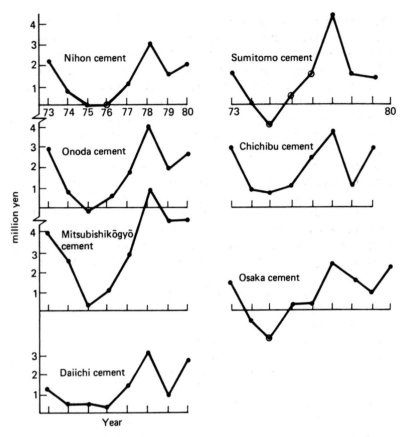

FIGURE 4.4   Relations between corporate deficits and redundancies (net profit/loss per employee in cement companies, 1973–80)

Source: Rōdōshō (Ministry of Labour) *Shiryō Rōdō Undōshi* (Documentary History of the Labour Movement)

was earlier reasoned that the loss would be higher to the extent that a worker's skills were specific and were sophisticated. Age has been adopted as a proxy for these variables, because our earlier discussion has demonstrated that there is an internal promotion system in large Japanese companies. Figures on redundancies by age are available in the Ministry of Labour's special survey on the labour force (*Rōdōryoku Tokubetsu Chōsa*) and Survey on Employment Structure (*Shūgyō Kōzō Kihon Chōsa*). As there is little to distinguish the trends appearing from the two sources, only the former survey's statistics have been shown in Figure 4.5.

TABLE 4.7 Relations between corporate performance and redundancies (electric machinery companies, 1973–80)

No. of employees		More than 10 000	5000–9999	1000–4999	500–999	–499
Deficits in two years	No redundancies	1		12		
	Redundancies			4		
Deficit in one year	No redundancies	1		9	3	
	Redundancies				1	
Low profitability	No redundancies			4		
	Redundancies			3	1	
Profitable	No redundancies	10	3	33	5	1
	Redundancies					

Source: 1. Rōdōshō (Ministry of Labour) *Shiryō Rōdō Undōshi* (Documentary History of the Labour Movement).
2. Okurashō (Ministry of Finance) *Yūkashōken Hōkoku Sho* (Balance sheets).

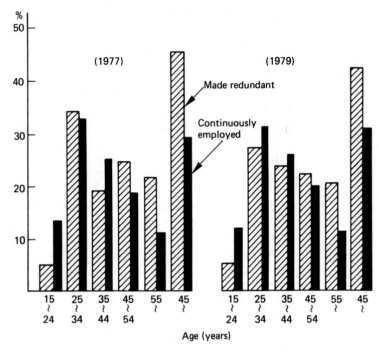

FIGURE 4.5　Redundancies by age of worker (males, 1977; 1979, percentage distribution by age)

Note: 'Those made redundant' are the persons who have been 'separated from a job since 1974' and whose reasons for separation are 'lay-offs' and 'bankruptcy', among 'the employed, the unemployed' and 'non-participants' in the survey.

Source: Rōdōshō (Ministry of Labour) *Rōdōryoku Tokubetsu Chōsa* (Special Report on the Labour Force Survey)

The Special Survey on the Labour Force has compiled figures on the reasons why workers have had to leave their places of employment at any time since 1974, because of factors such as personnel adjustments and the company's bankruptcy. The summed proportions by age have been contrasted in Figure 4.5 with the age composition of the employed labour force in two separate years. Among those under 45 years of age at the time of the survey, the number of workers who have been made redundant at some time since 1974 is lower than those who have remained in employment. The opposite pattern, however, pertains to those aged over 44 years, and particularly among workers aged 55 years and over the number who have suffered redundancy are much higher than the continuously employed. Figure 4.5 clearly shows the significant fact that workers for whom the loss in their investment in skills is high tend to be the ones made redundant. Because redundancy tends to be concentrated among those for whom the loss is high, the social tension arising from unemployment is quite severe relative to the actual numbers made redundant. This conclusion is subject to one reservation: since the figures in the labour force survey are not classified by company size, the situation in large companies alone needs to be observed more closely to make up for the absence of relevant statistical material.

4.6.4 Studies of Redundancy in Large Companies

Documentary History of the Labour Movement transcribes the statements made by both parties in the major labour disputes occurring each year. The periods chosen for discussion here are the three years from 1953–5, when there were frequent instances of redundancies among large company regular workers, and from 1972–8, which brings us up to the most recent reports. The amount of detail in the reports varies so much that just six out of the 36 redundancy cases whose development is followed in the first period, and 15 cases out of the 84 in the latter period can be used to classify which workers were actually made redundant.

Figures from the six redundancy cases in the 1953–5 period have been aggregated in Table 4.8. It should be noted that the figures are based on the criteria for personnel adjustments which were proposed by the management after the union had adamantly refused the initial invitation for voluntary redundancies. In the early 1950s even the apparently weak unions were so vigorously opposed to redundancies that they took lengthy strike action. But in most of the cases, because of a prolonged strike, the union's strength ebbed so much that in the final negotiations they could only agree to the originally proposed personnel adjustment criteria. Thus in almost all cases these criteria were more or less equivalent to the criteria for effecting redundancies.

Comments need to be made about two aspects which are evident from Table 4.8. Older workers aged over 45 years tended to be made redundant, though the associated loss would be higher than in the case of inexperienced workers. The second aspect concerns some of the other criteria for redundancy which, because of their ambiguity, were easily open to dispute. Especially among the criteria related to performance, making workers redundant on the basis that they lack

TABLE 4.8   Criteria for redundancies (Large companies in Japan, 1953–5)

	No. of cases where criteria mentioned *(Total = 6 cases)*
Older worker $\left(\begin{array}{l}\text{over 45}\\\text{over 50}\end{array}\right)$ years	5
Absenteeism	
irregular attendance	4
long absenteeism	4
long leave	3
taking sick leave too often	6
Income reasons	
two salaried members in one household	3
alternative income source	4
Performance	
inadequate performance	6
frequent mistakes	2
lacking cooperation	2
contravening work regulations	2

Source: Rōdōshō (Ministry of Labour) *Shiryō Rōdō Undōshi* (Documentary History of the Labour Movement).

cooperation must have been a highly subjective judgement: any union which was not wholly lethargic would engage in an industrial dispute over the proposed redundancies. Indeed in the early 1950s prolonged industrial action over six months or more was not uncommon.

Industrial disputes in the 1970s were governed by the memory of the bitter experiences in the early 1950s when unions failed to prevent redundancies in spite of lengthy strike action. Both parties now became more amenable to the idea of voluntary redundancy. The management had learned to act more circumspectly in inviting workers to retire on the basis of various guidelines whose acceptability to the union depended on their not being mandatory. Consequently the reports could only roughly show what guidelines were used in choosing workers for voluntary redundancy. And when these guidelines are aggregated in Table 4.9, the most conspicuous is that relating to older workers. Since the workers with longest service in a company are generally the older workers, the associated loss on their being made redundant can be concluded as being relatively large. Incidentally, despite the management having learned to act more tactfully with the unions in the 1970s, the strike weapon was not abandoned. It can be estimated that in about 20 per cent of the cases

TABLE 4.9   Guidelines for voluntary redundancy (Large companies in Japan, 1972–8)

	No. of cases where guidelines mentioned (Total = 15 cases)
Older worker (over 50 years)	13
Husband and wife in same company	4
Inadequate performance	3
Absenteeism	1

Source: See Table 4.8.

where large companies enforced redundancies, the union took strike action.

It may be thus generally concluded that large Japanese companies do not guarantee their workers security of permanent employment, as has been commonly believed. The true picture is that those workers for whom the potential loss is relatively high are the ones being made redundant. Consequently, the accompanying social strain is relatively high, though the numbers involved are relatively few. This distortion is a significant contemporary issue in the context of industrial relations in Japan.

4.7   RETIREMENT

Another contemporary issue which is relevant to industrial relations is the way in which large Japanese companies make their employees retire at the comparatively young age of 60 years or less. From the beginning of the twentieth century, when average life expectancy was much shorter than now, until the 1970s, the ruling retirement age was maintained at 55 years. The reason usually cited for the low retirement age is that Japanese wages are uniquely based on seniority. It is argued that a large company cannot continue to bear the burden of rising wage costs for older worker whose physical strength is inferior to that of younger workers. Yet the discussion in Chapter 1 has shown that West European white-collar employees, whose ruling retirement age is usually 65 years, also have a wage profile which rises with seniority. So why is it that the mandatory retirement age set by a large company (*teinen*) is lower in Japan than in West Europe?

The point of departure in answering this question is an apparent paradox: the participation rate of elderly Japanese in the labour force is much higher than in West Europe. Estimates of participation rates – especially in the case of the older age groups – do vary depending on the definitions employed. The EC does, however, carry out a uniform survey on the labour force every other year, whose approach resembles that of the Japanese and US surveys (though there are a few remaining discrepancies in survey methods). A comparison between Japan and EC countries of labour force participation rates is made in Table 4.10. Undoubtedly old people in Japan stay in the labour force for much longer than their counterparts in West Europe. The older the age group the wider are the differences in participation rates. By the late sixties age group participation in the labour force among the Japanese is still fairly high at almost 70 per cent, whereas in West Europe the corresponding rates are around 20 per cent, apart from 31.4 per cent in Britain and 49.1 per cent in Denmark. Why, therefore, does there appear in Japan to be a contradiction between a high labour force participation rate and a low mandatory retirement age in large companies?

The answer is straight forward: the mandatory retirement age does not imply that someone actually stops working. Instead, the workers leaves the company where he has been employed for a long time and enters a smaller enterprise. This pattern is apparent from Figure 4.6, which shows that more than one-third of workers in their early fifties are employed in large companies. Then a sharp drop in the proportion occurs so that the corresponding figure is barely 9 per cent among those aged over 60 years. Meanwhile more than 62 per cent of workers aged over 60 years are employed in small companies with between 10 and 99 employees, though in the early fifties age group the proportion at just over one-third is about the same as that of employed workers in large companies.

Older Japanese workers have either always been employed in a small or medium-sized company, or else they have changed their place of employment from a large to a smaller company. Even though the *teinen* system does exist in some small companies, it is not as strictly enforced as in the larger companies. Our interest here lies in the worker who moves from a large to a smaller company, which results in a substantial cut in his wage. This, essentially, is the reason why the wage profiles depicted in Figures 1.1 and 1.2 (Chapter 1) dropped so steeply for elderly Japanese workers. The question may be asked why those who change their place of employment have to suffer a wage cut, while the continuously employed can still receive

TABLE 4.10   Participation rates of males in labour force, Japan–EC comparison, 1975

Age (years)	50–54	55–59	Unit: % 60–64	65–69	70–
Japan	97.5	94.7	85.4	69.3	36.0
West Germany	94.0	87.0	62.4	17.2	6.3
France	93.0	82.6	55.3	20.5	7.2
Italy	88.1	76.8	42.4	17.6	5.0
Netherlands	89.8	80.9	65.4	17.2	4.0
Belgium	88.7	82.2	58.3	12.4	2.3
Britain	96.3	93.9	84.3	31.4	8.8
Denmark	91.8	87.1	77.6	49.1	6.3

Sources: Japan, *Shōwa 50-nen Kokusei Chōsa* (1975 Census) EC, *Labour Force Sample Survey* (1975).

relatively high wages. A clue to the answer is provided in Figure 1.1, where the shape of the wage profile shows that the average wage of those aged over 60 years is approximately equivalent to the average wage of the early twenties age group. The wage level of Japanese aged less than 25 years is extremely close to the ruling wage for unskilled workers, whose wage profile tends to run horizontally over all age groups. Thus the wage profile of older workers after rising then displays a significant fall, until their market wage ranks with the wage for unskilled workers.

The employees whose age is approaching *teinen* in large Japanese companies have had the most years of experience with that company. Among workers in their early fifties, 20 or more years of service have been given by 85 per cent of the white-collar workers with high school qualifications, and by 70 per cent of the blue-collar workers. Almost all of these long service employees have to seek work in other companies when they reach the age of retirement. But as conditions in the labour market are particularly severe for older workers, there is only a low probability of obtaining work which is appropriate for the individual's already acquired skills. Most of the workers moving to smaller companies eventually have to make a fresh start in unaccustomed work, where they are inevitably inexperienced. Thus they almost always have to take a cut in their wages down to the level of wages for unskilled workers.

There is no doubt that the practice of mandatory retirement systems in large Japanese companies effectively wastes the skills which employees have, as discussed earlier in this chapter, built up to

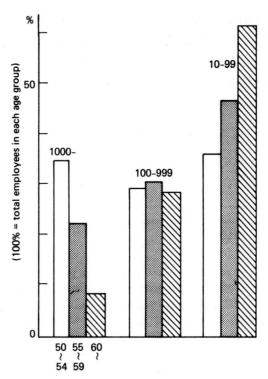

FIGURE 4.6   Distribution of older workers by company size (All industries, 1977)

Source: Rōdōshō (Ministry of Labour) *Shōwa 52-nen Chingin Kōzō Kichon Tōkei Chōsa* (1977 Wage Structure Survey)

an advanced level over many years of service. These intellectually-based skills do not diminish as a worker becomes older. The deficiency lies, instead, in the attitude which presumes that Japanese seniority wages are peculiar and hence that older workers are paid too much and must be retired from the company. One of the most important unresolved issues in Japanese management–labour relations is how to reform the practice of *teinen* so that workers can continue until their mid-sixties to utilize their skills in the workplace where they have provided long service.

4.8   CONCLUSIONS FROM CHAPTERS 3 AND 4

The comparison of blue-collar careers in large Japanese and US companies has indicated both similarities and contrasts. The major common feature is that internal labour markets have been established on the basis of skills being acquired within the company through on-the-job training.

The most evident dissimilarity is that blue-collar workers in large Japanese companies have broader careers than their counterparts in US companies. The Japanese worker's consequent understanding of the production process enables him to find ways of improving productivity, which suggests that he has really acquired the characteristics of a white-collar technician. This white-collarization of blue-collar workers in large Japanese companies is a special feature to which more attention should be paid. One of the important consequences is that the productivity gains effected by QC circles contribute to the growth of employment as well as to a more rapid upgrading of employees. Secondly, output can be made more responsive to fluctuations in demand. The employees who can handle a range of machines have the potential to be temporarily reassigned, which thereby minimises the higher average costs associated with a trough in demand. A third consequence of white-collarization stems from its influence on how the wage bill is distributed. Wage differentials between white- and blue-collar workers in large Japanese companies are narrower than in other countries. Egalitarian ideas have thus been nurtured, on which basis the growth of the Japanese economy has been supported.

But the workings of any economy are subject to some deficiencies. In the case of large Japanese companies, a major deficiency in their industrial relations is the treatment meted out to older workers. Redundancies tend to be concentrated among those in their late fifties. And, in any case, the older workers have to make a fresh start in unaccustomed work at a lower wage rate because the retirement (*teinen*) system requires them to retire from the large company and join a small or medium-sized one.

NOTES

1. Rōdōshō (Ministry of Labour), *Rōdō Kyōyaku Jittai Chōsa* (Survey on Collective Agreements) 1st edn (1962), 2nd edn (1967) and 3rd edn (1975) (Tokyo: Rōdōshō) and Chūō Rōdō Iinkai (Central Labour Relations Committee) *Rōdō Kyōyaku Chōsa* (Survey on Collective Agreements) 1st edn (1952), 2nd edn (1970) (Tokyo: Chūō Rōdō Iinkai).
2. Ōkōchi, Ujihara and Fujita (eds) (1959); Nitta (1981) demonstrates how effectively a Japanese labour union operates.

3. Ōkōchi *et al.* (eds) pp. 105, 108–9, 130ff.
4. Ōkōchi *et al.* (eds) pp. 384–91.
5. Dōryokusha Rōdō Kumiai (Locomotive Engineers Union) *Dōryokusha Undōshi* (A History of Locomotive Engineers Union) (Tokyo: Dōryokusha Rōdō Kumiai, 1962); and *Dōryokusha 20 Nenshi* (20 years History of a Locomotive Engineers Union) (Tokyo: Dōryokusha Rōdō Kumiai, 1973) 2 vols.
6. Ōkōchi *et al.* (eds) pp. 203–6.
7. Derber and Chalmers (1965) p. 21.
8. Ōkōchi *et al.* (eds) p. 76.
9. Shinnittetsu Rōdōkumiai Kyōgikai (Nippon Steel Confederation of Trade Unions) *Chōsa Jihō* (Bulletin) August 1971.
10. Tsuda (1959); Kōshirō (1959); Takanashi (1967). Also Totsuka and Takahashi (1961).
11. I also made this point in Koike (1960). See also Doeringer and Piore (1971) Chapter 4 and Becker (1964). Doeringer and Piore and Becker overlook the monopolistic conditions enjoyed by large companies.
12. Almost the only source for comparing the proportions of regular and inplant subcontract workers is from a survey carried out by Tekkō Rōren. In official sources, subcontract workers and companies incorporated among the employees of small and medium-sized. Tekkō Rōren (Japanese Federation of Steel Workers Union) *Tekkō Rōdō Handbook* (Steel Labour handbook) (Tokyo: Tekkō Rōren) yearly.
13. Accurate figures on the proportion of pool workers in the total company workforce could not be obtained.
14. The detailed case study report can be found in: Koike, Muramatsu and Yamamoto (1975).
15. *Rōdō Kyōyaku Jittai Chōsa* (1967).
16. Whitehill and Takazawa (1968).
17. Derber and Chalmers (1965) p. 21.
18. Ōkōchi *et al.* (eds) pp. 203–6.
19. Nitta, Michio, Tekkōgyo ni okeru Rōshi Kyōgi no Seido to Jittai (Joint Labour–Management Consultation Conference in the Japanese Steel Industry) *Shakai Kagaku Kenkyū*, 32, 5 and 6 (1981).
20. Rōdōshō (Ministry of Labour) *Koyō Kanri Chōsa, 1976* (Personnel Administration Survey for 1976) (Rōdōshō, 1977) and Rōdōshō, Shokugyō Kunren Kyoku (Ministry of Labour, Bureau of Vocational Training) *Jigyō nai Kyōiku Kunren Jittai Chōsa* (Survey on In-House Vocational Training) (Rōdōshō, 1982).

REFERENCES

Becker, Grays. (1964) *Human Capital* (New York: National Bureau of Economic Research).
Derber, Milton and Chalmers, William Ellison (1965) *Plant Union–Management Relations: From Practice to Theory* (Illinois: Institute of Labor and Industrial Relations).

Doeringer, Peter B. and Piore, Michael (1971) *Internal Labor Markets and Manpower Analysis* (Lexington, Mass.: D.C. Heath).

Koike, Kazuo (1960) 'Chingin Rōdō Jyōken Kanri no Jitta Bunseki' (An Analysis of Wage Administration and Working Conditions) in Susuki, Shinichi, and Ujihara, Shōjirō (eds) *Rōmukanri* (Personnel Management) (Tokyo: Kōbundō).

Koike, Kazuo, Muramatsu, Kuramitsu and Yamamoto, Ikurō (1975) Kōjō no Nakano Idō to Kōjō no Rōdō Kumiai (Internal Mobility and Plant-Level Union) *Chōsa to Shiryō* 58 (Bulletin) (Nagoya: Nagoya University, Dept of Economics).

Kōshirō, Kazuyoshi (1959) 'Nōritsukyū to Kanri Soshiki' (Payments by Result and Administrative Organization) in Okōchi *et al.* (eds).

Nitta, Michio (1981) 'Tekkōgyō ni okeru Rōshi Kyōgi no Seido to Jittai' (Joint Labour–Management Consultation Conference in the Steel Industry) *Shakai Kagaku Kenkyū*, 32, 5 and 6.

Ōkōchi, Kazuo, Ujihara, Shōjirō, Fujita, Wakao (eds) (1959) *Rōdō Kumiai no Kōyō to Kinō* (Structure and Functions of Trade Unions) (Tokyo: Tokyo University Press).

Takanashi, Akira (1967) *Nihon Tekkōgyō no Rōshi Kankei* (Industrial Relations in the Japanese Steel Industry) (Tokyo: Tokyo University Press).

Totsuka, Hideo, and Takahashi, Kō (1961) 'Gōrika to Shokuba Chitsujo' (Rationalization and Job-ladders in a Workshop) in Meiji University (ed) *Tekkōgyō no Gōrika to Rōdō* (Rationalization and Labour in the Steel Industry) (Tokyo: Hakutō Shobō).

Tsuda, Masumi (1959) *Rōdō Mondai to Rōmu Kanri* (Labour Problems and Personnel Management) (Kyoto: Mineruba).

Whitehill, Arthur N. Jr and Takazawa, Shinichi (1968) *The Other Worker* (Honolulu: East–West Center, Hawaii University).

5 Workers' Careers in Small Japanese Companies

Only a minority of Japanese workers are employed in large companies, where, as Chapter 4 has shown, the internal promotion system prevails. But what kind of skills are acquired by the majority of workers, who are employed in small and medium-sized companies? These workers, despite being employed in small companies, have a steeper wage profile than that for West European blue-collar workers (see Figure 1.1). This suggests that the acquisition of a wide range of skills by workers in large Japanese companies is a feature also of some workers in small and medium-sized companies. The effectiveness of the internal promotion approach to skill formation depends upon there being a prospect of continuous employment over a long period, but in small and medium-sized companies there is not such a long term prospect as in large companies. Of course, internal training is not the only path for skill formation. When there are limited prospects for continued employment, an alternative path may be adopted, whereby experienced workers who have acquired their skills externally are recruited. This chapter will focus on the actual conditions in small and medium-sized companies which lead to the choice of one of the alternative paths for skill formation.

The first wide scale survey on the issue of skill formation in small and medium-sized companies was carried out in 1978 by the Chūshō Kigyō Kinyūkōkō (Small and Medium-Sized Enterprises Finance Corporation). Only companies to which loans had been extended and which were located in the three major metropolitan zones (Tokyo, Nagoya and Osaka) were sampled. The sample was stratified to reflect the proportions of different industries in the three zones which were borrowing funds. Since companies from which information could reliably be obtained at regular intervals were deliberately selected, the sample would appear to have been biased towards the somewhat superior small and medium-sized companies. The size of the companies surveyed ranged from close to 30 employees up to 300 employees, and 384 companies responded out of the 670 surveyed (a response rate of 57 per cent). The questionnaire is reproduced as Appendix B (pp. 293–5). Any analysis of the survey's results should begin with an inspection of non-response. In particular, the respondents' care in filling out the questionnaire has to be assessed, and the pertinence of the questions to the topic being surveyed has to be judged so as to discern the quality of the data. Among the companies which returned the questionnaire, the non-response rate to questions which could have been answered was extremely low at around 0.5 per cent. Evidently almost all the companies were diligent in filling out the questionnaire. And Question 7 (Q7), which is the pivot of this chapter's discussion, had fairly low non-response rates of 0.8–1.0 per cent in the case of responses pertaining to blue-collar workers and of 2.3–2.9 per cent in the case of white-collar workers. There are, however, some misgivings about whether Q7's approach to the topic of worker's movements within the workshop really encompassed the situation. Since the non-response rate to almost all the questions was maintained at below 3 per cent, the questionnaire method can overall be judged as having been appropriate. It may be assumed that 0.5 percentage points of a non-response rate arises from companies not being in possession of the necessary facts to reply; and additional percentage points should be interpreted as indicating a negative response to the question. The parameters of the percentages calculated in this chapter are therefore the total figures rather than the response figures, unless any usage of the latter is explicitly noted.

5.1   EXTERNAL SKILL FORMATION APPROACH

5.1.1   Few Workers Trained Outside the Company

Skill formation among a company's employees may be divided into two main groups with two further subdivisions:

E   External skill formation:

1. Formal – school, training institute, etc.

2. Informal – experience in other companies.

I   Internal skill formation.

1. Formal – training programme set up within the company
2. Informal – experience within the company.

Since there were hardly any questions pertinent to $E1$ in the survey, our discussion has to begin with $E2$. The substance of skills will have been formed externally when the worker has had experience in another company over some years. Q6 thus asked: (1) What proportion of the employees have had three or more years' experience in a similar occupation outside the company? (2) How does their level of skills compare with those who have become experienced within the company? (3) What recruitment policy does the company now intend to use?

Figure 5.1 shows that in the majority of companies, less than 10 per cent of the employees have had three or more years occupational experience elsewhere. In the case of blue-collar workers the figure is 64 per cent of companies, and for white-collar workers it is 56 per cent. In contrast, only around 15 per cent of companies in the blue-collar case are in the combined categories where the majority or half of the employees have had substantial experience elsewhere. The larger the company size, the fewer are the workers who were recruited in mid-career. All of the companies with 300 or more employees are in the class where less than 10 per cent of the blue-collar workers have become experienced elsewhere. And even more than half of the smallest companies with less than 50 employees fall into this class. In summary, very few small and medium-sized companies rely on the external skill formation approach, especially among the larger companies. In half of the smallest companies with less than 50 employees there are still very few employees with substantial experience outside the company.

The question then arises of whether the skills in which a worker becomes experienced outside the company are inappropriate. In fact, there does not appear to be any tendency to firms positively to evaluate the skills of workers with experience in other companies, with the consequence that companies is generally prefer to rely on employees who entered the company in their youth.

A preference for internal training is also evident in the response to the survey's Q3. Whereas Q6 was posed in rather general terms, Q3

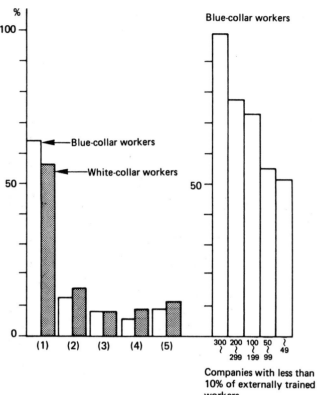

FIGURE 5.1   Ratio of externally trained workers (the ratio of employees
with three or more years of similar work experience in other
companies, manufacturing, percentage of small and medium-sized
companies, 1978)

Note: (1) Less than 10%
      (2) Around one-third
      (3) Nearly one-half
      (4) Majority
      (5) Unclear.

Source: Koike (1981).

applied only to essential skilled personnel. Figure 5.2 demonstrates
that in an overwhelming majority of companies most of the personnel
had been inexperienced when they entered the company. When the
blue-collar worker case includes the category of those who had
received some level of technical training at an educational institution,

184

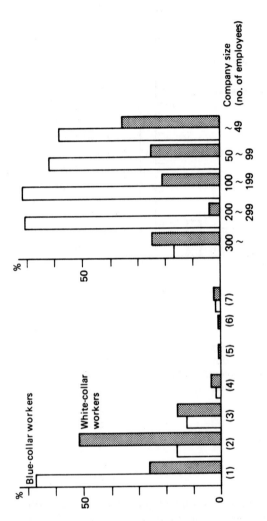

FIGURE 5.2 Essential skilled personnel on the shopfloor (manufacturing, percentage of small and medium-sized companies)

Note: (1) Inexperienced when entered the company and have had in-house experience
(2) Inexperienced, but had had technical training when entered the company and have had in-house experience
(3) Experienced when entered the company in mid-career from other similar small companies
(4) Experienced when entered the company in mid-career from similar or related large companies
(5) Transferred from a parent company
(6) Others
(7) Not clear.

Source: See Figure 5.1.

the proportion of companies reaches 85 per cent. In the case of companies where most had entered when inexperienced, the proportions are higher the larger are the companies, though there is only a slight distinction. It should be noted that in more than half of the companies with less than 50 employees most of the blue-collar employees were unskilled when they were recruited. In summary:

1. Even in a small or medium-sized company, very few of the workers will have acquired their skills externally. Few companies seek employees with experience elsewhere, and company policies indicate that even less will do so. Instead the general trend is to adopt the *I* (internal skill formation) approach.
2. This trend is more pervasive among the larger companies.
3. Yet half of even the smallest companies with less than 50 employees have adopted the *I* approach for their essential skilled personnel; and the majority of these small companies intend to adopt it.
4. The *E* approach is used by only about 15 per cent of the companies in all sizes, and most of these companies are in the categories for companies with less than 100 employees. Even in companies with less than 50 employees, of which as few as 20 per cent look on the *E* approach as an ultimately positive measure, its adoption has usually been out of necessity.

5.1.2 Training Approach a Function of the Industry?

Is the adoption of either the *E* or the *I* approach a function of the industry? The extent to which companies by industry depend on the *I* approach is displayed in Figure 5.3. One axis shows the response to Q6 (1) where less than 10 per cent of the employees have had three or more years' outside experience. On the vertical axis is the proportion of companies responding affirmatively to Q3, which asked whether inexperienced workers were recruited and trained in skills within the company. The following deductions may be made from Figure 5.3:

1. Both indicators suggest that the *I* approach is widely practised in the majority of industries.
2. There are, however, a number of deviations. First, in the non-manufacturing industries of construction and transportation as well as in printing and publishing, the *I* approach appears on both indicators to be practised by less than 40 per cent of the companies. Secondly, the indicators for the industrial electrical machinery and

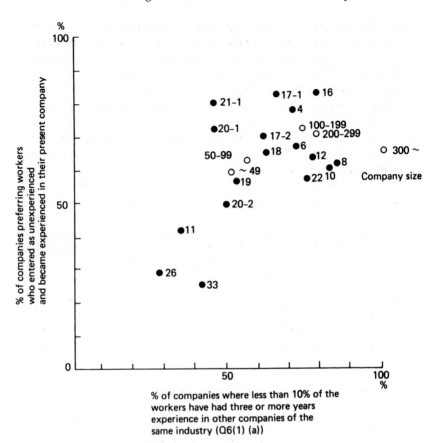

FIGURE 5.3   Extent of in-house training by industry

Note: 4: Food
         6: Textiles
         8: Lumber
        10: Paper and pulp
        11: Printing and publishing
        12: Chemicals
        15: Stone, clay
        17–1: Non ferrous metals
        17–2 Iron and steel
        18: Fabricated metals
        19: Machinery
        20–1: Electrical appliances for home use
        20–2: Electrical machinery for industry
        21–1: Automobiles
        22: Instruments
        26: Transportation
        33: Construction.

Source: See Figure 5.1.

the general machinery industries are, at around 50 per cent, rather lower than in the remaining industries, which suggests the influence of technological conditions, because in both these industries non-mass production is prevalent. Still there is a general tendency for companies using non-mass production technologies, as well as those based on mass production, to favour policies directed towards the *I* approach. To answer the question of why companies give so much emphasis to policies under which their employees form their skills within the company, it is necessary to observe how the *I* approach actually operates.

5.2 INTERNAL SKILL FORMATION APPROACH

Consideration of the *I* approach usually conjures up the image of a formal training programme set up by the company. The survey's Q5 was directed towards this programme which represents the company's deliberate efforts, while the bulk of training takes place in other ways. The companies where there are 'organized and regular' programmes are as few as 16 per cent for induction training and 13 per cent for in-service training. But many companies implement programmes 'when required', amounted to 43 per cent for induction training and 50 per cent for in-service training. Both categories may appropriately be combined, which yields around 60 per cent of companies where training programmes are being implemented.

Nevertheless, the discussion on large companies in Chapter 4 has demonstrated that the nucleus of the *I* approach is not formal training programmes, but on-the-job training. Workers attain proficiency by sequentially experiencing a grouped range of related jobs, so that skills are formed while working. Skill acquisition is determined by which jobs are undertaken over a long time period. The extent of skill formation can thus be revealed from the question relating to movements in workers' assignments.

5.2.1 Movement Within the Workshop

Movements between assignments within the workshop were the subject of Q7. The first indicator in Figure 5.4 shows the response to Q7 (1) as to whether workers change their assignments and, if so, whether the movements occur at regular intervals. The incidence and frequency of movements, however, gives no indication of their extent – whether a worker experiences most of the workshop's assignments.

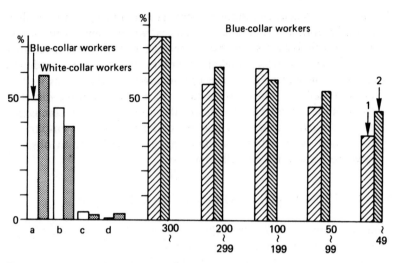

FIGURE 5.4   Intra-workshop mobility (Manufacturing, percentage of small and medium-sized companies)

Note: a: Assignment rarely changed
      b: Changed intermittently
      c: Changed regularly
      d: Unclear.

Source: See Figure 5.1.

1. Total of assignments
   'Changed intermittently'
   'Changed regularly'
2. Long serving workers have usually experienced most positions in one work-shop.

Q7 (2) has thus provided a second indicator, showing companies where workers employed for at least five years have experienced most of the workshop's assignments. The first bar chart based on the first indicator demonstrates that although very few companies change their workers' assignments at regular intervals, when combined with the response of intermittent changes the movement of blue-collar workers between assignments can be recognized in almost half of the companies surveyed. The clearly recognizable trend in Figure 5.4 is that the proportion of companies where blue-collar workers change their assignments rises in line with the company size category. Whereas movement occurs in 75 per cent of companies with 300 or more employees, the corresponding proportion is only 35 per cent in companies with less than 50 employees. This trend is also evident from the response to Q7 (2) on long serving workers. There is a distinctly positive relationship between company size and the proportion of companies where long servers have experienced most of the assignments in one workshop. There is a discrepancy with the first indicator in that the proportion of companies with widely experienced long servers is higher than the proportion where assignments are changed, especially in the smaller companies. In the larger companies with 300 or more employees, the two indicators are consistently high at 75 per cent. But the distance between the two proportions widens as company size decreases. Whereas movement in blue-collar assignments takes place in 35 per cent of companies with less than 50 employees, the proportion where long servers experience most of the workshop's assignments reaches 45 per cent. This discrepancy could have arisen on account of labour mobility between small companies being relatively high.

A high rate of labour mobility does not imply that most workers are mobile, but rather that there is a group of workers who often change their place of employment, which is relatively larger than the immobile group. The custom of moving workers between assignments cannot easily be fostered among the group of mobile workers. Thus only 35 per cent of the smallest companies could respond positively to Q7(1). But of the higher positive response to Q7(2) suggests that the group of immobile workers, though relatively few in number, do tend to experience most of one workshop's assignments. Thus any discrepancy in the responses to Q7(1) and Q7(2) is apparently due to the differing proportions that the two groups of mobile and immobile labour occupy in a company's workforce.

5.2.2 The Purpose of Movement Within the Workshop

The motives underlying changes in workshop assignments and the company's relevant policy plans were surveyed in Q7(3) and Q7(4). The companies were asked to select and rank as appropriate two of the motives displayed in Figure 5.5, where the recorded responses have been aggregated without regard to their rank so as to simplify presentation. Since those companies where assignments were not changed would have omitted this question, the non-response rate was high. Of the seven motives, the one most positively and deliberately directed towards skill formation would be to provide experience so as to widen skill acquisition. Here, movement between assignments would presumably be directed and would range widely. This motive was secondary, having been selected by 42 per cent of the companies in respect of blue-collar workers and by 38 per cent for white-collar workers. The most common motive – 60 per cent for blue-collar

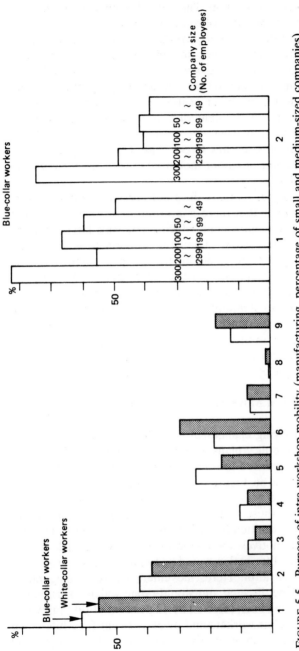

FIGURE 5.5 Purpose of intra-workshop mobility (manufacturing, percentage of small and medium-sized companies)

Note: (1) To jobs corresponding to abilities and aptitude
(2) To provide wide range of experience
(3) Worker's own wishes
(4) To improve human relations
(5) To adjust to fluctuations in the volume of output
(6) To accompany changes in machines and job content
(7) To fill vacancies caused by separation
(8) Other
(9) Unclear.

Source: See Figure 5.1.

workers and 55 per cent for white-collar workers – is for moving workers to assignments which correspond to their abilities and aptitude. Even though this suggests some concern with skill formation, any deliberate approach of moving workers widely between assignments is not implied. Nor are any of the other motives directed towards skill formation. Around 40 per cent of the companies have chosen reasons which relate to rearrangements of assignments in response to fluctuations in operational levels and changes in the organization of work.

The motive which is most pertinent to our discussion – 'to provide experience so as to widen skill acquisition' – has been broken down by company size in Figure 5.5. For companies with 300 or more employees, the proportion reached 75 per cent, whereas only 40–50 per cent of other companies chose this motive.

In summary, the *I* approach – in which workers are deliberately moved between a wide range of assignments so as to acquire broad skills – can be recognized in between 40 and 50 per cent of companies with less than 300 employees. Since there is hardly any distinction depending on industry or on company size, apart from companies with 300 or more employees, a factor such as managerial initiative must be of more significance than the technological conditions.

5.2.3 Adoption of I Approach by More Companies

How managers evaluate the practice of moving workers between assignments is indicated by their prospective policies. Figure 5.6 shows the proportions of companies who have chosen one of the responses: 'not practised until now, but do intend to do so', or 'practised until now but intend to continue more positively'. A keen interest in the practice of movement within the workshop can be surmised from there being extremely few non-respondents, which amounted to only 1.8 per cent in respect of blue-collar movement and 3.8 per cent for white-collar movement. The wholly negative evaluation – practised until now, but intend to cease doing so' – has not been chosen by even one company. The converse evaluation – 'not practised until now, but do intend to do so' – has, on the other hand, been subscribed to by around 20 per cent of the companies. And the other positive response – 'intend to continue more positively' – accounts for around 5 per cent. Companies which place a positive value on moving workers between assignments are, evidently, increasing in number.

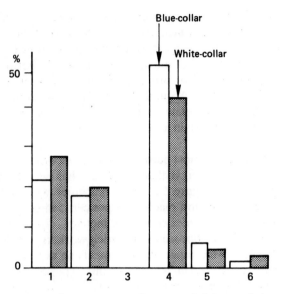

FIGURE 5.6   Prospective company policy towards intra-workshop mobility (manufacturing, percentage of small and medium-sized companies)

Note: (1) Neither practised until now, nor intend to do so
      (2) Not practised until now, but do intend to do so
      (3) Practised until now, but intend to cease doing so
      (4) Practised until now, and intend to continue
      (5) Practised until now, but intend to continue more positively
      (6) Unclear.

Source: See Figure 5.1.

5.2.4   Movement Between 'Familiar' Workshops not Unusual

When the main approach to skill formation is through a wide experience or related jobs, movement between assignments need not necessarily be confined to one workshop. Jobs requiring closely related skills can transcend one workshop's boundaries. The survey's Q8(1), therefore, asked whether male workers were often moved between workshops and, if so, whether the movements were at regular intervals or intermittently. Figure 5.7 demonstrates that while in more than 50 per cent of companies workers are rarely moved to different workshops, many companies do move workers intermittently: for blue-collar workers 43 per cent of companies, and for white-collar workers 41 per cent. When the few companies which move workers at regular intervals are added, movement of blue-collar workers between workshops occurs in 44 per cent of companies

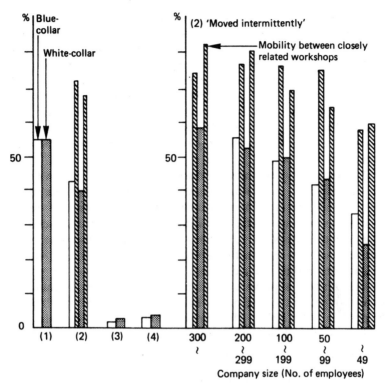

FIGURE 5.7   Extent of inter-workshop mobility (manufacturing,
percentage of small and medium-sized companies)

Note: (1) Rarely
      (2) Moved intermittently
      (3) Moved regularly
      (4) Unclear

Source: See Figure 5.1.

and white-collar movement in 43 per cent. The usual pattern, in which the proportions are higher in line with company size continues to hold. Nonetheless, in around one-quarter of the companies with less than 50 employees, workers are moved between workshops; and this proportion reaches over 40 per cent of companies with 50 – 99 employees.

All the above figures apply to movement between any kinds of workshops. Whether workers were moved between workshops with closely related skills was asked by Q8(2). The results (in the form of narrow bars) have been incorporated in Figure 5.7. Paradoxically movement between 'familiar' workshops appears to occur in more companies than general movement between workshops, apart from in the case of blue-collar movement in companies with 300 or more employees. The paradox might be explained by a respondent's attitude in giving a negative response when the workers were only rarely moved between workshops. But the same company could have given a positive response to Q8(2), if the rare movements were between 'familiar' workshops. The figures obtained from Q8(1) should thus be chosen as a better reflection of the real extent of movement between workshops.

The motive most commonly subscribed to is – as shown in Figure 5.8 – to move the worker to a workshop which is appropriate for his abilities and aptitude. The next ranking choice is to provide experience so as to widen skill acquisition, followed by the need for adjustments in response to various changes. The same ordering of motives has been seen in the motives for moving workers between assignments within the workshop. But the weight of the second ranking motive – to provide experience so as to widen skill acquisition – has dropped in the case of movement between workhops to below 40 per cent. Moreover, when broken down by company size, the companies subscribing to this motive of a deliberate approach to skill formation are a majority only in the category for companies with 300 or more employees. Thus, while many companies with 300 or more employees do move workers between 'familiar' workshops with the intention of imparting wide ranging skills, in smaller companies any motivation of nurturing skills through this approach is rather weak.

So as to assess the management's evaluation of movement between workshops, the survey asked whether this policy would be practised in the future. The wholly negative evaluation – practised until now, but intend to cease doing so – has not been chosen by any company in the case of blue-collar movement, while a mere 0.3 per cent of companies have assented for white-collar movement. In contrast, the positive evaluations – 'not practised until now, but do intend to do so', or 'practised until now, but intend to practise more positively' – have been subscribed to by about one-quarter of the companies. This positive evaluation is more prevalent in the larger companies, but the difference depending on company size is quite small.

5.2.5 Summary

The above discussion has provided various indicators for assessing the diffusion of the *I* approach. The main results in respect of blue-collar workers have been collated in Figure 5.9. The adoption of the *I* approach requires that workers should move between assignments in the workshop. The proportion of all companies engaging in this practice is shown by indicator (1) to be less than 50 per cent, but the figure rises in line with company size: it applies to 35 per cent of companies with less than 50 employees, but to 75 per cent of companies with 300 or more employees. Indicator (2) shows the proportion of companies where workers move between workshops. thereby experiencing a greater variety of related jobs. Although the proportion is lower than in the case of movement within the workshop, the difference is fairly small, and movement between workshops is not unusual.

How deliberate and positive is the *I* approach – for movement within or between workshops – is a function of whether the managerial motive is to provide experience and widen skills. Indicators (3) and (4) show that the proportion of companies subscribing to this motive is below indicators (1) and (2), but the difference is less than might have been expected. It thus appears that the majority of companies to which indicators (1) and (2) apply do deliberately implement the *I* approach. The distinction depending on company size is negligible. Indicators (3) and (4) are below (1) and (2) in the middle categories, whereas in the categories for companies with less than 50 employees and for companies with more than 300 employees, there is barely any difference between the two sets of indicators. All the larger companies which have adopted the *I* approach have done so deliberately. And, though a minority, the smallest companies practising the *I* approach do so deliberately.

The above figures do not distinguish between long serving employees and the mobile group who often change their place of employment. Indicator (5) shows the proportion of companies which provide a wide range of experience in different assignments to long servers. Another important distinction concerns whether the essential skilled personnel are trained within the company, which is shown by indicator (6). Both indicators (5) and (6) are higher than the proportions in (1) and (2). Over all company sizes indicator (5) is applicable to 53 per cent of companies and indicator (6) to 80 per cent. And even in the category for companies with less than 50 employees, indicator (5) registers 45 per cent and indicator (6) reaches 70 per cent. Thus the core of essential skilled workers is usually formed under the *I* approach, even in the smallest companies.

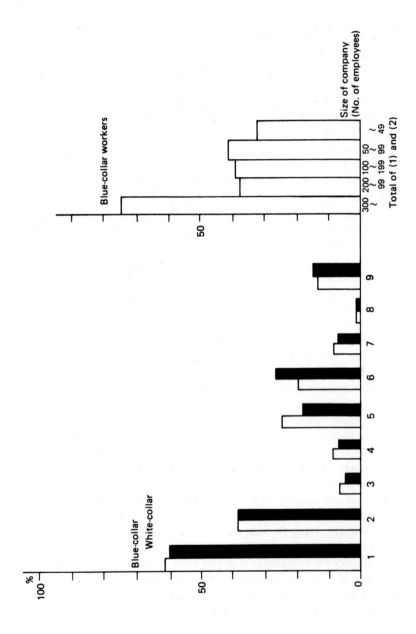

FIGURE 5.8 Purpose of inter-workshop mobility (manufacturing, percentage of small and medium-sized companies)

Note: (1) To jobs corresponding to abilities and aptitude
(2) To provide wide range of experience
(3) Worker's own wishes
(4) To improve human relations
(5) To adjust to fluctuations in the volume of output
(6) To accompany changes in machines and job content
(7) To fill vacancies caused by separation
(8) Other
(9) Unclear.

Source: See Figure 5.1.

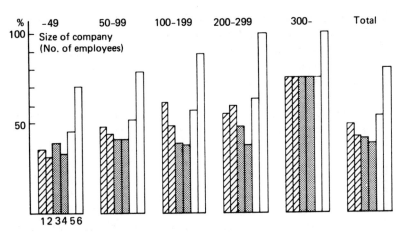

FIGURE 5.9　Indicators of internal skill formation systems (percentage of small and medium-sized companies)

Note: (1) With intra-workshop mobility: total of 'assignments changed intermittently' and 'regularly'
(2) With inter-workshop mobility: total of 'moved intermittently' and 'regularly'
(3) With the purpose of intra-workshop mobility, being 'to provide wide range of experience'
(4) With the purpose of inter-workshop mobility, being 'to provide wide range of experience,
(5) With long-serving workers usually experienced most positions in one workshop
(6) With preference for in-house training of essential skilled personnel on the shopfloor.

Source: See Figure 5.1.

5.3　FACTORS ENGENDERING THE *I* APPROACH

What factors underlie the *I* approach? The diffusion of the *I* approach does not appear to vary by type of industry, nor with the profitability of industry, nor even in proportion to the numbers of long serving workers. Thus, neither technological nor economic factors can satisfactorily account for the presence of the *I* approach.

5.3.1　The Part Played by Labour Unions

The presence of a labour union in a small or medium-sized company is in itself influential. Labour unions are prevalent in large companies and their presence is accepted as normal, but in only 27 per cent of the small and medium-sized companies surveyed were there labour unions. Even so, this figure is rather higher than the usual estimate of the rate for organized labour in these companies. This lack of unionization is, however, compensated to some extent by 'employee social clubs' (*jūgyōin shinbokukai*). In the past, these clubs were usually formed for the purpose of recreation and mutual benefit projects, but nowadays they play some part in negotiations on wages and labour conditions. Nonetheless a social club, whose members include not only supervisory workers, but also the section heads (*kachō*), is not recognized as a labour union under the Labour Union Law. Nor is there any superstructure to which a social club could be affiliated, and it would hardly ever resort to strike action. Yet there are social clubs whose determination in frequently presenting demands and in negotiating is enough to embarass the management. Since such clubs are effectively functioning as labour unions their existence should not be overlooked, and social clubs existed in just under 40 per cent of the companies surveyed. In around one-third of the companies, there was neither a labour union nor a social club. What is the impact of unions or social clubs on the *I* approach, particularly as manifested in movement within the workshop?

Because changes in assignments would have had a detrimental effect on the skills of the traditional kind of artisan, the classical notion views unions as being opposed to movement between assignments. The artisan would have benefited more from changing his place of employment than from moving to a different assignment. But it appears from Figure 5.10 that movement of blue-collar workers within the workshop is most prevalent in the companies where there is a labour union. The lowest proportion of companies with movement of workers are in the category for companies where there is neither a labour union nor a social club. This trend is applicable even in the case of workers moving between workshops, which might potentially be thought disadvantageous for the worker and thus subject to union opposition. It should be noted, however, that the relationship between movement of workers and the presence of a union or a social club falls apart in the case of white-collar workers.

The survey's results do not provide any answer to the question of why blue-collar worker movement is more prevalent in companies with a union or club. One may conjecture that the presence of a labour union requires a more deliberate pursuance by management of the policy of moving workers. Consequently they would have to give more consideration to a long term and pragmatic approach. Even from the worker's point of view alone, the acquisition of a wide range of skills through movement in assignments under the *I*

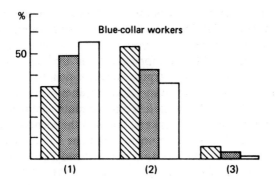

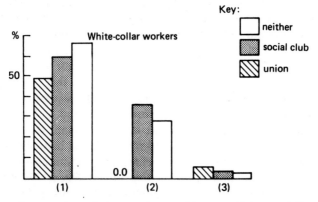

FIGURE 5.10   Labour unions and intra-workshop mobility
(manufacturing, percentage of small and medium-sized companies)

Note: (1) Rarely change assignments
(2) Change intermittently
(3) Change regularly.

Source: See Figure 5.1.

approach should nowadays be regarded as an asset. The promotion of this practice by unions and social clubs thus appears to have evolved naturally.

5.3.2   Managerial Attitudes as a Factor

Our discussion so far has focussed on possible technological, economic and social factors, none of which has appeared completely to determine the practice of moving workers between assignments.

Even under the assumption of environmental conditions being constant between companies, the degree to which movement within the workshop occurs would differ.

Intermediate variables must, therefore, be presumed to have a role: especially the attitude of management towards skill formation. This variable can be roughly approximated from the response to the survey's question on the field in which the company president has had most experience. As is clear from Figures 5.11, movement within the workshop is most prevalent in companies where the president is experienced in personnel affairs or labour management. The relevant proportion of companies is about 70 per cent in the case of blue-collar movement and 80 per cent for white-collar movement. Evidently there is some correlation between adoption of the *I* approach and managerial attitudes and initiative. This dependency has an effect even when technical and other conditions are constant.

5.4 Summary

5.4.1 *I* Approach Widespread in Small and Medium-sized Companies

Our discussion has brought out the noteworthy point that the *I* (internal skill formation) approach is fairly well dispersed throughout small and medium-sized companies. It is rather common knowledge that large Japanese companies have generally adopted the *I* approach in preference to the *E* (external skill formation) approach for training their employees. Large companies are particularly favoured with the conditions required for efficiently carrying out the *I* approach: a low separation rate among employees, and the feasibility of a long term approach to planning. In contrast, the popular notion of small and medium-sized companies presumes their employees are highly mobile and that their financial base does not permit a long term view. Nonetheless our analyses of the Chūshō Kigyō Kinyūkōko survey results have indicated that almost half of these companies have adopted the *I* approach. As might have been expected, the proportion of companies falls as the company size becomes smaller. But even among companies with less than 50 employees, one third practise the *I* approach and an even higher proportion of companies have adopted the *I* approach for training the core of essential skilled labour. Thus in small and medium-sized companies the *I* approach appears to be the most pervasive method for training their employees.

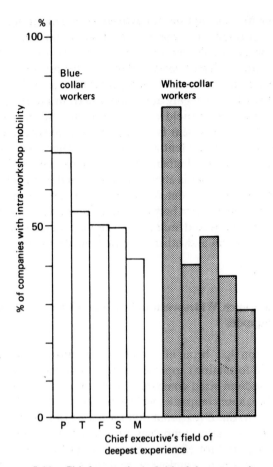

FIGURE 5.11   Chief executive's field of deep experience and
intraworkshop mobility (manufacturing, percentage of
small and medium-sized companies)

Note: P   Personnel
     T   Technology
     F   Finance
     S   Sales or administration
     M   Manufacturing

Source: See Figure 5.1.

This result is surprising in view of the conditions required, which are
more typical of large companies.

    The other side of the coin is the small fraction, amounting to
roughly one-sixth of the surveyed companies, where the *E* approach
has been adopted. The proportion is higher in the smallest com-

panies, though reaching only a quarter of the companies with less than 50 employees. It is remarkable that so few companies have adopted the *E* approach, which is the one commonly referred to in textbooks concerned with skill formation. This result, therefore, has valuable implications for improving the effectiveness of vocational training, employment placement and other schemes, which have tended to be based on the classical view of skill formation.

The subsequent question would ask what factors determine which of the two approaches a company adopts for imparting skills. Almost all of the survey's results have shown a remarkable interdependence with company size. As the company size category enlarges, the proportion of companies implementing the *I* approach rises, while those using the *E* approach become relatively fewer. There is, in contrast, only a small distinction in respect of which of the two approaches is adopted by different industries. Movement within the workshop appears to occur more prominently in industries which may be broadly defined as utilizing mass production technologies, but the correlation is quite weak with a large margin left unexplained. The correlation with company size could be explained by economic factors. The conditions under which the *I* approach may operate efficiently are, as discussed earlier, a relatively immobile workforce and economic feasibility permitting a long term perspective. These factors would become more attainable as the size of the company increased, although the survey's results do not provide sufficient evidence for us to accept the hypothesis for certain.

But the analysis has revealed that labour unions and employee social clubs exert a substantial influence. Certainly the presence of such organizations is likely to increase with company size. Close observation, however, reveals that movement within the workshop is a function of a labour organization being present even in the same company size category. The presence of a labour organization in a company incontrovertibly increases the probability of there being movement within the workshop. One explanation is that a labour organization represents a countervailing power to managers, who have therefore to be aware of labour's role under a long term perspective. Another factor which has a significant impact on the realization of the *I* approach is the attitude of management.

5.4.2 Corroborative Results From an Interview Survey

The content of the *I* approach as practised in small and medium-sized companies has been observed through a supplementary interview survey.[1] For the core of skilled labour, a pattern similar to that in large companies, as seen in Chapter 4, could be recognized from the interview responses. These workers acquire wide ranging skills through experiencing assignments in the main workshops of a plant, in addition to going through most of one workshop's positions. What is dissimilar to the large company pattern is that whereas in a large company a majority of male blue-collar workers possess wide ranging skills, only a part of the small and medium-sized company work force is given this opportunity.

This is but one aspect of the fact that the workers in small and medium-sized companies comprise diverse groups. One group consists of those who possess a wide range of skills comparable to the skill acquisition of large company regular workers. Some of this group would be promoted as far as section head (*kachō*) and higher ranking positions in small and medium-sized companies, because the promotion pattern is not as institutionalized as in large companies where blue-collar workers would rarely progress beyond the position of foreman. The status of this group is recognized in its wage profile being comparable to that for regular workers in large companies. The second group comprises those with many years of experience, but in just one workshop. The workers in this group do not have any further opportunity to widen their range of skills because the workshops are generally smaller than in a large company. This group – for which an appropriate label might be 'shallow internalization type' – accounts for the majority of workers in small and medium-sized companies. The distinction between this group and the first group begins when management tends two to three years after the recruitment of comparable workers to make a division primarily through assessments of work performance. The second group's wage profile is flatter and, in particular, shows only a small gain after ten years of service, because the workers' skill range is narrower. There is, finally, a third group which comprises the unskilled and part-time workers.

The average wage profile over all three groups of workers in small and medium-sized companies falls below that for large company employees, once the mid-thirties age group with ten or more years of service has been reached. Nonetheless the profile remains steeper than that for EC blue-collar workers, because the *I* approach permits these workers – apart from those in the third group – to acquire a broad range of skills, although the skills of the majority, who are in the second group, are shallower.

NOTE

1. See Koike (1981) chapter 2.

REFERENCE

Koike, Kazuo (1981) *Chūshō Kigȳo no Jukuren* (Skill Formation in Small and Medium-Sized Businesses) (Tokyo: Dōbunkan).

6 White-collar Careers in Large Japanese Companies

6.1 ATTAINMENT OF EXECUTIVE POSITIONS AND LENGTH OF SERVICE

Chapters 4 and 5 have looked at the careers of large company blue-collar workers and of small and medium-sized company employees. But it is actually the careers of the remaining group – white-collar employees of large companies – which are perceived to be bound by the classical type of seniority system. The usual view is that promotion is strictly in line with seniority in years of service and age. Consequently the worker's job performance would be of no significance, because the order of promotion would have already been determined at the time and even before he entered the company. Whatever his ability, he could not overtake anyone who was recruited before him. The stereotyped conclusion must therefore be that promotion is non-competitive, which would be expected to result in highly inefficient work performance. Yet the business performance of large Japanese companies is hardly inefficient. Why Japanese companies do not operate inefficiently in spite of non-competitive internal labour markets has been popularly explained by the culturalist thesis of a unique Japanese society. Emphasis has been laid on the bizarre explanation that strong loyalty to the company as a group has engendered efficiency.

This explanation of group loyalty has now been demonstrated to be inappropriate for the case of blue-collar workers in large companies. The analysis of this issue in Chapters 3 and 4 should ideally be extended to incorporate white-collar workers.

Unfortunately, however, there is a paucity of empirical research on white-collar promotion. Nonetheless, good quality data on executive posts and length of service have been compiled in Japan's *Wage Structure Survey* and the 1972 European survey (Chapter 1, pp. 17–18). This material does at least permit some grasp of the issue of whether or not promotion in Japan is actually in line with seniority and, hence, non-competitive.

In both the surveys, age distributions and years of service distributions have been aggregated for executive grades. If white-collar promotion in large Japanese companies were bound simply by seniority, the different executive levels should have a high correlation with length of service and with age. Since the perfectly strict seniority system does not, of course, exist, the strength of the relationship will have to be judged by a comparison with the EC countries. In other words, the data should display in the case of Japan a remarkable convergence of each post into a specific age group and a specific length of service group.

Every year since 1970 the *Wage Structure Survey* has compiled length of service, age and educational qualifications figures by size of company for department heads, section heads and subsection heads.[1] Since the lowest ranking of these posts is rather easily attainable, it will be disregarded here. Thus the focus will be on department and section heads in 1976, when the survey scale was relatively large. The 1972 European survey has divided white-collar workers into five groups. Despite the ambiguity of the European definitions, the relative proportions in each group suggest that group 1 ('management executives') and the upper levels of group 2 ('executives') correspond to department heads in Japan, while the middle and lower levels of group 2 are roughly equivalent to section heads. Incidentally group 1 has been further divided by the European survey into two levels. But the numbers occupying the upper 1A group are much too few to make any contrast with department heads meaningful. In comparing the distributions the wider age groups of 10 or 15 years used in the European survey have required that the Japanese figures be further aggregated beyond the original detailed aggregation of five year intervals.

6.1.1 Age on Attaining Executive Posts Does Vary

We shall begin by simply looking at the relationship between age and attainment of executive posts. Figure 6.1 shows that in Japan roughly two-thirds of section heads are concentrated in the 30–44 year age group; there is also close to a 60 per cent concentration of department

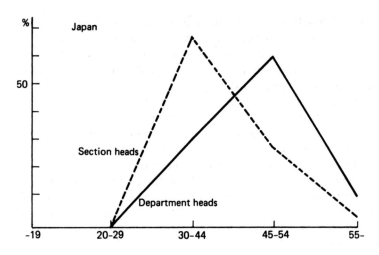

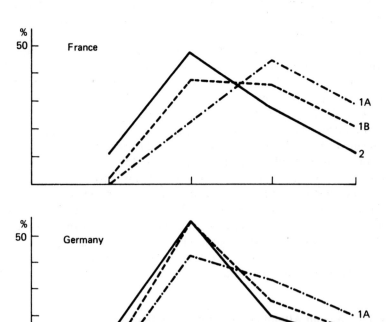

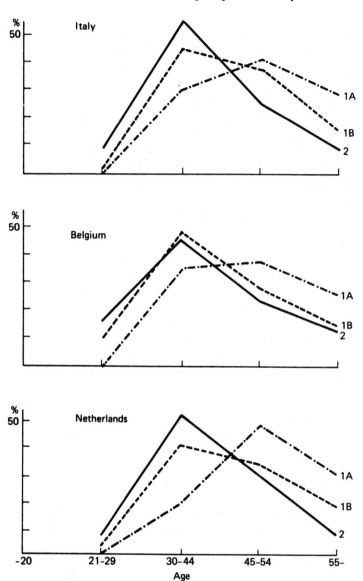

FIGURE 6.1   Percentage distribution of executives by age in Japan and the
EC (1972; 1976 by executive position)

Sources: EC, *Structure of Earnings in Industry*, 1972; 1975–6. Japan, Rōdōshō (Ministry of Labour) *Shōwa 51-nen Chingin Kōzō Kihon Tōkei Chōsa* (1976
Wage Structure Survey).

heads in the 45–54 year age group. Some concentration can also be seen in the EC countries, but to a much lower degree than in Japan. Apart from in West Germany, around 45 per cent of group 1A are aged between 45 and 54 years, which is a much lower degree of concentration than the 60 per cent of department heads. Nor is the 45 per cent degree of concentration in the 30–44 year age group of group 1B, where West Germany is again the exception, at all commensurate with the concentration of department heads. Similarly the concentration of group 2, which does generally reach as high as 50 per cent among those aged between 30 and 44 years, is still well below the almost 70 per cent concentration of section heads in the same age group.

The general conclusions from Figure 6.1 are as follows:

1. The common notion of non-competitive promotion in Japan receives some superficial support from the fact that holders of executive posts are relatively highly concentrated in specific age groups
2. Nevertheless in the EC countries also some concentration, though not to the same degree as in Japan, can be discerned
3. Moreover, there is the feature (common to both Japan and the EC) that the degree of concentration tends to be greater for higher ranking posts, even though this trend is subject to some significant divergences.

In general, therefore, the seniority system can be said to operate to some extent in the EC countries, but its influence is much less pervasive than in Japan.

6.1.2 Weight Given to Length of Service

What is significantly different between Japan and the EC becomes much clearer once the length of service distributions over executive posts are compared. Insofar as there is some correlation between age and length of service, the age factor appears to be influential because of the importance attached to length of service. The distributions displayed in Figure 6.2 show that length of service is much more significant in attaining executive posts in Japan than in the EC. The distribution for department heads in Japan displays an upward slope right up to 20 or more years of service, whereas in the EC countries it is only group 1A which in general has a rising trend. (The exception in the case of the 1B group occurs in France.)

Moreover, the degree of concentration for 20 or more years of service is around 40 per cent of group 1A in the EC, but is close to 60 per cent of department heads. In the case of the EC's group 1B, the peak concentration of around 30–35 per cent occurs among those with 10–19 years of service – apart from in France. Nor is the peak of group 2, which registers around 30 per cent in the EC, commensurate with the 50 per cent of section heads in Japan concentrated in the same 10–19 years of service group.

The sharp peaks in Japan's distributions illustrate another special feature: an executive position is largely unattainable without having given years of continuous service to one company. There are extremely few department or section heads with less than 10 years of service; merely 8 per cent of section heads and 6 per cent of department heads have served for 5–9 years. But these figures suddenly jump once more than 10 years of service have passed; over 50 per cent of section heads are in the group for 10–19 years of service. The graph describes a promotion route in which the section head level is hardly ever attained with less than 10 years of service, and then the next step after 20 years of service is to become a department head. How does this pattern – in which long service is required to reach executive level – correspond to the situation in the EC countries? There is a complete contrast, in that more than a few Europeans have reached executive positions after relatively short service; one-quarter to one-third of group 1A have served for less than 10 years, with the relevant proportion extending to one-half of group 1B. Thus in the EC a picture is drawn of a fast promotion route for a number of young employees or those with short length of service, although some consideration is given to length of service. This route requires that promoted workers overtake their seniors, whereas the picture in Japan suggests an orderly promotion with the primary weight being attached to length of service. These contrasting pictures apparently provide substantial proof to support the common notion of non-competitive promotion in Japan.

6.1.3 Is Giving Weight to Length of Service Non-competitive?

It has been agreed that promotion in Japan gives more weight to length of service than in Europe. But this fact should not immediately be linked with the proposition that promotion procedures in Japan are non-competitive. If promotion at all levels were to follow the length of service ranking, that would indeed be non-competitive. But the feasibility of that procedure necessitates an improbable precondition:

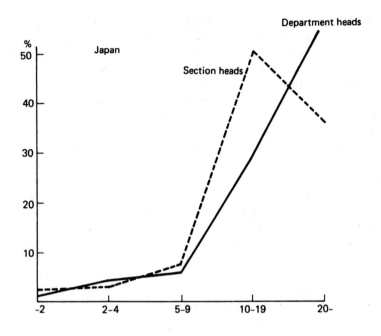

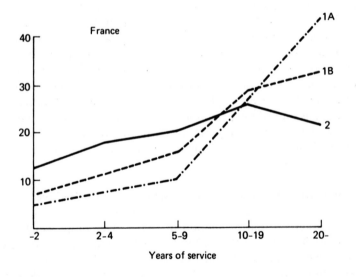

Years of service

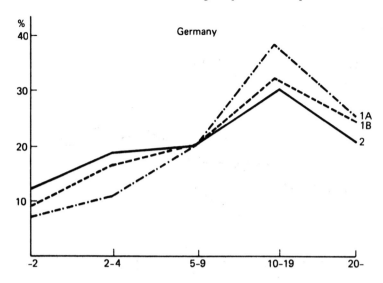

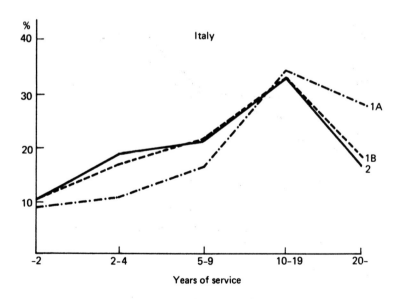

Years of service

Continued on p. 214

FIGURE 6.2 *continued*

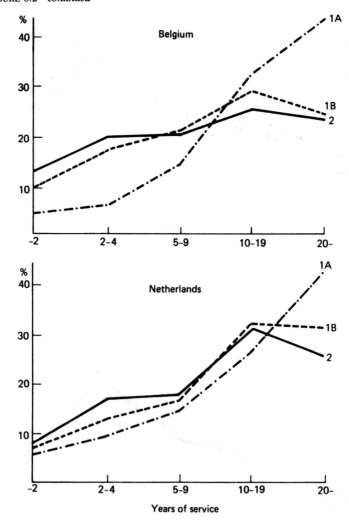

FIGURE 6.2   Percentage distribution of executives by length of service in
Japan and the EC (1972; 1976 by executive position)

Sources: See Figure 6.1.

that the number of posts in an organization should not decrease even
at the highest administrative levels. Unless this assumption were
fulfilled, the majority could not be promoted at all levels, however
many years of service each had accumulated. Since the number of

posts has to become fewer as the rank rises – whatever kind of large company and in whatever country it may be – selective promotion cannot be avoided. Thus the proposition that cumulative years of service is the only factor determining promotion in Japan is in reality not feasible.

What is the meaning, therefore, of the importance attached to length of service? The implication should be that the target group from whom a number will be selected for promotion is concentrated in a certain length of service category. For example, Figure 6.2 indicates that the selection of section heads in Japan is made from among employees with 10 or more years of service. This procedure is still open to an interpretation of being non-competitive, because the limits to competition have been set by the narrow boundaries of the target group. Suppose, instead, that section heads were selected from those with less than 10 years of service. Then those who have not been promoted to section head would be disappointed early in their career. The likely consequence would be a lowering of morale. One beneficial aspect, however, would be that the early selection of management trainees could permit a planned programme of experience in various important jobs over a long period. The different advantages and drawbacks of each of the two approaches – an early or a delayed selection for promotion – render any judgement on which is more efficient open to dispute. Later on in this chapter the opinions of those with experience in these matters will be heard.

The contention that giving weight to length of service need not be non-competitive receives further support from Figure 6.2. The distribution of years of service for Japan shows that in the group with 20 or more years of service, not only are there department heads, but also many section heads. And in the same group – though the distribution is not displayed here – there would also be a fair number of assistants and clerical staff. This issue may be investigated further by using the *Wage Structure Survey* for data on executive posts classified by educational qualifications and by company size. There is strong adherence to the notion that status in Japanese society is governed by educational qualifications (*gakureki shakai*).[2] The next stage in our discussion is to see, therefore, whether there is a large variation in educational qualifications for executives in the same age group.

6.1.4 Are Educational Qualifications Important?

The proportions of white-collar males holding executive positions by age and by educational qualifications are displayed in Figure 6.3. The

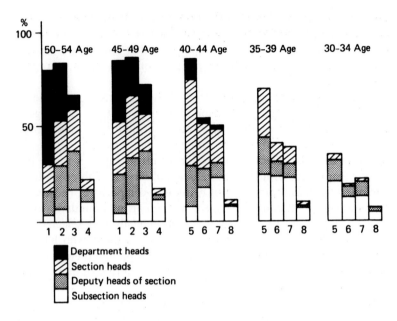

FIGURE 6.3   Percentage distribution of executives by rank and by age
(by educational grade, male, 1976, large companies with 1000
and more employees, all industries)

Note: (1) University graduates (old system)
       (2) Technical college graduated (old system)
       (3) Middle school leavers (old system)
       (4) Primary school leavers (old system)
       (5) University graduates (present system)
       (6) Junior college graduate (present system)
       (7) High school leavers (present system)
       (8) Junior high school leavers (present system)

Source: Rōdōshō (Ministry of Labour) Shōwa 51-nen *Chingin Kōzō Kihon Tōkei
         Chōsa* (1976 Wage Structure Survey).

figures are confined to companies with 1000 or more employees,
because our present concern is with promotion in large companies. It
is reasonably assumed that executives are very rarely demoted before
the mandatory retirement age, which was usually between 55 and 60
years in the 1970s. Thus the posts held by those in their early fifties
represent the final level of white-collar workers' careers. This age
group were all educated under the old educational system prior to its
overhaul in the late 1940s, which will be designated below by the use
of 'former'.[3]

6.1.4.1 Comparison of former university graduates with former college (technical high school) graduates

1. When looking at all executive posts former college graduates despite three years less formal education, appear to have been a little more successful. Whereas executive level has been attained by 84 per cent of former college graduates, the corresponding proportion is 80 per cent of former university graduates.
2. There is, nonetheless, a considerable discrepancy in the proportions reaching the highest executive post of department head: 50 per cent of former university graduates as opposed to 30 per cent of former college graduates.
3. At lower levels, the discrepancy is reversed. The proportion of former college graduates occupying section head and lower executive posts is relatively high.

In summarizing the above points, one can see a divergence of which, however, only a part is consistently explained by educational qualifications. The most that can be said is that former university graduates have a higher probability of becoming department heads than former college graduates, for whom, nonetheless, promotion to that level is not impossible.

6.1.4.2 Comparison of former university graduates with former middle school leavers, where the first group have had as many as six more years of education

1. The proportion of former middle school leavers attaining executive level is 67 per cent, in contrast to the 80 per cent of former university graduates.
2. The 50 per cent of former university graduates reaching department head level is decisively higher than the mere 8 per cent of former middle school leavers, although 8 per cent can hardly be considered negligible.

A minute proportion of former elementary school leavers attain executive level. Since white-collar employees of large companies who are elementary school leavers are, however, exceptional, no importance should be attached to these figures in explaining overall trends.

Overall, there are two points which can be stressed:

(a) Clear divergences in the attainment of different executive posts depending on educational qualifications can be discerned.

(b) Nevertheless, these divergences are far from being decisive; educational qualifications are merely one factor among several in determining promotion. Thus, some 15 per cent of former university graduates have remained at the level of assistants or clerical staff right up to retirement, and about 4 per cent are only subsection heads with 13 per cent at the intermediate levels; a further 13 per cent have progressed just as far as section head. On the other side of the coin, we have seen that two-thirds of middle school leavers attain executive posts, and the conclusion must be that educational qualifications are certainly not given a large weight as a factor in promotion, and may actually be relatively small in importance.

There remains the possibility, however, that the career progression of individual workers may indeed have been influenced by the educational qualifications. Perhaps university graduates are promoted more quickly than school leavers, although the latter may eventually catch up. Perhaps also those in their early fifties in 1976 were educated at a time when there was a low diffusion of tertiary education, the importance of factors underlying promotion may have changed once a much greater proportion of employees had been graduates of tertiary level institutions.

6.1.4.3 The early thirties group

To investigate these issues, the early thirties age group on Figure 6.3 should be observed. This group would have left high school in the mid-1960s and would have graduated from university in the late 1960s, when the diffusion rate for high school attendance was between 70 per cent and 75 per cent, and for university attendance around 20 per cent.

Comparison of university graduates with high school leavers shows two things:

1. 35 per cent of university graduates and 22 per cent of high school leavers have reached executive level by their early thirties; it is hence common to both groups that only a minority have attained executive level and, while two-thirds of university graduates are still at assistant or clerical levels, more than one-fifth of high school leavers have reached executive level.
2. Looking at each of the executive posts below department head

level, the proportions for university graduates are higher, but the differences are small. Thus 3 per cent of university graduates and 2 per cent of high school leavers are section heads; in the intermediate grades the proportions are 12 per cent and 7 per cent, while 20 per cent of university graduates and 13 per cent of high school leavers are subsection heads. Thus the picture presented by the early fifties age group is largely repeated here. What is strikingly dissimilar is the status of two-year college graduates. Under the old educational system the role of colleges was quite close to that of universities. But under the present system two-year college graduates appear to be no more successful in promotion than high school leavers. This pattern can also be discerned in the case of the other age groups.

The substance of the above analysis turns out to be that there is little difference in the speed of promotion depending on educational qualifications. Confirmation is provided by Figure 6.4, which compares the age distributions by educational level for holders of executive posts. If the university graduates' distribution were to peak earlier than the high school leavers' distribution, a faster promotion route on account of higher educational qualifications would be implied. In fact, however, the modal groups more or less coincide whichever of the distribution sets for university graduates and high school leavers is taken. These distribution sets have the common features of the department head peak occurring in the late forties age group, the section head peak in the early forties, and the subsection head peak in the early thirties. The modal groups for middle school leavers occur among older age groups, but, as in the case of former elementary school leavers, their presence among white-collar employees of large companies is exceptional. The distributions for university graduates are more skewed to the left – in other words, a higher frequency of younger men hold executive posts, which means that university graduates do tend to be promoted somewhat earlier than high school leavers. Nonetheless this divergence in the speed of promotion cannot be large since the modal groups do coincide.

6.2 LONG RANGE EVALUATION OF CANDIDATES

The above discussion has suffered from being based on aggregated data. Over the whole body of manufacturing companies competition

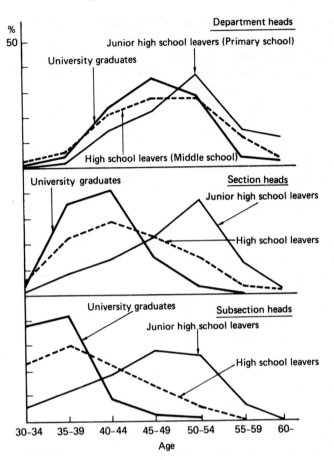

FIGURE 6.4   Percentage distribution of executives by age (by educational grade, 1976, large companies with 1000 and more employees, male, all industries, Japan)

Source: See Figure 6.3.

in promotion has been seen to operate insofar as white-collar workers in the same age group, same length of service group and with the same educational qualifications occupy a variety of executive, assistant and clerical positions. But, suppose that within individual companies the only factor determining promotion were in fact length of service; then data aggregated over both growing companies and depressed companies could still give an overall appearance of competition in promotion. The analysis in section 6.1 above should, therefore, be supported with observation of how promotion takes place in individual large companies before concluding that Japanese promotion procedures are competitive. The information gained from interviews with a number of personnel managers can provide necessary support.

6.2.1 Promotion by Selection Occurs Late

Let us begin from the common place proposition that the higher ranking is a job, the more complex are its demands. The qualifications required for promotion to a simple job can be set out quite clearly. But the job content of the department and section head posts is intricate, involving various disciplines, with the result that the qualificatiᵥns required are neither simple nor plain. Consequently the standard for promotion has to be a composite judgement on a variety of factors. When personnel managers are questioned on this issue, their replies reflect an anxiety lest an equivocal response might be misunderstood by an outsider. For similar reasons, even were there any written rules for promotion, the actual procedures could not be accurately recorded. Thus the only approach left is to find out the customary procedures from the aspects which can be easily observed.

The following observable aspects will be considered:

1. The proportion of candidates who are promoted by selection
2. The time period over which selection is made
3. The number who are involved in evaluating the candidates.

The proportion of candidates selected differs, of course, depending on the executive post's ranking. Our attention will be directed to where the majority are promoted, and to where a minority are selected. The latter, obviously, has to occur for promotion to the higher executive posts. The second aspect to be observed concerns, therefore, whether the minority are selected fairly soon after recruitment or else after many years of service.

The invariable response of experienced managers in large Japanese companies to our questions shows the adoption of the 'late selection for promotion' approach. Even after 10 to 15 years of service there is barely any difference in the wages and status of employees who entered the company at the same time. Although a number will have begun to lag behind, the majority are clustered together on one rising line, which might invite a casual perception of promotion largely depending on relative lengths of service. That, however, is only a part of the whole story; selective procedures then suddenly exert pressure to permit only a minority to go on to higher levels. What are the actual features of this late selection for promotion after 10 to 15 years of service?

Whatever other comments there may be, the most striking feature is the care taken over selection. During the long period when the majority are, on the surface, being treated as equal, selection procedures are already underway, in that a merit rating takes place every six or twelve months. This short term rating is not immediately implemented in promotion decisions, but it becomes part of a meticulous evaluation of work performance in the long term. The long time period, moreover, permits a worker whose work has on one occasion been deficient to retain hope for promotion.

The second significant feature is the number of people involved in evaluating candidates for promotion. The length of the time period naturally means that not just one but quite a few people make an evaluation. When posts change hands about every three years (as is quite common in large Japanese companies), over a period of 15 years, during which the supervisory personnel also change, there would be about 10 different people evaluating one candidate. Nor is there necessarily at one point in time just one evaluation; the evaluation made by one section head is supplemented with the opinions of heads in related sections, and of the department head. No objective standard could arise in the course of the original evaluation, because a subjective appraisal is necessitated by the nature of white-collar work in a large company. A simple job could, in contrast, be evaluated quite mechanically by, for example, the number of completed units or number of errors. In the case of complex work one step towards lessening the bias arising from a subjective appraisal is to have more than one evaluation. This permits the setting of a standard evaluation in a way similar to the establishment of a market price through the actions of multiple buyers and sellers. Furthermore those making the evaluation are themselves evaluated. Suppose that someone receives a very low evaluation on one occasion, but is highly rated in the subsequent two periods. This discrepancy would lead to the original evaluation being queried. This process results over time in a more or less objective and standard evaluation being made of the worker's performance.

6.2.2 'Strategic Ability' and 'Combative Strength' Factors

The most significant issue in selecting candidates for promotion is how certain aspects of ability are evaluated more highly than others; a worker's performance could vary in accordance with which standards are used for the merit rating. Just as a runner's approach would differ between a 100 metre sprint and a 5 kilometre race, so would a different kind of work performance be required depending on the nature of the job. The appraisal of required abilities is easy in the case of a simple job, but – at the risk of being repetitive – such simple jobs are rarely in the sphere of large company regular employees. Under the merit rating form set up by the personnel affairs section there are a surprising number of items, each of which is in substance so abstract that even those making evaluations must be perplexed.

When questioned on this issue, those who have had long experience in a large company tend to give vague replies, which could however be summed up as: 'It boils down to a candidate's personality'. This appears to be a modest requirement, but the words must actually imply a high level of ability. The content of a white-collar job in a large company with its diverse internal groups consists not just of standard tasks; there is also a discretionary element which becomes more significant as the worker accumulates experience. The way in which an ordinary white-collar employee in his early thirties or an executive approaches an important planning task may illustrate the kind of personality required. The more important is his plan, the more are the sections with which he has to maintain and mobilize good contacts. First he must be capable of gathering information which is not readily available through formal channels. Valuable information, in particular, is most efficiently found through personal contact with both superiors and subordinate colleagues. Since few would volunteer important information to anyone on whom they did not rely, an attractive and reliable personality is crucial. Next, he should have the capability of conceiving a good plan and then of persuading his colleagues of its desirability. Finally, and most importantly, he must have a keen insight into his own complicated organization, including in particular the informal structure as well as the formal one. To put his plan into effect, he needs to know who will be the key persons in its implementation, and where to begin prior consultation on his plan. This process of prior consultation and interaction between managerial personnel is known in Japan as *nemawashi* (literally: digging round the roots). But, as far as is shown by my observations and interviews, such prior consultation is certainly not unique to Japan. When executives in West Germany, for example, were asked about systems for management participation, they replied that prior consultation at all levels was normal and natural, because organizations and meetings where people of different persuasions were gathered together could not otherwise function effectively. Such consultation is doubtless characteristic of any sophisticated organization. A favourable assessment for promotion tends to be given to those who have the kinds of capabilities mentioned above. Such capabilities, which range widely from strategic ability to combative strength, are so highly integrated that they can often be indicated only by the 'total personality'.

One more special feature of promotion procedures in a large Japanese company is, as mentioned earlier, the long period of time for evaluation. Promotion procedures are greatly enhanced by there being someone keeping a long term surveillance, which may counteract the dazzling impact made at the time of selection by the candidate's performance. Because of the prominent role of large companies in Japanese industry, the issue of whether the successors to executives are those who are aware of long term strategies is serious. This point does seem to be given due consideration in the procedures for selective promotion in large Japanese companies.

To sum up: the majority advance together on one path as far as the point where selective promotion of a minority begins. Denoting this procedure as a seniority system disguises the reality of what should be seen as a neck and neck race. Because the candidate's performance is thoroughly observed over a long term period, rapid selective promotion towards the end of the period becomes feasible. This reality is sharply divorced from the popular idea which suggests that promotion procedures in large Japanese companies are hardly at all competitive.

NOTES

1. These three positions do not cover all of the named executive posts in large Japanese companies. In addition there are many other titles, including *bujichō* (vice-department head), *buchōdairi* (acting department head), *kachōhosa* (assistant section head), *shunin* (manager), *eigyōshochō* (office manager), *shitenchō* (branch manager). At the same time the posts of *buchō*, *kachō*, and *kakarichō* are the most representative titles, which can be found in all companies. Since there are differences in the content of

the other named posts depending on the company, statistical aggregation would not be feasible. It would be possible to make a rough estimate of the numbers holding these other posts, but they lie between (and are much fewer than) those in the positions of *buchō*, *kachō* and *kakarichō*. Since the latter three do encompass the major executive positions, their inclusion is sufficient to reveal the essence of our discussion.

2. One of the best analyses written in English is Dore (1976). Entrance to schools and universities with a high status in Japan is highly competitive, because career prospects are generally perceived to be determined within the educational system. It is arguable, however, whether large Japanese companies place more weight on educational status than, in particular, French companies. This question among others is examined in Koike and Watanabe (1979).

3. It would be useful to give here a brief outline of the structure of Japan's educational system prior to its overhaul after defeat in 1945. After six years in primary school, roughly 80 per cent completed their education with a further two years at a senior primary level. The remainder attended a middle school for five years, from which a minority entered either a college or an elite high school for three years. Only the graduates of elite high schools had the opportunity of progressing further into one of the imperial universities.

REFERENCES

Dore, Ronald P. (1970) *The Diploma Disease* (London: George Allen & Unwin).

Koike, Kazuo and Watanabe, Yukirō (1979) *Gakureki Shakai no Kyozō* (Is Japan Governed by Educational Qualifications?) (Tokyo: Tōyōkeizai).

7 'Enterprise Unionism'

7.1 INDUSTRIAL DISPUTES

In the preceding chapters the legends of permanent employment and seniority wages have crumbled. The remaining legend pertaining to Japanese industrial relations is that of enterprise-based unions, whose essential meaning should be that:

1. Labour unions are separately organized in each firm, from which is derived the fact that
2. The function of these unions is to cooperate in the firm's operations, and their voice in various issues is weak and ineffectual.

A labour union's strength in negotiations is essentially based on its control of the supply of labour. The usual argument is that an effective control of the labour supply requires that a labour union should be organized across companies so as to cover the whole labour market in each occupation and in each industry. This argument goes on to allege that conversely a union which is organized within a company inevitably lacks strength in negotiations and has a weak voice. The resulting consensus between the union and management is all the more unavoidable where enterprise unions are founded on the group loyalty to the company which is presumed to prevail in Japan.

This argument, however, emanates wholly from the theoretical depiction which is based on the premise that all workers possess only general skills. Yet the acknowledged reality is that in most careers skills are enterprise specific. Internal labour markets have been established and the internal promotion system is widespread in large companies. Consequently an enterprise-based union whose sphere encompasses the relevant labour market can be powerful; this characteristic may be commonly perceived in spite of the special features and differences between countries. It can thus be reasoned that the basic organizational unit of Japanese labour unions being each company is not an aberration, nor does it immediately follow that their voice is weak. To arrive at a legitimate conclusion the strength of the union voice in different industrialized countries should be compared. There are various ways in which the strength of unions could be interpreted and measured. The best approach would be to observe the unions' say in the issues which are of particular concern to union members. Under the presumption of labour markets being internalized to some degree, these issues would be redundancy, promotion, transfers and the wage rates for each job, because of their impact on skill development and, hence, on the employment and livelihood of union members. There is no simple way, however, of measuring the strength of the union voice in these matters. The lack of any directly relevant data means that recourse will have to be made to a rudimentary observation, which cannot help but leave a margin of doubt. To reduce the area of ambiguity a start will be made by comparing data on industrial disputes, which, though not directly relevant, are at least unambiguous.

The way in which industrial disputes show the capacity of a union's negotiating strength and influence is not however, at all clear. On the whole it is considered that there is a positive relationship between the frequency of industrial disputes and the strength of the union voice. At the same time, there is the contrary argument that a really powerful union does not have to resort to strike action in order to force acceptance of its demands. Still the assumption here will be that the general tendency is towards a positive relationship, which is, however, indirect.

7.1.1. Defining 'Industrial Dispute'

The International Labour Organization (ILO) has collected each country's official statistics on industrial disputes under the following headings:

1. Number of disputes with work stoppage
2. Number of workers involved
3. Number of working days lost in disputes.

One problem is that there are some differences in the way each country defines 'industrial disputes'. In particular, some countries' official statistics do not include small scale strikes or those of short duration.[1] Since the major definitional difference concerns the size and the length of strikes, the resulting errors in an international comparison can be minimized by using the number of working days lost. This statistic is, moreover, the most appropriate indicator of the extent to which industrial disputes have a detrimental impact on the economy. To make a legitimate comparison between countries with different working populations, the calculation of working days lost per 1000 employees has been used here. Some of the extreme yearly fluctuations have been smoothed out by taking averages over five years. And, finally, a logarithmic scale has been used on the vertical axis of Figure 7.1, because otherwise the large differences between some countries would preclude a graphic observation.

7.1.2   Industrial Disputes in Japan Rank With Those in France

The results shown on Figure 7.1 permit several groups to be distinguished:

1. The group with a relatively high proportion of days lost: Italy, the USA, and – since the 1970s – the UK. In Italy the days lost per 1000 employees have tended to increase, whereas in the USA there has been more or less a stable trend. The UK's statistic rose sharply to reach the US level during the early 1970s.
2. The middle group: France, Japan, and – in the 1950s and 1960s – the UK. It should be remarked that, despite a fall in Japan's statistic in the late 1970s, Japan has generally been lying among the middle group and so cannot be thought of as a country with notably few working days lost in strikes.
3. The low group: West Germany and Sweden. By the late 1970s, however, Sweden's continually rising trend since the late 1960s had resulted in its statistic surpassing Japan to reach the level of France.

The revelation of Japan not being a country with particularly few strikes (and the figures used refer both to official and unofficial strikes), but instead lying quite close to France and the UK in its level of industrial disputes, is quite contrary to the conventional wisdom. Certainly some large and well-known firms in Japan have very few strikes, but for other firms this is not the case. The image of the Japanese economy as suffering little impact from industrial disputes because of their short duration should, therefore, be open to question. The average duration of strikes has been estimated from the ILO data by dividing the working days lost (i.e., total of length of strike × number of workers involved) by the number of workers involved. The results shown in Figure 7.2 suggest that the average duration of strikes in Japan is relatively short. Nevertheless the Japanese statistic is comparable to Italy, the UK in the 1960s, and to West Germany since the late 1960s. Moreover the average duration of strikes in Japan is longer than in France. There is no reason, therefore, to conclude that Japan is exceptional in its relative average duration of industrial disputes.

The stereotype of Japanese unions has been undermined by the comparative data on industrial disputes. The next step should then be to reexamine the image of what is the appropriate unit of organization for labour unions.

7.2 LOCALS IN THE USA

The study of union organization needs to be approached from two directions. One of the paths is obviously to examine the organization of Japanese labour unions. It has to be demonstrated that, while one organizational unit is the plant or company, there are also umbrella organizations functioning at the industry and national levels. The other path requires a comparative study with the labour organizations in Western Europe and the USA. There is an unfortunate tendency to equate labour unions with industry-level organizations because of the latter's prominence in reporting by the mass media. The consequence has been a misunderstanding of how labour unions in the West actually do function. Nowadays the issues which are of most concern to shopfloor workers – redundancy, promotion and transfers – are undoubtedly negotiated and monitored by the workplace unions. Thus the breaking down of misleading stereotypes should be carried out in the case of the West as well as Japan. That is the justification for making a fairly detailed study of European and US labour organizations in a book whose topic is Japan.

In Western Europe and the USA there are three major types of workplace union or labour organization at the plant or company level:

1. Formal labour unions, e.g. locals in the USA
2. Informal labour union organizations, e.g. shop stewards' committees or workshop committees in Britain

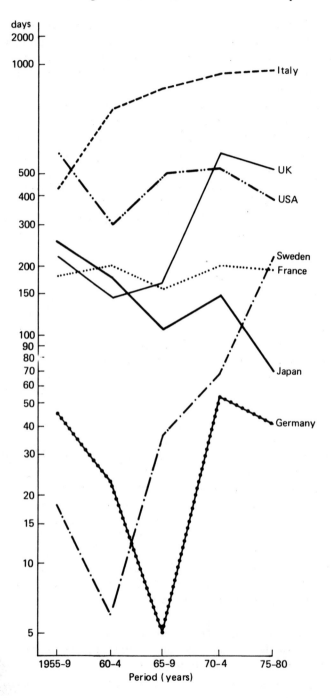

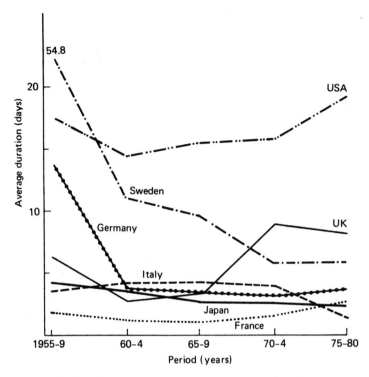

FIGURE 7.2   Duration of industrial disputes, international comparison

Source: See Figure 7.1

3. Employee organizations under legal provisions for participative management; Works councils in West Germany are the classic example, but similar organizations can be widely seen in European continental countries.

The US locals (1) and the West German works councils (3) will be observed here as a basis of comparison for evaluating the organization and functions of Japanese enterprise unions. If there were no international comparison, there would be a risk of wrongly emphasizing the alleged peculiarities of Japan.

FIGURE 7.1   Scale of industrial disputes, international comparison (average yearly working days lost through industrial disputes per 1000 employees, 1955–80)

Source: ILO (International Labour Office) *Year Book of Labour Statistics.*

7.2.1   How Widespread are Locals?

Members of labour unions in the USA amounted to 19.4 million in 1970[2], and with the addition of employees' associations[3], which more or less correspond to labour unions, total membership reached 21.25 million. The rate for organized labour was thus 30.1 per cent of all employees.[4] The vast majority, surpassing 21 million, were members of 185 national unions (industrial unions) and 23 employee associations. Organized labour – apart from a very small portion – is concentrated in large scale unions, since three of the national unions and one of the employees' associations each accounted for more than 1 million members. And more than half of total union membership was amassed in 14 national unions, each of which accounted for more than 400 000 members. Overall, 85 per cent of members were in 48 national unions, whose membership was more than 100 000 each. In Japan, only the All Japan Prefectural and Municipal Workers Union (Jichirō) has more than 1 million members. Nevertheless the concentration in large scale unions is comparable, in that 58 per cent of Japanese union members in 1973 were in 14 national unions whose membership was over 200 000 each; and 76 per cent were accounted for by 26 national unions of 100 000 or more members each. The resemblance in concentration is shown in Figure 7.3, where the scale distributions of national unions in Japan and the USA both peak twice at 100 000–200 000 members and at more than 500 000 members. These corresponding peaks suggest that there may be 'economic scales' for membership of national unions.

The lower level labour organizations, which are affiliated to the national unions in the USA, are known as locals, or sometimes as lodges.[5] The Bureau of Labour Statistics (BLS) survey held in 1970 counted 76 792 locals. The designation 'local' is commonly perceived as referring only to area locals – i.e., labour organizations across companies which cover separate industries and occupations within an area. But closer observation would reveal the existence of another kind of local which bears a resemblance to a Japanese labour union; this is a plant local – i.e., an integrated labour organization which encompasses most of the occupations within a plant or company. The extent to which each kind of local prevails has not been directly addressed by any statistical series, the author has not come across any meticulous research which is relevant to this issue. In the studies which I have carried out both types, along with various subtypes, have appeared:

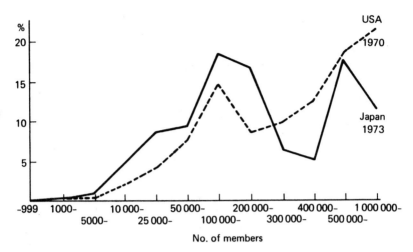

FIGURE 7.3 Size of national unions, USA–Japan comparison (percentage distribution of industrial unions by number of members, 1971; 1973)

Sources: USA, US Department of Labor, Bureau of Labor Statistics, *Directory of National Unions and Employees' Associations, 1971.*
Japan, Rōdōshō (Ministry of Labour) *Rōdōkumiai Kihon Chōsa* (Survey of Labour Unions).

(a)1 Locals of craft unions which grimly protect apprenticeship systems as well as strictly regulating recruitment and entry into their trades. This subtype is epitomized by the unions for carpenters, plumbers, etc. in the building trades. Their functions are to make labour contracts with the regional employers' association in the industry and, nowadays, to administer the apprenticeship system in concert with the employers' association. Through its complete control of the 'hiring hall', the local of a craft union can undoubtedly establish a monopoly in labour supply.

(a)2 Locals for unskilled workers which, though controlling the hiring halls, have no apprenticeship systems – e.g., longshoremen (dockers) unions.[6]

(a)3 Area locals for factory workers, especially those who frequently change their place of employment between small companies. Many of these area locals act as an umbrella to labour organizations located within each plant – e.g., the Garment Workers' Union.[7]

(b)1 Integrated labour organizations encompassing most of the occupations within a plant or company. These plant locals are indisputably like many of the Japanese enterprise unions.

(b)2   Amalgamated plant locals covering several plants or companies regardless of occupation. When there are too few workers in a small company's plant to justify there being a full time union official or even an effective union, the workers in several plants or companies may combine to form a local with one full time official. In this case, however, labour contracts are still separately concluded with each company, and the unit of union activity remains the single plant or company.

Owing to the lack of directly relevant data, it is impossible to know how many of the 21 million union members in the USA belong to each of the above types of local. Nor would it be reasonable to make any *a priori* judgement from the names of the national unions. The locals of the carpenters' national union (the sixth largest with 820 000 members) clearly fall into the (a)1 type, and the locals of the two national unions for longshoremen must be of the (a)2 type. But any judgement about the other unions is more or less impossible. There are cases of both the (a) and (b) types coexisting in the same national union. The fact that both types of local are affiliated to the International Brotherhood of Electrical Workers (fourth largest of the major unions) was apparent even under the limitations of my field work. There are craft locals ((a)1 type) scattered through most areas for electricians in the building trades; at the same time quite a lot of plant locals ((b) type) in the electrical machinery industry are certainly affiliated to the International Brotherhood of Electrical Workers. Similarly, there are two different types of local affiliated to the Sheet Metal Workers' Union even within the same provincial city with a population of 170 000. One is a craft local ((a)1) for the sheet metal workers in the building trades and the other is an amalgamated plant local ((b)2 type). Despite both types of local being affiliated to the same national union, no similarities in functions can be recognized nor is there any collaboration.

Probably the only way, even indirectly, to obtain a picture of the distribution of the different types of local is through the statistics displayed in Figure 7.4. This bar chart does not actually show the spread of locals; instead it merely indicates the extent to which the parties to collective agreements were single plants or companies. This indirect approach to estimating the prevalence of plant locals is reasonable, because US collective agreements, which are – as noted

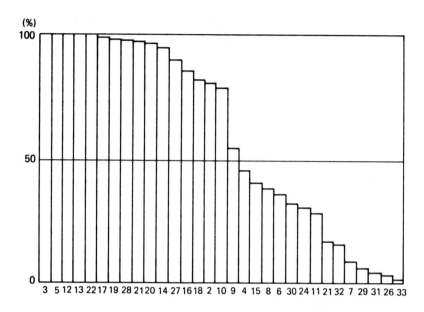

FIGURE 7.4 Collective agreements covering 1000 employees and more made with a single employer (percentage of workers covered, USA, 1971)

Note:

Manufacturing	2	Fabricated metal products	18
		Machinery, except electrical	19
Ordnance and accessories	3	Electrical machinery, equipment,	
Food and kindred products	4	and supplies	20
Tobacco manufacturers	5	Transportation equipment	21
Textile mill products	6	Instruments and related products	22
Apparel and other finished products	7	Miscellaneous manufacturing	
Lumber and wood products, except		industries	23
furniture	8		
Furniture and fixtures	9	Non-manufacturing	24
Paper and allied products	10		
Printing, publishing, and allied		Mining, crude petroleum, and	
industries	11	natural gas production	25
Chemical and allied products	12	Transportation	26
Petroleum refining and related		Communications	27
industries	13	Utilities: electric and gas	28
Rubber and miscellaneous plastics		Wholesale trade	29
products	14	Retail trade	30
Leather and leather products	15	Hotels and restaurants	31
Stone, clay, and glass products	16	Services	32
Primary metal industries	17	Construction	33

Source: US Bureau of Labor Statistics, *Characteristics of Agreements covering 1000 Employees or More, Bulletin* 1822, July 1973.

in Chapter 3 – much more detailed than in Japan or Britain, quite accurately reflect the actual situation. The following conclusions may, therefore, be gleaned from figure 7.4:

1. Agreements with single employers cover 56 per cent of all indus-trial workers and 80 per cent of manufacturing workers alone. It should be noted that the BLS survey was confined to agreements covering 1000 or more employees, and therefore the amalgamated plant locals ((b)2 type) probably would not have been fully rep-resented in the survey target. The widening of the survey to include all agreements might have resulted in a higher proportion of workers than displayed here being covered by agreements concluded between plant locals and single employers. Though the scale of craft locals might have been expected to be small, they do tend to be quite large in numbers.
2. Plant or company locals concluding separate agreements are par-ticularly prevalent in the heavy and chemical industries and in the gas, electricity, water and communication industries. More than 95 per cent of workers in most of these industries are covered by agreements with single plants or companies. The proportion falls below 95 per cent in the paper and applied goods, metal manufac-tures, stone and clay, and communication industries, but still remains at above 80 per cent.
3. Where only around 30–35 per cent of workers are covered by separate plant or company agreements is in the remaining manu-facturing industries – light manufacturing. One exception is the apparel industry, which falls into the next group.
4. In addition to the apparel industry, the non-manufacturing indus-tries – especially transportation and construction – display ex-tremely low figures for separate agreements. The main unions involved are the craft unions in the building trades, the Teamsters' Union, the two longshoremen unions, the Hotel and Restaurant Employees' Union and the Ladies' Garment Workers' Union.

It should be remembered, however, that the above figures apply to collective agreements made with a single plant or company. Under this category cases may have been included where there was more than one labour organization for different occupational groups in a plant, each of which concluded separate agreements with the one company. This point cannot apparently be confirmed statistically. But the plant local did appear from my observations to be on the whole an integrated labour organization covering most occupations in a similar way to the Japanese enterprise union. The situation where there is more than one local in a plant arises only when just a few workers in the maintenance department form their own local; the main plant local still accounts for the overwhelming majority of workers. Thus the overall conclusion remains: there is a close resemblance between the ways in which Japanese and US workers are organized, because about 80 per cent of US union members in manufacturing industries – with a higher proportion in the heavy and chemical industries – belong to integrated plant labour organizations regardless of occupation.

7.2.2 A Wide Lower Boundary to Membership of a Local

The dissimilarities between US locals and Japanese enterprise unions begin to emerge once their respective spheres of membership are observed in more detail. The three major distinctions are as follows:

1. It is already well known that white-collar workers tend to be excluded from membership of US locals. The locals which I observed were all confined to blue-collar workers. Even though in the major steel plants there are cases of white-collar workers being organized and belonging to the same national union as the blue-collar workers, the locals for the two groups of workers are separate. The US locals in this respect resemble the pre-1940 Japanese labour unions and the post-1945 mining unions.
2. The second major distinction is that in the USA foremen do not belong to the local. It should be noted that in this case foremen are considered to be those wholly engaged in supervising; those in the supervisory positions where they themselves also operate machines – group leaders, leadmen, etc. – are union members. The intention is to avoid the situation where a union member would be giving orders to other union members. But in Japan and West Germany foremen are usually union members. Many US locals have, moreover, adopted a policy in which foremen are not only required to break off their union membership, but also have to sever all their connections with the union. This means that even though a foreman may return to a rank and file position, all the seniority rights which he had gained while previously a union member are forfeited. The union regulations in practice require that once a member becomes a foreman, he cannot return to the union as a rank and file worker, unless he is willing to make a completely fresh start. Accordingly, while the majority of foremen

have emerged from among blue-collar workers, their links with the union are completely broken. Consequently there is among labour a powerful consciousness of foremen as being on the 'opposing side'. And a foreman has barely any employment protection, because if by any chance he is in conflict with management, he is on his own. The resulting phenomenon is that more than a few workers decline promotion to be a foreman, whereupon the management are obliged to allot some of these positions to new university graduates. This trend, (which cannot be demonstrated statistically, however) was apparent in much of my fieldwork.

3. The above two distinctions were concerned with the upper boundaries to union membership, where the US plant local is narrower than a Japanese enterprise union. The local's lower boundaries are, on the other hand, much wider than in the case of Japan. The relevant clauses are straightforward: all of those who have passed through the probationary employment period, which is usually 90 days, are required to become union members, and in practice they do so. In that all the plant's employees are union members there is no difference to the Japanese union, except that in the USA actual plant employees occupy a wider lower boundary, since some of the work which in Japan would be done by temporary workers and by parts manufacturers is in the USA carried out by the large company's employees. Indeed the definition of integrated labour organizations covering most occupations, which is commonly applied to Japanese enterprise unions, may be more appropriate for the USA plant locals.

With respect to union officials, the most outstanding difference appears to be in the percentage of their salaries borne by the company. There is no appropriate set of statistics, but my inquiries have revealed that the percentage borne by union funds in the USA is to a surprising extent smaller than in Japan. For a union official in Japan to receive a company salary while engaged in union activities would violate the Trade Union Act, because of the implied intimacy with management. The relatively large amount used up for union personnel expenses results in the part left over in union funds for strike compensation being less than in the USA. What would in Japan be in violation of the Trade Union Act is quite customary in the case of the US plant locals. There are few full time officials of locals whose salaries are wholly borne by union funds. But there are a lot of part time officials, who receive part of their salaries from the company and who in practice behave as full time officials. A common example is that of a company paying half the salary of a union official in acknowledgement of his union activities taking up four hours a day, amounting to 20 hours a week out of working hours. He is a part time official by reason of working in the union office for these 20 hours, while the rest of the time he does an operative's work. The union could pay the other half of his salary, to let him become a full time official. The relative number of union officials, when these *de facto* full time officials are included in the count, appears to be close to the number of full time officials in a Japanese enterprise union. The Japanese full time officials are paid the whole amount of their salaries from union funds.

7.2.3 Power of Locals Rooted in Rigid Rules

To what extent does a local have a say in the important matters of redundancy, promotion and transfers? A yardstick for measuring the extent of union control needs to be provided, and the method adopted here is to observe in the procedures for promotion, transfers and redundancy (a) whether the labour organization does have a voice, and (b) to what extent it has established rigid rules. A rigid rule is defined as being when there is an unalterable standard, whoever formally makes the decision. Examples of rigid rules are the seniority ranking of employees by their date of entry and regular rotation systems; with such rigidity, any merit rating made by management loses its significance. Thus there is little scope for discretion, which means, for example, that the management has no freedom in deciding whom to promote. The existence of such rules may be seen, therefore, as a yardstick, giving the union a most powerful voice. At the other extreme is the plant labour organization which has absolutely no say at all in decisions concerning promotion and other important matters, which would indicate the weakest kind of voice. Between these two extremes there are a variety of forms: the case where the management merely gives prior notice of whom it will promote; the case where there is consultation after notice has been given, but the final decision remains with the management; the case where the labour organization's actual consent is necessary. Which of these different forms is practised may be ascertained by inquiring into the actual procedures for consultative decisions.

To summarize this section:

1. The US labour unions are formally based on workplace unions (known as locals) which, at the very least, are prevalent in the large companies of the heavy and chemical industries. In this respect US labour organizations do not differ from the Japanese unions, which will be examined later in this chapter. Indeed, once internal labour markets have been formed, the presence of integrated plant unions is inevitable.
2. At the same time the US locals do have a powerful voice. In the matters of most concern to blue-collar workers, procedures are governed by the rigid rule of strict seniority, which has more or less precluded any managerial discretion.

7.3   WORKS COUNCILS IN WEST GERMANY

The employee organizations for participation in management in West Germany and France are legally different to labour unions, and taking strike action is prohibited. Nonetheless, because they are labour organizations which generally have a say in wage rates, promotion, transfers and redundancy, there is little real difference from formal labour unions. Concerning the issues of promotion, transfers and redundancy there exists, as far as I know, only scanty material which shows the functioning of labour–management relations at the plant level in West Germany. Nonetheless on the basis of two sets of relevant material, the actual procedures for participation in management will here be considered.

Use will first be made of Otto Blume's survey (1964), which covered the major industries apart from steel and coal[8]. Research on industrial relations has for the most part tended to pursue formal labour unions without reaching as far as conditions at plant level. While there are indeed several other German surveys on the actual procedures for participation in management, they have mostly concentrated in some way on the more 'splendid' aspects. Thus the participation of labour representatives on the board of directors has received ample attention, whereas the functioning of plant employee organizations – the other pillar of participative management – has tended to be ignored. Otto Blume's survey is unusual, therefore, in providing material which is relevant to the issues being examined here, even though his research was conducted some time ago. The survey target was plants or establishments with 200 or more employees in the construction, metals, chemicals, printing, textiles and foodstuffs industries. A regionally stratified sample of 432 establishments was selected, and interviews were conducted with the chairman and one member – for a total of two in each establishment – of the works council (*Betriebsrat*). The interview was composed of set questions, which we will call the 'questionnaire survey'. In addition, further interviews were held with the chairmen of works councils in 46 establishments with 1000 or more employees, which we will call the 'interview survey'. The survey was held over a period of two years from 1961. Its usefulness to our area of concern is confined at best to the information on redundancy procedures, since promotion and transfers were not a survey object. Still the Blume survey does seem to provide much more information than other surveys in this field. The other set of material is the results of interviews which I conducted in West Germany, although the cases were few and the duration of each interview was rather short.[9]

7.3.1 How Works Councils are Organized

Since there are legal provisions requiring the establishment of works councils, our discussion will begin by examining the relevant laws. All enterprises with five or more employees are required by law to set up works councils; but their actual diffusion cannot be estimated as there are neither penal regulations nor any completely accurate data. It appears that works councils are prevalent in establishments with 200 or more employees, and their diffusion in small and medium-sized enterprises may be only slightly greater than in the case of Japanese labour unions. Under the law, the establishment's blue-collar and white-collar workers should each elect their own council representatives, whose numbers are in proportion to the total work-force. For example, there would be 15 works council members representing 1001–2000 workers, and 29 members for 5001–7000 workers. The size of the works council lies above that of the union executive committee at plant level in Japan and below that of the central committee at company level. Even though white-collar workers are said to be represented in the works council, in fact this applies only to those below the executive level which apparently corresponds to section heads and above (*leitende Angestellte*). The council's representation thus roughly matches the membership of Japanese labour unions. The West German law goes so far as to stipulate the number of full time officials for a works council. Legally there should be at least one official in an establishment with 300–600 employees, three for 1001–2000 employees and seven for 5001–6000 employees. As, in practice, there could be more full time officials, the number are close to the usual number of full time officials in a Japanese plant union. In various respects, therefore, the structure of a works council bears a close resemblance to a Japanese enterprise union. The one major difference is that by law the works council is neither recognized as a trade union nor permitted to strike. Nonetheless there have in fact been occasions, particularly since the late 1960s, when the works council was the centre of strike action. Under the law, union funds cannot be raised, so all the works council's expenses for activities, which include personnel expenses for full time officials, office space and expenses, are borne by the company.

What, if any, is the relation between the works councils and the labour unions? In the autumn of 1976, I was able to carry out five case studies in West Germany. One representative study shall be discussed here. On the spacious premises of the plant adjacent to a huge chemical company's head office, there is in one corner a neat single-storey building surrounded by lawns: it is the works council office, where I interviewed the vice-chairman and five council members. The office's location and size give one the impression of visiting an enterprise union in a large Japanese company. The company is one of West Germany's largest and oldest chemical concerns. And out of a total of 33 000 employees there are 14 000 working in this extremely large scale chemical plant. At the time of my visit there were 35 council members, whose number corresponded to the legal requirement. The chairman and the vice-chairman presided over two separate committees. The works committee was made up of 11 people, all of whom were full time officials. They retained the status of company employees and their wage rates were quite high because of being skilled blue-collar workers. The works committee roughly corresponds to the executive committee of a Japanese plant level union. The other committee had responsibility for economic matters. This economic committee, which has to be set up under the law in enterprises with 100 or more employees, roughly corresponds to the labour members of the labour–management consultation committee associated with a Japanese enterprise union. The members constituting each of the two committees almost all overlapped. Below the works committee, there were specialist subcommittees, whose chairman and vice-chairman positions were mostly occupied by full time officials and whose members were the ordinary works council members. The works council, therefore, in organizational structure and in scale closely resembles an enterprise union in Japan. The major point of difference is that in West Germany the chemical company was bearing the expenses for the 11 full time officials, two secretaries, office space and administration.

About 70 per cent of the blue-collar workers in this plant were members of the chemical industrial union (*I. G. Chemie*), and some of the rest were affiliated members of the Christian labour union. Around 10 per cent of the white-collar workers were union members. The production workers in each workshop elected shop stewards (*Vertrauensleute*), from whom the shop stewards' committee (*Vertrauenskorper*) was composed. And all the works council members representing blue-collar workers were shop stewards. The works council vice-chairman told me that there was a long tradition for the activities of shop stewards. When labour unions were reconstructed after defeat in 1945, shop stewards, who were elected from each workshop and department, became the nucleus of union activities. The vice-chairman thought that it was, therefore, natural for the works council, which takes on similar activities, to be composed of shop stewards. Activities in plant labour organizations were thus essentially based on the work of shop stewards prior to the guarantees given by the 1952 Plant Organization Act (*Betriebsverfassunggesetz*).

In the other case studies also, I was told by the personnel managers that the shop stewards' committee comprised and controlled the works council. The overall conclusion should be that in West Germany the nucleus of the labour side in plant-level industrial relations is the works council, which is independent of the formal labour union outside the plant and instead is maintained by the informal labour organization within the plant, namely the shop stewards' committee.

7.3.2 Labour's Voice in Redundancy Issues

The 1969 Act for limiting redundancies (*Kündigungsschutzgessetz*) distinguishes between individual discharges (*einzelne Entlassungen*) and mass redundancies (*massen Entlassungen*). Actual examples of individual discharges are mostly in the category of disciplinary discharges; it is mass redundancies which are related to economic contract laws. Formalities for mass redundancy must, under the 1969 Act, be a subject of consultation between the company and the works council, but the latter's consent need not be obtained. The opinions of the works council are, however, attached in the company's submission to the Labour Office (*Arbeitzamt*).

The 1969 Act has also set up, in outline, provisions on who should be made redundant. The Act stipulates that consideration must be given to 'social aspects' (*soziale Gesichtpunkte*) such as the number and age of any dependants, any spouse's income, the years of service, any prior intention to quit the company, any impairment to health because of the job, being a youth organization's delegate, etc. Should litigation occur, the works council's opinions on these social aspects are appended to the court's proceedings. Since there is a relatively high proportion of youths among the unemployed in West Germany (Figure 2.4, p. 71) the stipulations concerning social aspects in the Redundancy Act do seem to have some impact. Nonetheless the Act's considerable ambiguities leave certain questions quite open: How should the above social factors be ranked in importance? How should each individual be ranked in terms of each factor – for example, the ranking of those with neither spouse nor dependants? So as to understand how in practice such questions are addressed, reference will be made to material provided in Otto Blume's survey.

Concerning the issue of mass redundancies, the questionnaire survey covered 74 works councils in companies where there had been redundancies at some time between 1952 and the time of the survey in 1961. The reply that they had been given an adequate say in the redundancy plans was given by 49 of the chairmen, accounting for 66 per cent of the total. 44 per cent of works councils were consulted on the issue of which individuals to make redundant, and 41 per cent were consulted on the standards for selecting redundant workers. The amalgamation of these two groups results in 85 per cent of works councils having some say in the decision on whom to make redundant. But the survey does not refer to general criteria for selecting individuals to be made redundant.[10] However, the interview survey results suggest that intervention by works councils in the event of mass redundancies was an established principle. Explicit standards (which did not completely determine redundancy selection) were set out in two of the quoted cases. In the first case, recourse was made initially to shorten working hours. The management and works council then carried out negotiations on whom to make redundant, and the criteria adopted were (i) the unmarried workers, and then (ii) those in households with other wage earners. Thus in this case the two standards were clearly ranked. In the second case, working hours were not shortened. The management presented a prior list of redundancies, and then the works council negotiated curtailments in the list. The criteria adopted by the management were short length of service and lack of aptitude. The resulting list was cut back by the works council, according to its chairman, on the basis of 'social aspects' and membership of the union. The number of workers to be made redundant had previously been decided at 450; however which of these criteria were more stringently applied was not reported in the survey results.[11]

The preceding discussion may be summarized by the following points:

1. In large companies at least, negotiations on who should be made redundant are held between the management and works council
2. The criteria apparently used tend towards redundancies being concentrated among those with shorter length of service
3. Nonetheless, it is not clear where priority is given in ranking the various factors; this ambiguity could leave some scope for incorporating merit ratings into the decision: thus the procedures for redundancy have not gone so far as the form of rigid rules as in the USA, which more or less accords with what the author observed in the five case studies during the autumn of 1976.

7.3.3 Labour's Voice in Promotion Issues

Labour's say in the procedures for promotion and transfers was not covered in the Blume survey. Nor, as far as I know, is there any other substantial material on this issue. Recourse has to be made to the rather scanty interviews made by the author. Since similar trends emerged from the results of each of the five case studies in 1976, only one will be referred to here: the plant with 14 000 employees adjacent to the head office of a large chemical concern.

According to the vice-chairman of the works council, the differential between the highest and lowest basic wage rates in a workshop was a mere 15 per cent, and there were few transfers to other workshops, even within the same department. Thus there appears to have been little scope for promotion from the viewpoint of basic wages; nor does an internal labour market seem to have been well established. Nevertheless a tendency towards internal priority in promotion could be observed; although a line of progression such as in the US process industries was not apparent, vacancies arising in jobs with high basic wage rates were advertized inside the plant. The choice among the applicants for promotion was said to be a subject of consultation between management and the works council. And, even though the management had the prerogative to nominate workers for promotion, their 'qualifications' would be investigated by the works council member responsible for personnel affairs. 'Qualifications' comprise not only the certificates for completed training programmes, but also previous work experience with reference to work records and personal relations in the workplace.

The preceding report given by the works council's vice-chairman indicates reliance on an overall judgement, rather than on a rigid rule of seniority as in the USA. It may be conjectured, therefore, that, even though 'qualifications' are said to be investigated by the works council, they lack any clear-cut criteria for rejecting the management's nominees.

Even among jobs earning the same basic wage rate, there would in fact be various differences arising from some jobs being more difficult or arduous, and from the adoption of payments by results leading to income disparities. The decision on who should be assigned to each job lay with the foreman, and any objections were lodged with the works council. If the complaint was upheld by the personnel affairs member's investigation, then negotiations with the company would be opened. But I was told that such complaints had rarely occurred. One's overall impression is of priority in promotion at any rate being given internally and of the works council having some say in the procedure, but without going so far as the form of a rigid rule as in the USA.

7.3.4 Summary

The legal clauses which differentiate West German works councils from labour unions could lead to misunderstanding. There is actually a close resemblance with Japanese enterprise unions. Similarities are that a company's blue-collar and white-collar workers belong to one labour organization, and the relative number of full time officials who are as well the company's employees. Moreover, a works council does have a say in labour issues just like a labour union. Thus a works council should undoubtedly be viewed as a *de facto* plant-based union.

The strength of the works council's voice, however, does appear – as far as is shown by some rather inadequate research material – to be weaker than that of US locals. For procedures relating to blue-collar union members, US locals have established rigid rules, which preclude almost any scope for assessment ratings or managerial discretion. In contrast, while the West German works councils – and also the supporting shop steward committees – do have some say in the important issues for shopfloor workers, they are far from setting rigid rules, and so the management retains a significant amount of discretion. In these aspects also the works council resembles the way in which most Japanese enterprise unions function – as will be discussed later in this chapter.

The dissimilarities with enterprise unions are (i) that the law forbids a works council to take strike action, since it is not legally recognized as a labour union, and (ii) that the company bears the personnel expenses of full time officials and the office and administrative expenses. The significance of (i) is low, however, since resorting to strike action has been neither a natural or frequent habit of West German labour unions; some works councils, moreover, have actually been at the centre of strike action. The second dissimilarity is only relevant to the case of Japanese enterprise unions which are, internationally, the exception in not having their expenses borne by the company. The part time officials of a US local receive company wages while being engaged in union activities. Similarly in Britain there are more than a few examples of plant union convenors receiving company wages and being engaged in union activities. The West German works councils should thus surely be regarded as plant-level labour unions.

7.4 THE STRUCTURE AND FUNCTIONS OF JAPANESE ENTERPRISE UNIONS

7.4.1 Historical Developments since 1890

The idea that Japanese unions are extremely weak remains a persistent one, despite the contrary evidence displayed in ILO statistics on the number of working days lost in industrial disputes. This question must be approached by outlining the structure and functions of Japanese labour unions.

One common misconception is that Japanese unions were first set up under the postwar policies of the US occupying forces, producing the view that Japanese unions have a very shallow tradition. But even under the limiting definition that the worker groups should actually be known as labour unions, Japanese unions had made their appearance at the latest by the 1890s. Unions more or less emerged just after Japan's industrial revolution – in a pattern similar to their emergence in the West – when there was rapid increase in the establishment of factories during the 1880s.

In this early stage there were craft unions like those in the West during the nineteenth century. This comparability with the West can also be seen in the occupations which were unionized, with unions for engineering craftsmen, for locomotive engineers and firemen, and for printing workers prominent. In Western Europe, the golden age of craft unions had already passed and the period from 1890 until the First World War saw a trend towards industrial unions. During this transitional period in Japan, however, the recently formed craft unions evaporated, primarily because there was a rapid drop in the collection of union funds when the membership who could pay dues fell sharply. During the First World War, however, labour unions emerged and expanded. The labour shortages which accompanied upswings in the Japanese economy permitted unions to engage in disputes and acquire wage rises. The consequent gains in real wages were considerably above those in Western Europe at that time. The famous Yawata strike at the largest steelworks in 1919 won the workers an eight hour day; and the union which was organized has continued to function right up to the present. Apart from the construction industry, industrial unions were formed as superstructures to the labour organizations in plants and companies. The major distinction with post-Second World War unions was that then only blue-collar workers were organized. The peak of unionization at the beginning of the 1930s was when the rate for organized labour reached 8 per cent. But under the assumption that the ceiling is the present rate of around one-third in industrialized countries, then Japan had only about one quarter of it's potential unionization. The extent of unionization was similar to that in the USA just before the New Deal. Then as the war with China intensified during the 1930s the Japanese government imitated Nazi Germany in aiming to dissolve the unions. But the formal dissolution of all labour unions by 1940 did not mean that industrial disputes no longer occurred. Data show that there continued to be disputes right up to the closing stages of the Pacific War.

Within just 18 months of defeat in 1945, labour unions had rapidly sprung up, with the result that the rate of organization surpassed 50 per cent. One factor was the support of the US occupying forces, whose policies sought the non-militarization of the Japanese economy. But by far the most significant factor was that the war had left the economy in ruins and people were at starvation levels. Marxist ideology was consequently in the ascendancy. The restoration of better living standards was conversely accompanied by the gradual retreat of Marxism and a fall in unionization to a level of around one-third, which is comparable to that in the industrialized countries. Thus the rate of organization in Japan cannot be considered to be exceptionally low.

7.4.2 Industrial Unions and Enterprise Unions

Another significant misconception is that the organization of Japanese unions is confined only to the enterprise level, whereas in fact there are three levels:

1. The foundation is made up of the labour organizations in separate plants and companies. But, in addition, the craft occupations, such as carpenters, have naturally been organized on occupational and regional bases. The plant labour organizations are formal labour unions like the US locals; and union funds are collected, from which full time officials are paid salaries.
2. Enterprise unions have joined together to form federations, each of which more or less corresponds to a particular industry. As discussed earlier (p. 232) these industrial federations resemble the US national unions in scale.
3. There are several nationwide organizations with which the industrial federations are associated. The main ones are Sōhyō (which accounts for 37 per cent of all union members), Dōmei (for a little under 20 per cent), and Sōrengō (for 11 per cent).[12] These organizations at one time had ties with political parties, in which respect they bore some resemblance to French and Italian unions, but these ties have loosened recently. In addition, there has been a movement towards unification of the nationwide organizations.

A three-tiered union structure is common to both Japan and the West, and the functional divisions are also similar. In the case of Japan, we find that:

1. The labour organization at the plant or company level negotiates redundancies, promotion, transfers and wage rates (as discussed in Chapter 4). These functions are no different to those of the US locals.
2. Industrial federations of unions influence negotiations on the

overall rise in the wage bill. Even though in many cases the enterprise union sits at the negotiating table, the industrial federation has a stronger say in the content of the negotiations and in the final decision. Intensive consultations both among the unions and among the managers often take place across competing companies in the same industry; and the industrial union president also participates in informal negotiations. Thus identical responses can be given at the same time on the same day, with the eventual outcome being an identical average percentage wage rise and average amount of gain in one industry. It should be noted, moreover, that in some industries formal industrywide negotiations take place. And negotiations on general labour conditions are dealt with in a similar way to wages.[13] In these aspects, therefore, Japanese unions should not be viewed as functioning in a way greatly different to US unions.

3. The primary activities of the nationwide organizations are in elections and in negotiations with the government. These functions have become more important as the government takes on a more significant role in matters of economic policy and social security.

Thus the functions of the three tiers of the union structure in Japan are not dissimilar to the West. But are resources also distributed in a similar fashion? It is possible that the allocation of personnel and finance in Japan is skewed more towards the company and plant level organizations than in the West, but this cannot be statistically confirmed, and comparisons of the systems of organization are difficult. For example, in the case of the West German organizations for management participation, the relative number of full time officials is comparable to a Japanese union at plant level; but the West German officials' personnel expenses are borne by the company, which also pays the office expenses. Consequently, even though union resources may be skewed towards the plant level in Japan, the overall funds and human resources which can actually be made use of by labour are to that extent not skewed. There are similar problems in making comparisons with the US locals where officials' salaries are partly borne by the company. The feature which instead is special to contemporary Japanese unions is that a relatively high proportion of their expenses for union activities are independently covered. It is in such detailed aspects that the differences between Japanese and Western unions may lie.

Another conjecture might be that there are differences in the boundaries to union membership. Since all an enterprise's employees, regardless of occupation, are members of the one union, it had been supposed that Japanese unions were weak because of this economically heterogeneous membership. But US locals are, as discussed earlier, no different in that respect. An integrated plant-based union is the inevitable outcome once an internal labour market has been established. However, as we have seen, the membership of many Japanese unions includes foremen and white-collar workers up to the level of subsection heads. But it must be reiterated that this feature appeared only in the unions formed after the Pacific War, whereas in their earlier history Japanese unions were confined to blue-collar workers. In any case union membership covering white-collar workers and foremen is not unusual in Western Europe – for example, the West German labour unions.[14] Moreover, there is a close resemblance in membership between the German works councils, which are geared towards management participation, and Japanese unions. The membership of a works council comprises the whole spectrum from roughly subsection heads through lower ranking white-collar workers and foremen right down to blue-collar workers.

7.4.3 Involvement in a Wide Area of Managerial Affairs

May it be supposed that Japanese enterprise unions are functionally inferior? The discussion in Chapter 4 has shown that unions speak out often on the important matters of transfers, promotion, redundancies and wage rates. Especially in the case of transfers, which occur quite frequently, the unions intervene to settle the details.[15] Nonetheless unions in Japan have not gone so far as to make and establish rigid and indisputable rules. Strict seniority is not followed in determining whom to transfer. Nor is rotation commonly employed for temporary transfers. The extent of managerial discretion in Japan does suggest that Japanese unions do appear to function less effectively than the US locals. However, as far as the frequency of intervention in matters of importance is covered, then Japanese unions may be ranked with the West German works councils. And, as far as is apparent from some short interviews, Japanese unions function as effectively as Swedish unions.[16] In this respect, therefore, Japan should be seen as a middle or somewhat lower ranking country, and it would be hard to argue that Japanese unions have a particularly weak voice.

Insofar as there is any special characteristic belonging to Japanese unions, it lies in a different aspect: the union's interest and voice in a wide area of managerial affairs. Participation in management has been established through the adoption of the joint labour-management consultation system, which has been the object of numerous surveys. Here our focus will be on the Labour Ministry's 'Labour–Management Communication Survey (*Rōshi Komyunikēsyon Chōsa*), whose value lies in employees themselves responding to questionnaires, rather than being confined to a straightforward survey of enterprises. And the survey's high sampling rate permits statistically significant results. The survey was held on two occasions in 1972 and 1977, and it revealed communication channels which, though not being thought of as labour-management consultation schemes, did appear to be so in practice.

It is clear from Figure 7.5, drawn from the survey, that joint consultation channels are widespread throughout enterprises where there are labour unions. Particularly in establishments with 300 or more employees the figure reaches 85–90 per cent. Consultation channels are somewhat less prevalent in establishments with 100–299 employees, but even so they exist in 70 per cent of such establishments with a labour union. While consultation channels and labour unions do indeed usually coexist, the former appear to be more common. The statistic for establishments without unions shows a marked fall, but is still over 50 per cent in the case of establishments with 1000 or more employees, and even in the case of smaller establishments reaches one-third. Where there is no labour union, the consultation channels are evidently performing some union functions. The employee representatives in the discussions held under joint consultation channels are, according to this survey, invariably the union representatives when there is a labour union. And even if no union exists, the representatives are elected by the employees in two-thirds of the cases. Meetings are held once a month or more frequently in just under one-half of the establishments; and in more than two-thirds the rate is more than once every two months. Discussions between labour and management may thus be said to occur frequently.

Figure 7.6 looks at the issues taken up in the joint consultation channels. When any of the nine issues depicted on the horizontal axis were a topic of consultation, the 'Labour–Management Communication Survey' assessed the extent of the workers' influence as follows: (i) receiving only an explanation, (ii) only soliciting the workers'

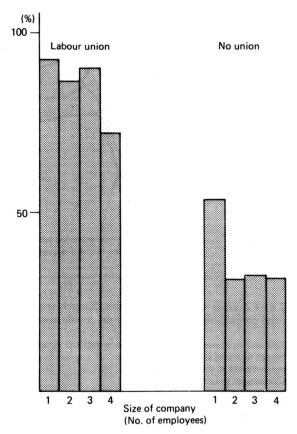

FIGURE 7.5   Percentage of establishments with joint consultation channels
(1974, all industries)

Note: 1. 1000–
      2. 500–999
      3. 300–499
      4. 100–299.

Source: Rōdōshō (Ministry of Labour) *Shōwa 47-nen Rōshi Communication Chōsa*
(Labour Management Communication Survey)

opinions, (iii) consultations taking place, (iv) workers' consent required.

By displaying the total of (i)–(iv) separately from the sum of (iii)
and (iv), where the latter represents workers having a powerful
voice, Figure 7.6 shows several points. First, it is clear that negotiations under the Japanese joint consultation schemes have a function

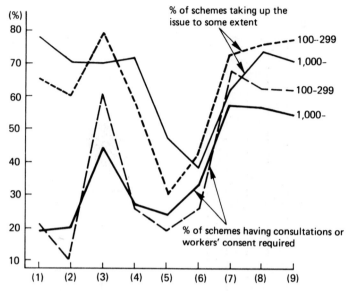

FIGURE 7.6   Coverage of joint consultation channels (percentage of
joint consultation channels taking up certain issues)

Note: (1) Plant and equipment investment and new product development
      (2) Present financial situation
      (3) Improvement in production methods
      (4) Recruitment policy
      (5) Company mergers
      (6) Training policy
      (7) Main conditions of labour
      (8) Shopfloor environment and safety
      (9) Fringe Benefits

Source: See Figure 7.5.

complementary to formal collective bargaining because of effectively
encompassing the workers' main areas of concern – conditions of
labour, shopfloor environment and safety and fringe benefits. And
the workers' influence in these matters is powerful. Secondly, management policy in the areas of plant and equipment investment, new
product development (present situation and plans), and present
financial situation is often taken up in joint consultations: in more
than 70 per cent of establishments with 1000 or more employees, and
reaching over 60 per cent even in establishments with 100–299 employees. The extent of consultation in about half of the cases where
plant and equipment investment and new product development are

topics is confined only to the workers receiving an explanation. But the workers' side also gives its opinion in over 20 per cent of the cases; and in around another 20 per cent consultations take place. In other words, although in around half of the establishments where these issues are taken up in joint consultation schemes the discussions are confined merely to hearing the management's case, in a little under half there are consultations, or at least a hearing is given to the employees' opinions. One cannot help but be impressed by this flow of information and exchange of opinions. The extent of the workers' say is lower in the case of the 'present financial situation', where in around two-thirds of the establishments they receive only an explanation; but this statistic is still remarkable in that financial information is being conveyed to the workers.

On the shopfloor also there is usually labour–management consultation through a fine mesh of information channels. Similar functions to the consultation system are provided by channels at all levels from the department down to the workshop. In some cases there is a formal labour–management consultation scheme based on the labour contract, while in others the policy has been initiated by the management. So as to cover all possible kinds, the survey asked the management: 'Has the company or plant set up sessions for the employees on the shopfloor to meet and discuss with the administration issues of progress in work, the working environment and safety, etc.?'

The diffusion of workplace consultative meetings appears from Figure 7.7 to be remarkable. And the high diffusion rate is not a function of whether there is a labour union. Such meetings take place in more than three-quarters of establishments with a labour union, regardless of the number of employees. Where there is no labour union, the meetings are rather more common the smaller the establishment: in more than 60 per cent of establishments with 1000 or more employees, and reaching 85 per cent of establishments with 300–499 employees. The statistic falls a little in the case of small establishments with 100–299 employees, but even so reaches 75 per cent. The diffusion of workplace meetings in establishments without a labour union rises well above that of joint labour–management consultation schemes. The workplace consultative meeting can here be seen to provide channels for conveying information into every corner of the establishment. In the workplaces which I have observed discussions were held through the medium of the joint labour–management consultation system and the workplace consultative meetings. Management explanations and workers' queries were addressed

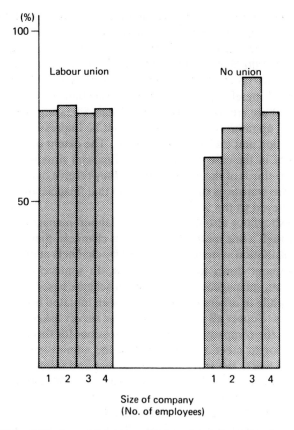

FIGURE 7.7   Diffusion of joint consultation channels at the department
level (percentage of establishment with channels)

Note: 1. 1000–
      2. 500–999
      3. 300–499
      4. 100–299.

Source: See Figure 7.5.

to the previous month's results and any divergence from the plan was
investigated. They went on to discuss that month's production targets
and what arrangements were necessary for their achievement through
decisions on the numbers of personnel to be transferred and between
which workshops. The discussions on the production plans and
financial prospects were, of course, based on the disclosure of company information. Although no appropriate data exists to permit a

comparison with Western countries, this abundant flow of information seems to be unmatched elsewhere.

7.4.4 A Strong Desire to Participate

A Japanese labour union's interest (and say) in managerial affairs depends upon the attitudes of the individual union members. As part of the 'Labour–Management Communication Survey' 10 000 workers gave their own responses to the following questions:

1. 'Do you wish to know about the management's plans and about the managerial situation?'. And 'How much do you actually know and by what means?' The responses here can be used as an index of the workers' 'desire to know'.
2. 'Do you think that there is a need for the wishes of rank and file workers to be reflected in some way in the management's plans?' The response can be taken as an index of the workers' 'desire to participate'.

Both of these indices, which are displayed in Figure 7.8, register high values of more than 85 per cent of workers in the major establishments with 1000 or more employees. Even though the indices fall slightly as the establishment size becomes smaller, their values still surpass two-thirds in the case of establishments with 100–299 employees.

So as to analyze the reasons for these high indices, the differences by sex, age and length of service are included in Figure 7.8. The desire to participate of male workers is undoubtedly higher than that of female workers, though the latter's index is still reasonably high. In the case of age differences, lower indices are registered among young workers and among workers aged over 54 years. But the most distinct trend appears in the case of length of service where the 'desire to participate' and the 'desire to know' indices are higher for more years of service. This trend can lead to consideration of the following hypothesis: the desire to participate should become stronger to the extent that workers have more years of service and their careers are internalized. Generally the proportion of workers whose careers have been internalized is higher among male workers than female and higher among the middle-aged than among youths. This hypothesis is also supported by the clarity of the functional relationship between length of service and the desire to participate. The good

258

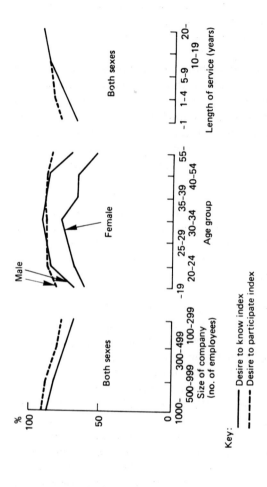

FIGURE 7.8 Desire to know and to participate (percentage of workers having the desire, 1974)

Source: See Figure 7.5.

fit of this hypothesis leads to the expectation that the desire to participate would be higher in Japan than in the West, because career internalization appears to be more prevalent in Japan than in the USA and Western Europe, and to be deeper than in Western Europe.

There are also in continental Europe various schemes for workers' participation in management. A typical example is in West Germany where workers' representatives are legally required to be sent to major companies' supervisory board. In practice, the workers' representative is usually the chairman of the works council. There are also legal guarantees to ensure that the management gives an explanation of its policies to the works council itself. The West German scheme thus appears to be a more formal arrangement than Japanese workers' participation in management. Nonetheless the workers' actual interest and say in managerial affairs are perhaps greater in Japan. This conjecture is primarily founded on the way in which joint labour–management consultation schemes take place at all levels from the workshop up to the section. The sheer quantity of information disclosed to workers also appears to be greater in Japan. Individual union members in Japan have a strong desire to participate, which seems to result from the deep internalization of their careers. In other words, the white-collarization of shopfloor workers has apparently engendered a greater interest and say in managerial affairs. It is, then, white-collarization which helps to explain the questions: Why is the desire to participate stronger? What is the impact on the wider area of industrial relations?

7.5 A MODEL OF TRADE UNIONS UNDER WHITE-COLLARIZATION

7.5.1 Internal Labour Markets Provide a Foundation

Internal labour markets more or less exist everywhere in the industrialized countries' major companies. A number of studies have examined the kind of industrial relations which have developed on the basis of internal labour markets, and these suggest that the labour union contributes towards higher productivity levels. This is, of course, contrary to simple textbook theory which suggests that rather than contributing to, labour unions detract from, productivity, because of their monopoly on the supply of labour. However, recently collated data have demonstrated that productivity is higher where there is a labour union. Considerable attention has been paid by US labour economists to Richard B. Freeman's results.[17] His work is an extension of the 'exit-voice model' which was originally formulated by Albert O. Hirschman.[18] Efficiency falls when there is dissatisfaction inside an organization. One solution – 'exit' – is for the dissatisfied workers to change their place of employment. The other solution is for the workers to remain in the company and use their 'voice' to improve their labour conditions. The consequent contribution to productivity which is made by the labour union 'voice' has been measured in several industries.

This model largely ignored the internal labour market factor; yet the cost of 'exit' for the workers (and hence the necessity of employing their 'voice') differ considerably depending on whether internalization of careers exist. The omission of this factor means that the relationship between productivity and the labour union is not explicit in the model. When careers are internalized, the company's vicissitudes have a considerable impact on progress or setbacks in the workers' careers; bouyancy may bring more rapid promotion, whereas recession may bring redundancy, which is extremely costly for workers where labour markets are internalized. Such workers naturally choose to cooperate in production so that their company remains competitive and their employment is thereby protected. It is not unusual in times of recession for US labour unions to cooperate in raising productivity and for them to accept QC circles. The difference between conditions in the USA and in Japan lies in the time scale, because the employment of long servers is protected over a longer interval in the USA, where redundancies are made in reverse order to length of service.

7.5.2 The Deep Internalization of Careers

The careers of white-collar workers and of production labour which has benefited from white-collarization are deeply internalized. A deep internalization of careers implies that channels exist within the company for promotion to higher status positions; and there are opportunities for experiencing a wide range of jobs, which permits workers to acquire a higher level of skills. Continued skill acquisition under an assumption of conditions being close to perfect competition should lead to a continual rise in wages, with the wage profile taking on the shape of a seniority curve: the 'high and late ceiling type'.[19]

By extending the earlier model a step further we can construct a model for industrial relations under the condition of a deep internalization of careers. The first point is that the cost of 'exit' becomes extemely high, because of the strength of the factor of enterprise specific skills. Except for the youngest workers, good prospects for promotion are implied by career internalization, as long as the worker has given – to some degree at least – continuous service. Thus the need for the workers to use their voice is heightened by the substantial losses they would bear if they were to move to another company. Whether the internalization of careers is shallow or deep, it is common to both industrial relations models that the workers' voice extends to the objective of enlarging the pie to be shared (the company's profits); but this aspect is particularly significant in the case of a deep internalization. Because the workers' own careers are deeply embedded in the company, whose vicissitudes consequently make a strong impact on their employment, they should have an influential voice in management affairs. Moreover workers whose careers are deeply internalized have a greater capability to make an effective contribution to managerial affairs, since the prospect of promotion to supervisory posts encourages workers to seek a better knowledge of the company's managerial affairs.

A further factor is that a deep internalization of careers does not mean that the possibility of redundancy is eliminated; and since the cost of redundancy is then extreme, the workers attach great significance to regulations governing redundancies. And transfers in response to business fluctuations may instead become more frequent. Careers which have been deeply internalized suffer considerable setbacks because of transfers, so that the need for their regulation becomes all the more significant. In the case of promotion also, the deep internalization of careers leads to intense competition between workers because the final prospects are so different. There is thus a real necessity for workers to have a voice in setting some kind of lowest guarantee, and the rules for competitive promotion. Similarly in the negotiations on wage rates, a group to speak out on behalf of the workers' voice is essential. In all these matters that group can in practice be only the labour union.

7.5.3 The Limits of Union Concern

Our model of industrial relations up to this point has not basically differed from the general theory of career internalization which had previously been developed. But when we examine the origins of the labour unions' negotiating strength, a significant difference appears: the labour union cannot take on responsibility for the whole of the occupational careers of union members. Deep internalization of careers requires that at least some workers have the prospect of moving into supervisory positions with middle or lower status. Often such promotion leads to workers giving up their union membership. Although in some countries white-collar managerical staff are said to be able to continue to hold union membership, in practice they would only pay union dues without any longer attending union meetings.

Under such conditions the capability of the labour union in negotiating with the management is weakened; strikes are hard to instigate, unless the dispute is widened to incorporate action by workers in competing companies. If the workers in just one company engage in a lengthy industrial dispute, then their employment is adversely affected because of the company being outstripped by its competitors. But the widening of disputes to other companies is hardly feasible, since disputes have to be internal for workers to be able to maintain their voice in important matters such as redundancy and transfers which are naturally dealt with separately by each company. These points show how a labour union could tend to accept the company's point of view. And this tendency is heightened in practice when careers are deeply internalized, whereas labour unions whose activities are centered on external labour markets may more easily set a 'market price' for a reasonable assessment of labour conditions and can, thereby, repudiate the management's viewpoint.

7.5.4 A Hypothesis for Industrial Democracy

Deep internalization of careers might be supposed to make it more difficult for a union to maintain a strong voice. But in our analysis it is the ability of the union to contribute to an enlargement of the pie (company projects) which determines the power of its voice. Deep internalization provides workers with a high level of skills, which in turn enlarge the scope for individual effort or 'X-efficiency'. There are great differences in workers' deployment of X-efficiency, depending on whether labour morale is high. The labour union and its members can inflict a substantial blow to the company's management by damaging profits. From the management's viewpoint, therefore, a high level of labour morale must be encouraged by giving the union the right to exercise its voice. This will be called the 'industrial democracy hypothesis'. In sum, high labour morale can be achieved by permitting workers to maintain a highly functional voice.

Industrial democracy is the general principle upon which lies the high labour morale and desire to participate of the white-collar group and of blue-collar workers who have entered white-collarization. Nevertheless, that morale needs to be continuously bolstered by giving the labour union a say in both the enlargement and the distribution of the pie. In the USA and Europe, where labour union membership rarely encompasses those who have entered white-collarization, circumstances have not encouraged the conception of this kind of hypothesis; relatively few white-collar workers are unionized and white-collarization of blue-collar workers has not yet been achieved. Japan has taken the lead in this respect, because the nucleus of the labour unions established after defeat in 1945 were those workers for whom white-collarization was being realized.

The above model of union behaviour should clarify the present position and issues relevant to Japanese unions. The features which are usually said to be peculiar are exactly those in which this model differs most from the simple textbook theory: a labour organization centred on the company, an interest and say in managerial affairs, cooperation in improving output, and thus high labour morale. These features would progressively become more common in the industrial relations of other countries if white-collarization were to become more prevalent with the support of labour unions. Japan can thus be considered as merely half a stride in advance on what is a general trend in industrialized countries. In other respects, this model can indicate the features of Japanese unions which are still inadequate. In particular, there is a need to consolidate the framework for further utilizing the workers' desire to participate arising from the internalization of their careers. And the workers' voice in the distribution of the pie should be heard more clearly.

NOTES

1. The main differences in how industrial disputes are defined can be seen as follows:

Japan: Excluding disputes lasting less than four hours, and excluding workers indirectly affected
US: Excluding disputes lasting less than one full day or shift
UK: Excluding political strikes, excluding disputes involving less than 10

workers, and including disputes lasting less than one day only if more than 100 working days lost
Germany: Including disputes lasting less than one day only if more than 100 working days lost
France: No restriction
Italy: Excluding political strikes
Sweden: No restriction

2. US Department of Labor, Bureau of Labor Statistics (BLS), *Directory of National Unions and Employees Associations* Washington, D.C. This biennial publication provides the basic data for assessing the scale of union membership. The directory corresponds to Japan's, *Rōdō Kumiai Kihon Chōsa* though with less detailed categories which do not go beyond displayed data on the number of locals in each national union and on union membership. Unless otherwise noted, the figures used here have been drawn from the BLS directory.

3. Employee associations, which have rapidly appeared on the scene of the white-collar professions, such as teachers and nurses, do in practice function as labour unions.

4. This rate for organized labour of 30.1 per cent does include the employees' associations, which are considered to function as labour unions. If employees' associations were excluded, the rate would fall to 27.4 per cent.

5. Between the national unions and locals there are organizations at regional level, many of which cover several states: see Barbash (1967) Chapter 5.

6. See Jensen (1964) and Larrowe (1955). 'Boston Harbour' locals which have complete control over employment entrance were among the locals which I observed.

7. One detailed historical study is Carpenter (1972).

8. Blume (1964).

9. These interview results have been reported and analyzed in Koike (1976).

10. Blume (1964) p. 123.

11. Blume (1964) p. 138.

12. Ministry of Labour, *Rōdō Kumiai Kikan Chōsa* (Survey on Trade Unions). This annual publication provides basic data on union membership and on the numbers comprising industrial unions and nationwide organizations.

13. A paper written in English on this is Koike (1980). A more detailed exposition in Japanese may be found in Koike (1962).

14. For a more detailed discussion, refer to Koike (1976).

15. A highly detailed observation of this aspect is provided in Nitta (1981).

16. See Koike (1976).

17. Freeman and Medoff (1979) is just one of his many contributions.

18. Hirschmann (1970).

19. Grinker, Coope and Kirsch (1970).

REFERENCES

Barbash, Jack (1967) *American Unions: Structure, Government and Politics* (New York: Random House).

Blume, Otto (1964) *Normen und Wirklichkeit einer Betriebsverfassung* (Tübingen: J. Mohr).

Carpenter, Jesse Thomas (1972) *Competition and Collective Bargaining in the Needle Trades 1910–1967* (Ithaca: New York State School of Industrial and Labor Relations, Cornell University Press).

Freeman, Richard B. and Medoff, James L. (1979) 'The Two Faces of Unionism', *Public Interest*, Winter, pp. 69–99.

Grinker, W., Coope, D. P. and Kirsch, A.W. (1970) *Climbing the Job Ladder: A Study of Employee Advancement in Eleven Industries* (New York: E. F. Shelley & Co.).

Hirschman, Albert O. (1970) *Exit, Voice and Loyalty* (Cambridge, Mass.: Harvard University Press).

Jensen, Vernon H. (1964) *Hiring of Dock Workers* (Cambridge, Mass.: Harvard University Press).

Koike, Kazuo (1962) *Nihon no Chingin Kōshō* (Collective Bargaining in Japan) (Tokyo: Tokyo University Press).

Koike, Kazuo (1976) *Rōdōsha no Keiei Sanka* (Workers' Participation in Management) (Tokyo: Nihon Hyōronsha).

Koike, Kazuo (1980) 'Inter-industry Wage Spillover in Japan – An Insight into "Shuntō"', *Keizai Kagaku*, 28, 2, December, pp. 30–3.

Larrowe, Charles P. (1955) *Shape-up and Hiring Hall* (Berkeley: University of California Press).

Nitta, Michio (1981) 'Tekkōgyō ni okeru Rōshi Kyōgi no Seido to Jittai' (Joint Labor-Management Consultation Conference in the Japanese Steel Industry) *Shakai Kagaku Kenkyū*, 32, 5 and 6.

8 A Typology of Labour to Explain Industrial Relations

8.1 SUMMARY OF DISCOVERIES: SIMILARITIES AND DISSIMILARITIES

8.1.1 White-Collarization

There has been the persistent belief that Japanese industrial relations are uniquely characterized by permanent employment, seniority wages and enterprise based unions, which are said to support Japan's high labour morale. But these assertions are found to be based on flimsy material. Nor have the believers in unique Japanese industrial relations made direct observations of actual conditions in the West, which has nevertheless been held up as the standard for judgement. Their beliefs have ended up as a misleading comparison of the actual situation in Japan with the textbook view of industrial relations in the West. Once a direct comparison of the actual situation in both Japan and the West is carried out, using the best data that are available, the supposedly unique features of Japanese industrial relations can be denied, on two counts.

The first is that the seniority curves for wages and for length of service are not applicable to the majority of Japanese workers; a persistently rising profile is confined to a minority. Continually rising wages are recognized to be centred only on the limited groups of white-collar males and large companies' blue-collar males, who do not exceed (even when generously defined) one-third of Japan's labour force. The validity of this contention holds still more strongly when a historical view is taken; the seniority curve for these limited groups has not been a consistent phenomenon since the beginning of industrialization in Japan. It is only since the First World War that a rising wage profile for large companies' blue-collar males can be recognized at all. And only after the Second World War did this phenomenon become notably more pervasive. From the limited available material on the major companies prior to 1914, it appears that blue-collar workers frequently moved between large companies to the extent that the annual separation rate sometimes surpassed 100 per cent and on occasion reached 200 per cent; nor was it likely that the wage profile for the large companies' blue-collar workers displayed a seniority curve.[1]

The second reason for denying the supposed uniqueness of permanent employment and seniority wages is that these features are held in common with white-collar groups in the USA and the EC. This comment applies mainly to males, although if more than a minority of women were employed continuously over a long time, they too would surely share these features. Morover in the case of the USA (but not of the EC) these features can be recognized to some degree among large companies' blue-collar males, who in this respect lie close to midway between Japan and the EC. In sum, it is the white-collarization of large companies' blue-collar males which should surely be seen as the special feature of present day Japanese workers.

8.1.2 A Wide Range of Skills

What does 'white-collarization' mean in practice? The most important issues for those who work concern skills, whose study has been the main topic of this book. The acquisition of skills is, nowadays, mostly through on-the-job-training. The cost of this may be minimized by workers becoming experienced as they pass through a grouped range of jobs which are deeply related to each other. One grouped range of jobs then comprises a career, whose length and width can be observed in order to assess the quality of skills attained during it. When such comparative observations were made in the heavy and chemical industries of Japan and the USA, both similarities and dissimilarities could be recognized. The major similarity is that even though young workers often change their place of employment, they thereafter remain for a long time in one company, where skills are acquired through on-the-job training. The dissimilarity lies in the relative widths of in-company careers, which are rather broader in Japan. Workers in large US companies may be either in places where most of the one workshop's main assignments are experienced, or else where only some of the jobs are passed around. All the more rare then are places where workers move between even closely related workshops. In contrast, the workers in large Japanese companies not only generally experience the main assignments in one workshop, but also have experience in other closely related workshops. This point should not, however, be misunderstood: commentators often remark that the movement of workers takes place between any workshops, which would indicate an absence of consideration for occupational careers. In practice, however, the formation of a career clearly takes place in only two or three closely related workshops. Apart from transfers to unrelated workshops which provide an escape hatch for avoiding redundancies (which occurs though to a lesser extent, in the USA as well), a Japanese worker usually experiences only two or three out of perhaps 50 workshops in one plant; and he would be reluctant to move to the majority of workshops, which lack any relation to the skills being formed in his career.

8.1.3   Worker Contribution to Enlargement of the Pie

It is the author's opinion that this formation of wide-ranging skills – which is the real essence of white-collarization – is the foundation for high labour morale in Japan. If workers' experience extends to related workshops then they have a good understanding of their department's production process, and this may enable them to initiate durable improvements in production and work methods. Such workers hold intellectual skills tantamount to a part of an engineer's qualifications, which justifies the use of the term 'white-collarization'. Since the range of skills widens and becomes more sophisticated for a worker employed for a long time, his long length of service synchronizes with the seniority curve for wages which usually applies to white-collar workers. Conversely, the work for which such wide-ranging skills are not required is handed over to inplant subcontract workers and outside workers, rather than being done by the company's regular workers. Not all the jobs denoted as being within the province of a large company are paid in correspondence with a seniority wage curve; a wider perspective shows how technology and skills crucially affect payments.

Another important quality emerges from the workers' understanding of the production process: the considerable scope for a flexible response to any changes. The persistent belief until now has been that the immobility of Japanese workers who stay with one company has limited the system's adaptability to economic fluctuations. But one of the most significant changes requiring a response would, for example, be the introduction of new machinery. The fundamental technological principles rarely differ even with the new machinery; so the possessors of wide-ranging skills, who have a good understanding of the production process, can take new machinery in their stride. A response to downward fluctuations – namely, a contraction in demand – is also within the system's capability. At a given moment there may be both workshops facing a demand expansion and others which are in decline within a single large company. When both types are related in terms of skills, then the workers who have acquired wide-ranging skills can transfer from the declining workshop to the area of growth and redundancies can thereby be minimized. And also within one workshop, detailed changes take place incessantly. For example, posts have to be reassigned in response to some workers being absent. The capability of the system to rearrange assignments differs enormously depending on the extent to which there are workers able to perform the tasks of any of the main assignments in the workshop. Slight changes in product specifications also arise, in response to which assignments have to be rearranged. In sum, the workers' possession of wide-ranging skills should be considered as having made a substantial contribution to Japan's economic growth or, in other words, the enlargement of the pie.

8.1.4 An Egalitarian Distribution of the Pie

The distribution of the pie is also influenced by wide ranging skills. Wage differentials in Japan are, as a general rule, relatively narrow, especially between white-collar and blue-collar employees. One outcome of the white-collarization of large companies' blue-collar workers is that their wage profile has conformed to the seniority curve in line with white-collar workers, and the wage differential between both groups has become narrower than in Western Europe and the USA. There is, on the other hand, a particularly wide wage differential in Japan between male and female workers aged over 30 years, which is another outcome of the white-collarization of blue-collar males. There is little difference between Japan and the EC in the wage curves for female workers; but in the case of blue-collar males, while those in large Japanese companies have a seniority curve, in the EC there is only a slight rise after the twenties age group. The corollary is that, although wage differentials by sex in Japan and the EC are comparable as far as the twenties age group, the differential in Japan has opened up widely for male and female workers in their thirties.

The distribution of the pie goes beyond renumeration in cash; how power is distributed is also extremely significant. Japanese blue-collar workers appear in practice to have little more power than their counterparts in the USA. How workers are assigned and their movements between assignments within the workshop are crucial to their skill formation. Even in the same Japanese plant there are various ways for making assignments and movements depending on the individual workshop, which suggests that the customs of the workshop are a determining factor; the implication is that the wishes of that workshop's workers are being implemented. This may be contrasted with the practice in large US companies, where postings and promotion are strictly determined by seniority; the regulations for postings and promotion are in practice decided on at a level higher than the workshop. Thus the US workshop's own authority must be somewhat less than in Japan.

Considering the work methods and routines may also permit an attempt to assess the comparative extent of authority. In both Japan and the USA standard work procedures are determined by those in the production control and industrial engineering departments. But the standard procedures end up being revised by Japanese shopfloor workers who set about demonstrating their own ideas for improving productivity. The practical authority held by Japanese shopfloor workers, which surpasses that of their US counterparts, should be considered as playing a part in strengthening worker morale.

8.1.5   Poor Treatment of Older Workers

There is no country where industrial relations are problem-free. In Japan, the most difficult issue concerns the cold treatment suffered by the senior workers who possess wide skills. One manifestation of this practice lies in redundancies being concentrated among middle-aged and older workers. The popular belief asserts that redundancies do not occur in Japan. But even in a large Japanese company workers are made redundant if the company's fortunes wane, and on such occassions the usual practice is for those aged around 50 years and older, who are generally long servers, to be made redundant. It is hard for these workers to find employment in other companies which sufficiently utilizes their wide-ranging and partly enterprise specific skills. Ultimately they land up in positions where their skills largely lie dormant, which represents a loss for the national economy as well as, of course, for the individual involved.

The second manifestation of cold treatment is the early mandatory retirement age (*teinen*) for workers in large Japanese companies, which in the early 1980s (being generally 60 years) is earlier than in Western Europe and the USA. Many workers do not withdraw from the labour market after mandatory retirement, but instead move to small and medium-sized companies where mandatory retirement either is not strictly enforced or else does not exist; so they continue to work until their late sixties. Although these workers' sophisticated skills which have been built up within the large company are still demonstrable, appropriate opportunities are few in the smaller companies to which the skilled workers have to move because of mandatory retirement, which is a euphemism for a strictly enforced redundancy. A comparison of these conditions with the USA where redundancies are made in reverse order to length of service shows that the loss is smaller in the USA, because the redundant workers who do not yet possess sophisticated skills can move to another company and start afresh. Also even before the provisions forbidding discrimination by age in the Equal Opportunities Law the retirement age of 65 years in the USA was later than in Japan. Similar trends, though less distinct, are apparent in Western Europe. In Japan, in contrast, redundancies are applied generally to those for whom the social cost of redundancy is high. The social stress is, therefore, enormous, despite the unemployment rate being relatively low.

This deficiency in Japanese labour practices has, if anything, been exacerbated by the erroneous perception of Japan as a country with permanent employment and seniority wages; to the extent that older and long serving workers are presumed to be excessively protected, then efficiency could be heightened by weakening their employment protection. This is but one example of the surprisingly harmful influence engendered by mistaken popular views.

8.2 A THEORY OF LABOUR TYPES

How can the similarities and dissimilarities between Japan and the West best be explained? For that purpose a theory of labour types will be proposed here. The labour type is a function of the character of the skills which the worker acquires during his career. Skill formation, which goes beyond what is initially determined by technology and machinery, depends either on on-the-job-training in companies or on the apprenticeship system and educational institutions. Each alternative is propagated by a social organization which as a social institution functions more or less independently of technology, in spite of there being some technological influences. Evidence has been provided by our limited comparative study of Japanese and US heavy and chemical industries, where careers display some differences in spite of technological similarities. Our theoretical explanation of differences in industrial relations will give attention to the social institutions reflected in labour types. The basic hypothesis is that the main labour types can be commonly seen to exist in all industrialized countries, but depending on their relative weights in each country, differences emerge in industrial relations.

The common emphasis on technological and economic conditions in determining the pattern of industrial relations is not disputed here. As an example, industrial relations in the construction industry are centred on the craft unions, which are indeed common to Japan, the USA and Europe; so the factor of technological conditions must operate powerfully across different countries. But focussing exclusively on such factors leaves one at a loss to explain dissimilarities in industrial relations, and often recourse has been made to 'cultural peculiarities', especially since neither technological nor economic conditions greatly differ between the same industries in industrialized countries. So as to avoid this pitfall, the intervening variable of labour type will be analyzed here. All of the four main labour types distinguished will be seen to exist to some extent in such industrialized country, which thereby lays the foundation for the universality of industrial relations. The relative weights of the four types, however, vary between different countries, which leads to dissimilarities in industrial relations. The explanation of our hypothesis now follows.

8.2.1 Four Basic Types of Labour

It goes without saying that labour type is a function of labour's ability; and the traditional classification of labour depends on whether those abilities – namely, skills – are high or low, which has led to the division between skilled and unskilled labour. This classification is supplemented in our theory by incorporating the element of time with a simple rule of thumb: whether or not labour ability has been heightened through accumulated experience. The traditional division of labour has ignored the obvious fact that labour's ability changes considerably, depending on the accumulation of experience. This may have been justified in the nineteenth-century world of craft skills and craft unions, but the simple division into skilled and unskilled labour is not compatible with contemporary industrial society. When the element of time is incorporated into the traditional division, the following four types of labour are obtained:

1. High and unchanging skills – craftsman or skilled type
2. Low and unchanging skills – labourer or unskilled type
3. Skills which become higher over a long time period – internal promotion type
4. Skills which become higher over a relatively short time period – semi-skilled type.

This typology sheds light on several issues: for example, the method of skill acquisition and the quality of skills. As well as skills being the most significant determinant of labour ability, their method of acquisition greatly influences ability. Under type 1 the periods for training and for working can be clearly distinguished, because the craftsman's skills barely change once he has completed his apprenticeship. A fairly concentrated training period, for which the apprenticeship system is most appropriate, is needed to attain the high skills required. Consequently skilled labour has often been defined as workers who have passed through apprenticeships. Since the skills are not acquired in a company training course, they remain as general skills rather than being enterprise specific.

Under the internal promotion type (3) skills are heightened along with experience, which means that training continues over a very long time period. On-the-job training is utilized in order to minimize training costs which would have been far more expensive if workers had been required to attend lengthy off-the-job training sessions. The most efficient way to implement on-the-job training, and thereby minimize training costs, requires that when a worker is beginning his career he should be doing the easiest job, from which he proceeds to a slightly more complicated job, and so on; and it is necessary that the present job and the next job should be technologically highly related. This approach permits the worker to be 'promoted' through a sequence of related jobs. The content of his skills will then be determined by the number and by the nature of the jobs which he experiences. The worker who fits into the internal promotion type will have done quite a lot of jobs over a long time period, whereas the semi-skilled type will have completed his career after doing relatively few jobs.

The approach to training under the internal promotion type results in skills becoming rather enterprise specific. There are careers which can be formed across different companies; but the worker must then be able to move freely between companies, which implies that he should not bear any loss in moving. To fulfill that condition there has to be a common assessment even halfway through his career of the skills which he has already acquired. As that assessment of career level would have to be standardized across companies, the degree of relationship between the jobs making up a career in one company would be lessened. Then the cost of skill acquisition through on-the-job training would become higher, because the conditions cited above for efficient on-the-job training would no longer be fulfilled. It is, therefore, inevitable that careers under the internal promotion system should be developed within a single company.

A career which evolves within a company naturally becomes, at least to some extent, enterprise specific. The content of the jobs which are done in that career will determine the skills of labour falling in the internal promotion type: in more detail, (a) the content of each job and (b) the boundaries to the grouped range of jobs which cover the career. There is no reason why either (a) or (b) should be shared in common across companies. Let us suppose that the machinery installed in a group of competing companies is the same in each company, and that the manufacturing operations are as a whole identical throughout the group. Even under this assumption there would be no guarantee that the content of all the jobs would be the same in each company. There would remain some flexibility as to how many workers are assigned to operating, and as to the number of jobs into which each process is divided. For example, the content of each job could be enlarged to encompass more operational units for a relatively proficient workforce, and vice versa. Thus the composition of the labour force not only varies between different companies in the same industry, but also shows continuous changes over time even within one company. In addition, there are changes in the company environment such as when, for example, output has to be suddenly raised beyond normal productive capacity. And the environment would change even more radically on account of technological innovations, some of which are almost an everyday occurrence.

In spite of the preceding factors, let us suppose that the content of individual jobs is invariable across a group of companies. There would still remain variety in the ways that careers are constructed, insofar as careers may be broad or narrow in their range of experience. The deeper is the promotion route – or, in other words, the greater are the number of jobs done in the career – then the stronger are these internal company characteristics, from which it follows that skills under labour type 3 easily tend to be enterprise specific. And since, on the other hand, the career of the semi-skilled worker in type 4 is shallow, any enterprise specificity of his skills would be hard to maintain.

At the same time there need be no justification for interpreting the quality of enterprise specificity as a total inability to realise those skills outside the one company. But, even though the skills could be utilized in another company in the same industry, a certain amount of supplementary training would be assumed to be required to ensure 100 per cent realization of enterprise specific skills elsewhere. The theory of labour types has up to this point established that the movement of labour type 3 to another company would always incur a cost.

8.2.2 The Different Forms of Regulations

When the differences in labour types are ignored, there is no way of grasping the dissimilarities in industrial relations which arise from the composition of the labour force. Our alternative theory is applied below by seeing how industrial relations are affected by different labour types when all other relevant factors are taken as given. Let us assume that industrial relations are the interactions between labour and management which are guided by the resulting 'web of rules'.[2] Each rule incorporates the following five elements:

1. What is being regulated – the object
2. Who is making the regulation – the subject
3. How the regulation is being applied – the method
4. Where the regulation is being enforced – the place
5. To what extent the regulation is being enforced – the extent.

The first four of these elements will naturally be variable depending on the labour type. Let us contrast the internal promotion type – since it has been newly established – with the skilled labour type from the traditional classification. Rather than attempting to examine all the regulations, our attention will be focussed on those which must be crucial to a career: namely, regulations which govern employment entrance, training, assignments and employment termination.

The case of the skilled labour type is clearly expressed in the functions of craft unions, whose membership are the epitome of skilled labour. The regulations which govern skill formation under the apprenticeship systems are in effect the regulations for entering employment and for training. Once workers have completed their apprenticeship, their skills are seen as being relatively immutable and as being appropriate for any job in their occupation. Therefore there is no need to regulate assignments which are not crucial in the formation of their skills. Consequently the best option for the skilled labour type is to endeavour to demarcate the boundaries of their profession, to limit the number of workers entering the craft and to enforce the requirements for entering the craft through the apprenticeship qualification. Terminating employment with one company implies nothing but the simple forfeiture of an employment opportunity; mobility between companies may occur on a large scale, because there would be no renunciation of opportunities to acquire skills and of promotion prospects. Thus the craft unions' provision of a framework for facilitating employment exchange mechanisms has been the focal point of their regulations.

In the case of the internal promotion type, on the other hand, employment entrance is generally confined to the lower ranking jobs with little importance being attached to technical qualifications; so labour unions do not feel any necessity to make regulations for entering employment. But, because skill formation depends upon assignments, it is promotion and transfers which are the primary focus of regulations. And employment termination is also an extremely important object of regulations, since not only is mobility between companies subject to severe restraints, but also leaving one company implies the renunciation of promotion prospects and, at times, the fear that the skills already acquired shall not have a chance to be utilized.

The above approach, which looked at the object of regulations, also serves to demonstrate the place and the organization monitoring the regulations. The career of the skilled labour type is widened outside the one company and, therefore, the object of regulations in each skilled occupation extends beyond the company. There is in each occupation active mobility between companies in each region, with rather less nationwide mobility. On that account the regional organization for each occupation, which belongs to a nationwide organization, is the primary monitoring body – i.e., the craft union. Under the internal promotion type, on the other hand, the plant or company has become the place for regulations, because assignments and promotion are internal issues. But there would be a loose relationship across companies in the same industry to the extent that the degree to which the career is enterprise specific may be small. Therefore, from the workers' viewpoint, the primary monitoring body should be the plant or company organization, but the industry union also plays a part. The relationship between the two levels of monitoring bodies is shown by close observation to be that the foundation of most industry unions are plant or company organizations.

The method of regulating also differs depending on the labour type. Under the skilled labour type, the main object of regulating skill acquisition is the apprenticeship system, where skilled workers, not managers, are the ones teaching techniques; it is labour which has taken the initiative in skill formation. Consequently the leadership of the workers has become powerful in the case also of regulations; the labour organization itself decides upon many of the important issues, as well as protecting the occupational boundaries, rather than decisions being taken in negotiations with management. If the management were to oppose the decision, then union members would withdraw their labour. Because, in sharp contrast, skill formation under the internal promotion type takes place within the company, the union has no alternative but to negotiate with the management in order to attain benefits for the union membership; the method of regulating lies mainly in negotiations between the two sides, namely collective bargaining.

The remaining element of regulations – the power – does also have a degree of flexibility, even under the same internal promotion type. Not only are there places where (as in the US heavy and chemical industries) the established regulations leave no room for managerial discretion, but also places where (as in Japan and many of the labour organizations of Western Europe) the seniority right is not strictly conceded, which means that the management's voice has more scope than in the USA. The power of regulations varies depending on the power relationship of both parties to the quasi-bilateral monopoly situation which emerges when a strong labour union is established and functions inside the company.

8.2.3   A Model of Unions Under White-collarization

At the present time the internal promotion type of labour should be given particular attention because of its increasing prominence globally, as well as its being in Japan the main current of organized labour. Therefore, the characteristics of the internal promotion type will now be considered in more depth. Even though a career's width is influenced by technological variables, those are not the sole determinant. Nor does the existence of internal promotion preclude any differences emerging in the width and depth of careers. The dissimilarities between steelworkers in the USA and Japan have been explained by the variety in career widths. Let us denote wide or deep careers, which characterize white-collar workers and shopfloor workers under white-collarization, as the 'deep internal type' of labour.

The model of industrial relations which has been established on this basis (Chapter 7, pp. 259–63) differs radically from the classical confrontation model in which the labour union takes strike action to raise the market wage, while ignoring other aspects of the company management. Under the assumption of market competition, the company invests in capital in order to survive, but in doing so faces risks because of competition. If the capital investment is successful, the management is rewarded with higher profits. And if, on the other hand, the investment is unproductive, the assumption of labour having general skills means that even in the case of resulting redundancies, workers can move to another company without bearing any losses in their acquired skills. Under such conditions, therefore, there is no reason why labour should have any interest in the company management.

There has, nevertheless, been a growing awareness that the classical confrontation model of industrial relations does not correspond to reality, at least in the industrialized countries. When careers are internalized to some extent, moving to another company does involve some loss. Company vicissitudes do reverberate on the employment and the skill development of union members. Despite this evidence, however, any theoretical development has been lacking. In any case, even though our analysis of the impact of a deep internalization of careers is self evident, in the USA and Western Europe unionization of white-collar workers, who do have deeply internalized careers, is still unusual. Only in Japan where white-collar workers entered the unions after the Second World War and where white-collarization has permeated large companies' blue-collar workers (who are the unions' main support) has this theory a substantial foundation.

When careers are deeply internalized the relationship between company management and the employment and skill development of union members is so strong that it can be said to be decisive. If the company were to expand, promotion would become faster and sophisticated skills would be acquired earlier. The reverse situation of a decline in business would lead to promotion being delayed and, in the extreme case, to redundancies. The cost associated with redundancy in the case of deeply internalized careers is considerable. Because in a competitive environment company management is always accompanied by risk, the workers whose careers are deeply internalized have to be prepared to bear the burden of losses whether they like it or not. Although the employees would have to bear a greater burden than small shareholders, the existence of large shareholders renders the situation different to that of a labour-managed or cooperative company. As long as the workers have to bear a share of the risk, it is only natural that they would want to have a say in company management. Workers are also capable of having a voice in management when they possess sophisticated skills; nor is their understanding of managerial affairs superficial. What is actually needed is for workers to have the opportunity of sending their own representatives to forums for managerial decision making, where their wishes can be communicated and debated. Unless this opportunity were provided, the continued maintenance of high labour morale would be problematical.

Nor, of course, should the labour union only have a say in managerial decision making, but its voice in the distribution of the pie also needs to be powerful; regulations governing promotion, transfers, redundancy and wage rates need to be established. Indeed the wider is the career, the more complex is the object of regulations and all the more imperative is the need for regulations. Invoking Hirschman's exit-voice model[3], the necessity of workers having a voice has become a stage greater, because the cost of exit is particularly high. The manifestation of this trend in Japanese industrial relations since the Second World War may be interpreted as being half a step ahead of the other industrialized countries, where neither the white-collarization of shopfloor workers nor the unionization of white-collar workers have yet taken place.

8.2.4   Internal Promotion Widespread in Japan

Now that the extent of the influence of labour types on industrial relations has been agreed to be considerable, the differences in the actual spheres covered by each labour type – and particularly the internal promotion type – need to be observed. Let us take up a wider area of observation than the organized sectors of the Japanese and US heavy and chemical industries, which have been examined earlier in this book. As relevant statistical material is lacking, there is no alternative but to rely on a few case studies, from which our conjectures cannot help but be rather inadequate.

The proportion of labour in the USA falling under the internal promotion type even in the unionized sector appears to be small, apart from in the heavy and chemical industries; this inference has been made from the analysis of separate plant and company collective agreements appearing in the BLS survey (Chapter 7, Figure 7.4). In large Japanese companies, on the other hand, the internal promotion system appears to be widespread throughout all the industries, as has been statistically demonstrated in Chapter 4 (section 4.1); and there is a high correlation between large companies and unionization. The general conclusion is that in the case of large companies the internal promotion system appears to be more widespread in Japan than in the USA.

Concerning the situation in the UK, the results of several case studies are available, from which it appears that the internal promotion type may be applicable to workers in the mainline departments of the iron and steel industry[4] and the chemical industry.[5] In the machinery industries, however, the skilled labour type is still prevalent, along with the semi-skilled labour type.[6] The internal promotion type would cover white-collar males on the evidence of their wage profiles and average length of service statistic seen earlier (Chapters 1 and 2). It should, moreover, be legitimate to view the UK and the other Western European countries as being more or less similar in these respects.

The internal promotion system can, in sum, be recognized as pertaining to white-collar males and to the process industries' production workers throughout Japan, the USA and the UK; its coverage of the workforce is widest in Japan, followed by the USA, while the narrowest coverage is in the UK.[7] The Japanese internal promotion system does, moreover, appear to be somewhat deeper and wider than in other countries. The point about the relative prominence of the internal promotion type in Japan should not be mis-understood; each of the other types – 1, 2, and 4 – do also account for substantial proportions, and the 3 type is left with only about one-quarter or (under the most lenient definition) one-third of the workforce. Even in Japan, workers who fall under the internal promotion type of labour are a minority. Any attempt at a time-series analysis is precluded by the paucity of statistical material, but the sphere of the internal promotion system may be considered to have widened over time. Even though there has been little change in the fairly deep internal promotion system pertaining to white-collar males, the appearance of the internal promotion type among produc-tion workers in Japan is only a post-First World War development. Generally this type can be seen to disappear, the further back one goes in time.

8.2.5 The Monopoly Stage and the Internal Promotion System

There is still the remaining question of why the internal promotion type of labour is more prevalent in Japan than in Western Europe and the USA. The causes for the emergence of the internal promo-tion type should be considered, though a convincing answer has not yet been reached. Thus, although penetrating empirical research into internal labour markets has been developed by Doeringer and others, the lack of any sufficiently dependable historical research has prevented them from explaining why a system of internal promotion emerges.[8]

The hypothesis which I proposed in 1960 suggested a close rela-tionship between the stage of economic development attained and the emergence of the internal promotion system. This hypothesis also included an explanation of the remarkable differences between coun-tries in the relative weights of labour types and of the factors which prevent a greater diffusion of the internal promotion system.[9] My initial suggestion for the emergence of the internal promotion system is that the monopoly stage of economic development in its concrete form of large scale fixed capital formation and oligopolistic product markets has been reached. The simple explanation is that the stabilization of markets permits a company to hold long term pros-pects, to which is linked the capability, when required, of employing workers for a long period.

The next factor is the great progress in the division of labour into the many specialized duties required for the efficient operation of large scale fixed capital, epitomized in the process industries of steel and chemicals. The resulting duties vary from the simple to the difficult. Workers can be assigned to a simple job without any need for apprenticeship training. Nor would any apprenticeship be needed for a difficult job as long as there were some connection to the simple job – e.g., both are concerned with operating the same machine – because in on-the-job training the worker moves from simple to more difficult jobs. And this approach to training is the most economical from the management's point of view. The workers' average years of service are prone to lengthen under on-the-job training which is facilitated (or, indeed, promoted) by the conditions of fixed capital formation and oligopolistic product markets. It is this environment which provides the setting for the emergence of the internal promotion system.

8.2.6   The Social Cost of Abandoning a Labour Type

The main factor which hinders the emergence of the internal promotion system has already been mentioned when we stressed that the formation of each labour type was related to a social institution. This point shall now be amplified further. The environmental conditions, especially technology and the product market, influence the emergence of a particular labour type. But once a labour type has been formed, it has an enduring existence as a social institution which is to some extent independent of environmental changes. It needs to be borne in mind that a labour type represents the kind of skill formation occurring over a worker's career; skills exist only in human beings. Therefore to assert that certain kinds of skills are no longer useful cannot justify the abandonment of the people holding those skills. Moreover as workers grow older, the acquiring of new skills and disposal of existing skills is, even though not impossible, both socially and psychologically difficult. Once a skill has been formed, it goes on to last at least a lifetime. In addition, skill formation is initially established by there being people who can teach skills as well as people who are learning. And this process takes place within the social organization of the company or apprenticeship system, which are complete organizations tending to persist independently. When the labour union intervenes to maintain this process of skill acquisition, which has become a stable social institution, technological and other environmental conditions tend to be irrelevant. The labour union has a vested interest in the protection of the process of skill acquisition in order to protect the union members who hold skills. It is for these reasons that the labour type tends to endure across generations and in spite of technological changes.

Assuming that the above analysis is correct, a theory of the historical development of the internal promotion system can be applied so as to permit the following explanation of differences between industrialized countries. The internal promotion system has been shown to be the labour type which is most appropriate for the monopoly stage of capital accumulation; and it is accompanied by an industrial relations system which is centered on the company level. On the other hand, there are other labour types which were most appropriate for earlier stages of capital accumulation, and on which were based various social institutions, such as the craft unions. When an earlier stage had prospered for a long time, the appropriate social systems were fully attained and established with deep roots. Consequently, even with the new stage of economic development, the previous stage's social system is inevitably hard to abandon. Changes in social systems do not occur as rapidly as changes in production processes. All the more, the cost of abandoning a social system which has been very well established would be high. This analysis is clearly shown by the strength of the craft unions and their resistance as a social system to change.

8.2.7 Japanese Industrial Relations in the Vanguard

Let us take the example of the UK, where craft unions became strong during the flourishing early stages of economic development. The craft unions' consequent ability to protect their territorial rights has severely hampered the diffusion of the internal promotion system. This factor also explains the differences by industry within the UK. Since the process industries, especially the chemical industry, emerged only in the twentieth century, there was no tradition of craft unions, which has thereby permitted a relatively greater diffusion of the internal promotion system than elsewhere in other UK industries. Similarly the internal promotion system can be recognized in the mainline departments of the iron and steel industry where powerful craft unions had not appeared. The internal promotion system is, conversely, least diffused in the machinery industries which have the most powerful craft unions.

But in countries where the earlier stages of economic development were relatively short, the appropriate social systems could not be firmly established and so their abandonment has not been difficult. Consequently the social institutions which are appropriate for the new stage have room to grow and flourish. Japan's late start in industrialization enabled some stages of economic development to be bypassed, with the result that the earlier stages' social systems were not well established. On that account the most recent period's system has become all the more fully and widely established. The implication may be, therefore, that Japanese industrial relations are at present in the vanguard. Similar reasoning shows that, since industrialization took place in the USA later than in the UK (but earlier than in Japan), the degree to which the USA internal promotion system is diffused lies between the other two countries.

Once the internal promotion system is premised as being in the vanguard, an explanation of other special features of Japanese industrial relations is facilitated: for example, the reason why a Japanese labour union is organized over a mixture of occupations, which includes white-collar workers. This feature has often be seen as a weakness in Japanese enterprise unions. Yet it is well known that in all industrialized countries white-collar workers are the group whose numbers have increased the most out of the whole labour force. It is for that reason that one of the main targets of labour unions in the West is to organise white-collar workers. But Japanese labour unions, which comprise a mixture of occupations, have made the most progress in achieving this target, for which the most important cause has been the fact that Japanese organized workers have a fair number of characteristics in common with the white-collar group. In other words, a wide internal promotion system has spread also to the large companies' regular workers, who have consequently taken on characteristics which basically resemble those of white-collar workers; and it is large companies' regular workers who have an important role in Japanese labour unions. Further contrasting evidence for the above analysis is provided by the example of miners, who because of the absence of an internal promotion system still have separate occupational unions, even though they are employed in large companies.

8.2.8   The Future of the Internal Promotion System

The final issue to be discussed concerns the future of the internal promotion type of labour. Doubts are at times expressed about whether this labour type might not decrease or collapse when faced with the recent developments in microelectronics. The first point to be noted is that research material has confirmed a consistent tendency since the nineteenth-century for the white-collar share of the workforce to expand in the industrialized countries. The question then becomes whether this universal current could be reversed by the technological revolution in microelectronics. Let us take the example of machine tools, where the skills required fall under the following three headings:

1. The ability to consider alternative plans, and so choose the best order of tasks in which to carry out a job is needed
2. For that purpose, knowledge and experience concerning the quality of the production materials and tools is necessary; knowledge and experience are also important for making an appropriate response when the tools become less accurate on account of their natural depreciation
3. Jobs have to be performed quickly and accurately.

It is only the third skill for which microelectronic machinery and tools have recently been able to provide a substitute. And the first and second skills – namely, the 'intellectual skills' – have become all the more necessary because the number of machines *per capita* are increasing. These skills could be acquired in various ways, but to the extent that the skills are highly intellectual, the approach through the internal promotion system becomes more efficient. Nor need the effectiveness of on-the-job training be diminished by short, though full time, supplementary training courses. This approach cannot be realized unless a long run view is held. The internal promotion system has the greatest possibility of enduring in large companies which can easily plan for the long term.

Even in the case of small and medium-sized companies, the internal promotion approach has been seen to exist for a core of workers in the mainline sections, though still being confined to a small minority. In the situation of competitive markets, employment in small and medium-sized companies must inevitably be subject to vicissitudes, and only a nucleus of workers can hold onto the prospect of long term employment. There is still some scope for the internal promotion system to become a little more widespread, because the promotion of high labour morale among small and medium-sized company employees who over the age of 30 years do, as a general rule, become immobile, requires the laying out of a career with attractive prospects. That must surely imply the eventual emergence of the internal promotion type of labour. The remaining group to be considered are the female employees, for whom there is a possibility of extending the internal promotion system. The structure by age of postwar Japan's female labour force rate has an 'M' shape; a high proportion of females are absent from the labour force from their late twenties to their mid-thirties, but they do reenter the labour market.[10] Thereupon a female could easily expect to be employed for a period of at least 20 years, which is of ample length for stepping onto a career. The feasibility of extending the internal promotion system must be great when one takes into account the considerable ability of female workers.

8.2.9 Transferability Overseas

The above analysis of labour systems in Japan should have demonstrated that there is but one remaining peculiar aspect: the characteristics which are seen among Western European white-collar workers have been extended to one section of blue-collar workers in Japan. I believe that because the essence of white-collarization lies in its appropriateness for enlarging industrial democracy, world trends dictate a high transferability to other countries on account of the compatibility of white-collarization with contemporary economic developments. But the human capital in which skill formation systems are embedded is quite different to physical capital like machinery and equipment; since skills exist only in the minds and bodies of human beings, they could not feasibly be discarded with the argument that they are no longer needed. Under a given social institution the method of forming some skills continues across generations, which means that the implementation of reforms takes time. Indeed there may perhaps appear in the far future a new system which will make the Japanese approach seem old fashioned and inappropriate: a development which would have to be accepted as being part of the flow of history.

NOTES

1. Hyōdō (1971) is just one of the many research studies.
2. See Dunlop (1958).
3. Hirschman (1970).

4. The existence of internal promotion systems can be inferred from Knowles *et al.* (1958) *and* Scott *et al.* (1956). In addition, see the recently published results of detailed Japanese case studies: Kikuchi (1982); Ishida (1981).
5. This inference in the case of the chemical industry is permissible in the light of Lerner *et al.* (1969) a study covering several industries.
6. The importance of the skilled labour type in the case of automobile industry may be surmised from Turner's work (1967), in spite of its failure to present clear research results. In the case of the electrical machinery industry, the results of my interview surveys support the inference emanating from Lupton (1963) and Hazama (1970).
7. The administrative careers in two large British companies which are depicted in Sofer (1970) are shown to be deeply internalized. See also Blackburn (1967).
8. See P. Doeringer and M. Poire (1971).
9. See K. Koike (1960).

REFERENCES

Blackburn, Robert M. (1967) *Union Character and Social Class* (London: Batsford).

Dunlop, John T. (1958) *Industrial Relations Systems* (New York: Holt).

Hazama, Hiroshi (1970) Igirisu Kōjōnai Rōshi Kankei (Industrial Relations at the Plant-Level in Britain) *Tōkyōdaigaku, Shakaikagaku Ronsū* 17.

Hirschman, Albert O. (1970) *Exit, Voice and Loyalty* (Cambridge, Mass.: Harvard University Press).

Hyōdō, Tsutomu (1971) *Nihon ni okeru Rōshi Kankei no Tenkai* (Developments in Industrial Relations in Japan) (Tokyo: Tokyo University Press).

Ishida, Mitsuo, (1981) 'Gendai Igirisu Tekkōgyō no Rōshi Kankei' (Industrial Relations in the Steel Industry in Contemporary Britain) *Rōdō Mondai Kenkyū*, 3, pp. 87–140.

Kikuchi, Kōzō (1982) 'Igirisu Tekkō Kōjō ni okeru Senninken Seido' (Seniority Systems in A British Steel Works) *Keizai Ronsō*, 129, 6, pp. 367–90.

K. G. J. C. Knowles, *et al.* 'Wage Differentials in a Large Steel Firm', *Oxford Institute of Statistics, Bulletin,* August.

Lerner, Shirley *et al.* (1969) *Workshop Wage Determination* (Oxford, New York: Pergamon Press).

Lupton, Tom (1963) *On the Shop-Floor* (Oxford: Pergamon Press).

Sofer, Cyril (1970) *Men in Mid-Career: A Study of British Managers and Technical Specialists* (Cambridge: Cambridge Univ.).

Scott, W. H. *et al.* (1956) *Technical Change and Industrial Relations* (Liverpool: Liverpool University Press).

Turner, Herken, Arthur (ed.) (1967) *Labour Relations in the Motor Industry, A Study of Unrest and an International Comparison* (London: Allen & Unwin).

APPENDIX A: STATISTICAL TABLES

TABLE A.1 Wage indices by age (EC (1972) and Japan (1976), male, manufacturing, wage indices with wage earnings for the age group 21–24 years being taken as 100)

Age		16–17 (–17)	18–20 (18–19)	21–24 (20–24)	25–29	30–34	35–39	40–44	45–49	50–54	55–59	60–
Japan Size of company (No. of employees)	10–	63	82	100	122	140	149	150	151	148	126	99
	1,000–	64	86	100	121	143	155	162	170	173	156	105
	100–999	65	83	100	124	145	155	157	156	154	136	107
	10–99	65	78	100	123	138	143	141	135	129	119	104
Blue-collar workers EC	West Germany	62	88	100	105	108	108	107	105	103	100	96
	France	71	87	100	109	113	114	113	112	110	106	103
	Italy	71	89	100	108	112	113	112	111	110	109	101
	Belgium	60	85	100	106	109	109	109	108	105	102	99
	Netherlands	46	69	100	112	116	117	117	116	114	112	108
	Luxemburg	47	89	100	105	109	111	111	110	107	105	98
	UK	49	78	100	110	115	115	112	112	106	106	98

	Size of company (No. of employees)										
Japan											
10–	63	79	100	129	162	184	200	212	218	185	136
1,000–	64	81	100	130	167	192	213	228	240	215	144
100–999	66	79	100	127	158	180	197	205	206	183	136
10–99	63	77	100	129	157	173	182	182	178	166	140
West Germany	61	73	100	130	148	155	157	151	148	144	143
France	61	72	100	133	162	176	186	188	183	174	176
Italy	–	78	100	127	159	176	189	195	195	199	220
EC Belgium	51	75	100	128	156	167	171	172	169	167	167
Netherlands	44	64	100	135	166	184	196	199	200	189	178
Luxemburg	–	80	100	128	151	164	166	166	168	177	187
UK	50	71	100	130	155	155	167	167	159	159	137

(White-collar workers)

Note: The age classifications in parentheses apply to the Japanese categories.
Sources: See Table 1.1 and Table 1.3.

290

TABLE A.2 Wage differentials by occupation and by age (The EC (1972), and Japan (1976), manufacturing, monthly wage earning indices with blue-collar wages being taken as 100)

	Age	20–24	25–29	30–34	35–39	40–44	45–49	50–54	55–59	60–	All age groups
Male	Japan	99	105	114	122	132	139	146	144	135	126
	West Germany	97	119	133	139	142	139	139	139	144	135
	France	116	143	167	180	190	192	194	190	199	181
	Italy	119	139	169	185	201	210	210	216	259	182
	Belgium	96	116	138	148	151	153	154	157	162	146
	Netherlands	92	111	132	146	155	158	161	133	152	146
	UK	90	107	122		134		134		125	123
Female	Japan	110	119	137	139	142	148	151	138	127	126
	West Germany	117	132	139	142	140	143	145	148	149	130
	France	115	130	144	151	152	155	155	153	160	139
	Italy	130	141	156	173	181	197	198	210	246	150
	Belgium	110	124	133	143	151	150	154	156	171	133
	Netherlands	111	123	140	153	158	167	163	167	142	121
	UK	111	126	131		132		134		132	122

Sources: See Table 1.1 and Table 1.3.

TABLE A.3 Wage differentials by size of company (By sex and by occupation, EC (1972) and Japan (1976), manufacturing, wage indices with wages for workers in companies with 1000 or more employees being taken as 100)

Size of company (No. of employees)		10–49	50–99	100–199	200–499	500–999	1000–
	White-collar						
	Male	91	94	94	94	95	100
West	Female	93	96	94	95	95	100
Germany	Blue-collar	92	93	93	94	90	100
		84	87	89	93	95	100
	White-collar	102	100	97	98	99	100
		93	93	91	93	96	100
France	Blue-collar	82	83	85	88	94	100
		80	81	83	87	92	100
	White-collar	68	75	85	92	98	100
		74	79	87	90	96	100
Italy	Blue-collar	70	77	83	89	95	100
		69	74	78	84	91	100
	White-collar	85	88	91	94	97	100
		80	81	85	88	91	100
Belgium	Blue-collar	74	76	80	83	89	100
		74	77	79	84	92	100
	White-collar	93	90	91	93	96	100
		83	84	84	88	94	100
Netherlands	Blue-collar	89	92	95	97	100	100
		81	84	87	96	97	100
	White-collar	84		88			100
		91		94			100
Japan	Blue-collar	83		89			100
		77		85			100

Sources: See Table 1.1.

TABLE A.4 Unemployment rates by age (EC and Japan (1977), male, percentage of labour force)

Age	Japan	West Germany	UK	France	Italy	Nether-lands	Belgium	Denmark	Ireland
14–19	5.6	5.2	10.4	13.5	18.8	7.1	8.4	9.1	21.8
20–24	3.6	4.4	8.0	6.9	14.6	6.1	6.4	9.5	13.6
25–29	2.1	3.4	5.9	2.9	4.9	4.1	2.7	7.7	10.5
30–34	1.5	2.3	4.1	2.0	1.3	2.7	1.8	4.5	8.9
35–39	1.4	1.7	3.6	1.8	0.9	2.1	2.1	2.8	7.5
40–44	1.4	1.6	3.7	2.0	1.0	2.8	1.8	2.9	8.3
45–49	1.3	1.7	3.4	2.3	1.0	2.0	2.3	4.9	7.2
50–54	1.6	1.6	3.4	2.4	1.2	1.8	2.6	4.2	7.0
55–59	3.3	2.1	3.6	2.6	0.9	2.4	3.5	5.2	8.3
60–64	4.6	2.2	5.1	5.0	–	4.8	4.6	6.5	8.5
Total	2.1	2.4	4.8	3.3	3.3	3.3	3.1	5.7	9.8

Sources: 1. EC, *Labour Force Sample Survey* (1977).
2. Japan, Sōrifu Tōkei Kyoku (Bureau of Statistics, The Office of Prime Minister) *Shōwa 52-nen Rōdōryoku Chōsa Nenpō* (1977 Year Book of Labour Force Survey).

Appendix B
Questionnaire on Skill Formation in Small and Medium Sized Companies

Q.3 This question concerns the personnel whose skills are essential.

(1) Choose one of the categories from 1. to 6. which is most applicable to your company's essential skilled personnel on the shopfloor. Then choose the category which is most applicable to the personnel in the administrative and research and development departments.

1. Those who were inexperienced when recruited, and then trained in your company;
2. Those who had received some technical education at a vocational high school technical college or university, but were then trained in your company;
3. Those who were already skilled when recruited in mid-career from another small or medium-sized company in the same or a similar industry;
4. Those who were already skilled when recruited in mid-career from a large company in the same or a similar industry;
5. Those who were transferred from a parent company or similar;
6. Others (please indicate).

Q.6 This question concerns the employees who have had three or more years experience in other companies doing similar work to what they are presently engaged in. Please give separate answers for (a) personnel on the shopfloor, and (b) personnel in the administrative and research and development departments.

(1) Which of the following proportions are accounted for by such employees?

1. Less than 10 per cent of the department's personnel (including no such employees);
2. About one third of the department's personnel;
3. About one half of the department's personnel;
4. The majority of the department's personnel.

(2) How does their level of skills compare with those workers who have become experienced wholly within your company?

1. Those who were trained in other companies generally have a higher level of skills;
2. Those who were trained in other companies generally have a lower level of skills;
3. Skill levels are roughly the same;
4. Unable to say either way.

(3) Choose one of the following which is closest to your prospective plans concerning the recruitment of personnel who have been trained in other companies.

1. A positive policy to recruit personnel who have had more than three years experience in other companies;
2. As far as possible to train personnel in own company;
3. Unable to say either way.

Q.7 This question concerns movements in assignments among male employees in your company.

Firstly concerning movements in assignments within the same workshop, please give separate answers for (a) personnel on the shopfloor, and (b) personnel in the administrative and research and development departments.

(1) Which of the following is the normal practice in your company in the case of male employees moving between assignments inside the same workshop?

1. Once they have received their assignments, they would rarely be changed.
2. Their assignments are changed intermittently, though not regularly.
3. Assignments are changed at regular intervals.

(2) Have the workers who have been in your company's employment for at least five years usually experienced most of their workshop's assignments?

1. Yes;
2. No.

(3) What are your company's main motives and reasons for moving male employees between assignments in the same workshop? Please choose and rank two of the following.

1. To move them to assignments which correspond to their abilities and aptitude;
2. To provide them with experience in a variety of assignments so as to widen their skill acquisition;
3. Depending on their wishes;
4. To improve personal relations in the workplace;
5. Movements accompany specific fluctuations in the amount of different assignments' output;
6. Movements accompany changes and restructuring in job content;
7. To substitute for workers who have left your company;
8. Others (please indicate –).

(4) In the light of your company's experience so far, what is your prospective policy concerning movements between assignments in the same workshop?

1. Neither practised until now, nor intend to do so;
2. Not practised until now, but do intend to do so;
3. Practised until now, but intend to cease doing so;

4. Practised until now, and intend to continue;

5. Practised until now, but intend to continue more positively.

Q.8 Following on from Q.7, this question concerns movements among male employees to other workshops. Please give separate answers for (a) personnel on the shopfloor, and (b) personnel in the administrative and research and development departments.

(1) Does it happen in your company that male employees are moved between workshops?

1. Once an employee is associated with a particular workshop, he would rarely be moved.

2. An employee is moved intermittently, though not regularly.

3. Male employees are moved between workshops at regular intervals.

(2) Which of the following apply in the case of male employees being moved between workshops?

1. Most of the movements are between workshops which are deeply related in technology and skills.

2. A fair amount of the movements are between workshops which are only weakly related in technology and skills.

(3) What are your company's main motives and reasons in the case of a male employee being moved to another workshop? Please choose and rank two of the following.

1. To move him to a workshop which is appropriate for his abilities and aptitude;

2. To provide him with experience in a variety of workshops so as to widen his acquisition of skills;

3. Depending on his wishes;

4. To improve personal relations in the workplace;

5. His movement accompanies specific fluctuations in the amount of different workshops' output;

6. His movement accompanies changes and restructuring in job content;

7. To substitute for workers who have left your company;

8. Others (please indicate –).

(4) In the light of your company's experience so far, what is your prospective policy concerning movements between workshops?

1. Neither practised until now, nor intend to do so;

2. Not practised until now, but do intend to do so;

3. Practised until now, but intend to cease doing so;

4. Practised until now, and intend to continue;

5. Practised until now, but intend to continue more positively.

Q.9 In which field is your company president most deeply experienced?

1. Technology or R & D;

2. Production;

3. Finance or accounting;

4. Administration or sales;

5. Personnel affairs or labour management;

6. Others

Bibliography

Abegglen, James C., *The Japanese Factory* (Glencoe, Ill.: The Free Press, 1958).

Abegglen, James C., *Management and Worker: The Japanese Solution* (Tokyo: Kōdansha International, 1973).

Aoki, Masahiko, *The Economic Analysis of the Japanese Firm* (Amsterdam: North-Holland, 1984).

Aoki, Masahiko, *The Cooperative Game Theory of the Firm* (Oxford: Clarendon Press, 1984).

Barbash, Jack, *American Unions: Structure, Government and Politics* (New York: Random House, 1967).

Becker, Gray S., *Human Capital* (New York: National Bureau of Economic Research, 1964).

Blackburn, Robert Martin, *Union Character and Social Class* (London: Batsford, 1967).

Blaug, Mark, *The Utilization of Educated Manpower* (Toronto: Toronto University Press, 1967).

Blume, Otto, *Normen und Wirklichkeit einer Betriebsverfassung* (Tübingen: J. Mohr, 1964).

Brooks, George W., and Gamm, Sara, 'The Practice of Seniority in Southern Pulp Mills', *Monthly Labor Review*, 78, 7, July 1955.

Bundesrepublik Deutschland, Statistische Bundesamt, *Gehalts-und Lohnstrukturerhebungen* for the year 1957, *Statistische Berichte*, vi–12 (1958).

Bureau of National Affairs, *Fair Employment Practice Cases*, yearly, (Washington D. C.: Bureau of National Affairs).

Carpenter, Jesse Thomas, *Competition and Collective Bargaining in the Needle Trades, 1910–1967* (Ithaca: New York State School of Industrial and Labor Relations, Cornell University Press, 1972).

Chūō Rōdō Iinkai (Central Labor Relations Committee) *Rōdō Kyōyaku Chōsa* (Survey on Collective Agreements) (Tokyo: Chūō Rōdō Iinkai, 1st edn 1952, 2nd edn 1970).

Clark, Rodney, *The Japanese Company* (London: Yale University Press, 1970).

Cole, Robert E., *Japanese Blue-Collar – The Changing Tradition* (Berkeley and Los Angeles: University of California Press, 1973).

Cole, Robert E., *Work, Mobility and Participation: A Comparative Study of American and Japanese Industry* (Berkeley: University of California Press, 1980).

Cook, Alice H., *An Introduction to Japanese Trade Unionism* (Ithaca, New York: Cornell University Press, 1966).

Derber, Milton, and Chalmers, William Ellison, *Plant Union–Management Relations: From Practice to Theory* (Illinois: Institute of Labor and Industrial Relations, 1965).

Doeringer, Peter B., and Poire, Michael, *Internal Labor Markets and Manpower Analysis* (Lexington, Mass.: D. C. Heath, 1971).

Dore, Ronald P., *British Factory – Japanese Factory* (Berkeley and Los Angeles: University of California Press, 1973).

Dore, Ronald P., *The Diploma Disease* (London, George Allen & Unwin, 1976).

Dōryokusha Rōdō Kumiai (Locomotive Engineers' Union) *Dōryokusha Undōshi (A History of Locomotive Engineers Union)* (Tokyo: Dōryokusha Rōdō Kumiai, 1962).

Dōryokusha 20 Nenshi (20 Years History of a Locomotive Engineers Union) (Tokyo: Dōryokusha Rōdō Kumiai, 1973) 2 vols.

Dunlop, John T., *Industrial Relations Systems* (New York: Holt, 1958).

European Community (EC), *Structure of Earnings in Industry* (Brussels: EC, 1975–6) 13 vols.

European Community (EC), *Labour Costs in Industry, 1972–75* (Brussels: EC, 1975).

Evans, Robert Jr, *The Labor Economies of Japan and the United States* (New York: Praeger Publishers, 1971).

Freeman, Richard B. and Medoff, James L., 'The Two Faces of Unionism', *Public Interest*, Winter 1979, pp. 69–99.

Galenson, Walter, and Odaka, Kōnosuke, 'The Japanese Labor Market', in Patrick, Hugh, *et al.* (eds), *Asia's New Giant: How Japanese Economy Works* (Washington D. C.: The Brookings Institution, 1979).

Grinker, W., Coope, D. P. and Kirsch, A. W., *Climbing the Job Ladder* (New York: Shelley & Co., 1970).

Hanami, Tadashi, *Labor Relations in Japan Today* (Tokyo: Kōdansha-International, 1979).

Hazama, Hiroshi, *Igirisu Kōjōnai Rōshi Kannei* (Industrial Relations at the Plant-Level in Britain) *Tōkyōdaigaku, Shakaikagaku Ronsū*, 17, 1970.

Hazama, Hiroshi, 'Historical Changes in the Life Style of Industrial Workers', Patrick, Hugh (ed.), *Japanese Industrialization and Its Social Consequences* (Berkeley: University of California Press, 1976).

Hirshman, Albert O., *Exit, Voice and Loyalty* (Cambridge, Mass.: Harvard University Press, 1970).

Hyōdō, Tsutomu, *Nihon ni okeru Rōshi Kankei no Tenkai* (Development in Industrial Relations in Japan) (Tokyo: Tokyo University Press, 1971).

Ishida, Hideo, *Nihon no Rōshi Kankei to Chingin Kettei* (Japanese Industrial Relations and Wage Determination) (Tokyo: Tōyō Keizai, 1976).

Ishida, Mitsuo, 'Gendai Igirisu Tekkōgyō no Rōshi Kankei' (Industrial Relations in Steel Industry in Contemporary Britain) *Rōdō Mondai Kenkyū*, 3, 1981, pp. 87–140.

Jensen, Vernon H., *Hiring of Dock Workers* (Cambridge, Mass.: Harvard University Press, 1964).

Kikuchi, Kōzō, 'Igirisu Tekkō Kōjō ni okeru Senninken Seido', (Seniority Systems in a British Steel Works) *Keizai Ronsō*, 129, 6, 1982, pp. 367–90.

Knowles, K. G. J. C., *et al.*, 'Wage Differentials in a Large Steel Firm', *Oxford Institute of Statistics, Bulletin*, August 1958.

Koike, Kazuo, Chingin Rōdō Jyōken Kanri no Jittai Bunseki (An Analysis of Wage Administration and Working Conditions) in Susuki Shinichi, *et al.* (eds) *Rōmukanri* (Personnel Management) (Tokyo: Kōbundō, 1960).

Koike, Kazuo, *Nihon no Chingin Kōshō* (Collective Bargaining in Japan) (Tokyo: Tokyo University Press, 1962).

Koike, Kazuo, *Rōdōsha-no-Keiei Sanka* (Workers' Participation in Management) (Tokyo: Nihon Hyōronsha, 1976).

Koike, Kazuo, *Shokuba no Rōdō Kumiai to Sanka – Rōshi Kankei no Nichibei Hikaku* (A Comparative Study of Industrial Relations on the Shopfloor in the United States and Japan) (Tokyo: Tōyōkeizai, 1977).

Koike, Kazuo, 'Inter-industry Wage Spillover in Japan – An Insight into "Shuntō"', *Keizai Kagaku*, 28, 2 December 1980, pp. 30–73.

Koike, Kazuo, 'A Japan–Europe Comparison of Female Labor-Force Participation and Male Differentials', *Japanese Economic Studies*, IX, 2, Winter 1980–1, pp. 3–27.

Koike, Kazuo, *Nihon no Jukuren* (Skill Formation Systems in Japan) (Tokyo: Yūhikaku, 1981).

Koike, Kazuo, *Chūshōkigyō no Jukuren* (Skill Formation in Small and Medium-Sized Businesses) (Tokyo: Dōbunkan, 1981).

Koike, Kazuo, 'Kaiko kara Mita Gendai Nihon no Rōshi-Kankei' (Redundancy in Contemporary Japanese Industrial Relations) in Moriguchi, *et al.* (eds) *Nihon Keizai no Kōzō Bunseki* (An Analysis of Contemporary Japanese Economy) (Tokyo: Sōbunsha, 1983).

Koike, Kazuo, Muramatsu, Kuramitsu, and Yamamoto, Ikurō, *Kōjō no Nakano Idō to Kōjō no Rōdō Kumiai* (Internal Mobility and Plant-Level Union) Chōsa to Shiryō, 58 (Bulletin) (Nagoya: Nagoya University, Department of Economics, 1975).

Koike, Kazuo, and Watanabe, Yukirō, *Gakureki Shakai no Kyozō* (Is Japan Governed by Educational Qualifications?) (Tokyo: Tōyōkeizai, 1979).

Kōshirō, Kazuyoshi, 'Nōritsukyū to Kanri Soshiki' (Payments by Result and Administrative Organization) in Ōkōchi *et al.*, *Rōdō Kumiai no Kōzō to Kinō* (The Structure and Functions of Trade Unions) (Tokyo: Tokyo University Press, 1959).

Larrowe, Charles P., *Shape-up and Hiring Hall* (Berkeley: University of California Press, 1955).

Lerner, Shirley, *et al.*, *Workshop Wage Determination* (Oxford, New York: Pergamon Press, 1969).

Levine, Solomon B., *Industrial Relations in Postwar Japan* (Urbana, Ill.: University of Illinois Press, 1958).

Livernash, Edward Robert, *Collective Bargaining in the Basic Steel Industry* (Washington D. C.: United States Department of Labour, 1961).

Lupton, Tom, *On the Shop Floor* (Oxford: Pergamon Press, 1963).

Macdonald, Robert M., *Collective Bargaining in the Automobile Industry* (New Haven: Yale University Press, 1963).

Marsh, Robert M., and Mannari, Hiroshi, *Modernization and the Japanese Factory* (Princeton, N. J.: Princeton University Press, 1976).

Minami, Ryōshin, *The Turning Point in Economic Development: Japanese Experience* (Tokyo: Kinokuniya, 1973).

Muramatsu, Kuramitsu, *Nihon no Rōdō-shijō Bunseki* (A Study on Japanese Labour Market) (Tokyo: Hakutō-shobō, 1983).

Nakayama, Ichirō, *Industrialization and Labour–Management Relations in Japan* (Tokyo: Japan Institute of Labour, 1975).

Nishikawa, Shunsaku, (ed.), *The Labor Market in Japan: Selected Readings* (Tokyo: Japan Foundation, 1980).

Nitta, Michio, 'Tekkōgyō ni okeru Rōshi Kyōgi no Seido to Jittai' (Joint Labour–management Consultation Conference in the Japanese Steel Industry) *Shakai Kagaku Kenkyū*, 32, 5 and 6, 1981.

Odaka, Kōnosuke, *Rōdō-shijō Bunseki* (An Analysis of Labour Market) (Tokyo: Iwanami, 1984).

Ōkōchi, Kazuo, Ujihara, Shōjirō and Fujita, Wakao (eds) *Rōdō Kumiai no Kōzō to Kinō* (Structure and Functions of Trade Unions) (Tokyo: Tokyo University Press, 1959).

Ōkōchi, Kazuo, Karsh, Bernard and Levine, Solomon B., (eds), *Workers and Employers in Japan* (Tokyo: Tokyo University Press and Princeton: Princeton University Press, 1973).

Organization for Economic Cooperation and Development (OECD), *The Development of Industrial Relations Systems: Some Implications of the Japanese Experience* (Paris: OECD, 1977).

Ouchi, William G., *Theory-Z: How American Business Can Meet the Japanese Challenge* (Reading, Mass.: Addison Wesley, 1981).

Rōdōshō (Ministry of Labour) *Chingin Kōzō Kihon Tōkei Chōsa* (Wage Structure Survey) (Tokyo: Rōdōshō) yearly, 1954–.

Rōdōshō (Ministry of Labour) *Koyō Dōkō Chōsa* (Labour Mobility Survey) (Tokyo: Rōdōshō) yearly, 1964–.

Rōdōshō (Ministry of Labour), *Okugai Rōdōsha Chingin Jittai Chōsa* (Wage Survey of Building, Trucking and Longshoremen's Trades (Tokyo: Rōdōshō) yearly.

Rōdōshō (Ministry of Labour), *Rōdō Kumiai Kikan Chōsa* (Survey on Trade Unions) (Tokyo: Rōdōshō) yearly.

Rōdōshō (Ministry of Labour), *Rōdō Kyōyaku Jittai Chōsa* (Survey on Collective Agreements) (Tokyo: Rōdōshō, 1st edn, 1962, 2nd edn 1967, 3rd edn 1975).

Rōdōshō (Ministry of Labour), *Shiryō Rōdō Undōshi* (Documentary History of the Labour Movement) (Tokyo: Rōmu Gyōsei Kenkyū-jo) yearly, 1945–.

Rohlen, Thomas P., *For Harmony and Strength – Japanese White-Collar Organization in Anthropological Perspective* (Berkeley and Los Angeles: University of California Press, 1974).

Sano, Yōko; Koike, Kazuo; and Ishida, Hideo, (eds), *Chingin Kōshō no Kōdō Kagaku* (The Behavioural Science of Wage Negotiation) (Tokyo: Tōyō Keizai, 1969).

Scott, W. H., *et al.*, *Technical Change and Industrial Relations* (Liverpool: Liverpool University Press, 1956).

Shiba, Shōji, *A Cross-National Comparison of Labour Management–with Reference to Technology Transfer*, IDE occasional papers series, 11 (Tokyo: Institute of Developing Economies, 1973).

Shimada, Haruo, *Earnings Structure and Human Investment: A Comparison Between the United States and Japan* (Tokyo: Kōgakusha, 1981).

Shinnittetsu Rōdōkumiai Kyōgikai (Nippon Steel Confederation of Trade Unions) *Chōsa Jihō* (Bulletin) August 1971.

Shinotsuka, Eiko, and Ishihara, Emiko, 'Oil-shock igo no Koyō Chōsei – 4 kakoku hikaku to Nihon no kibokan hikaku' (Employment Adjustment After Oil Shock – An International Comparison Between Large Firms and Smaller Firms in Japan) *Nihon Keizai Kenkyū*, 6, August 1977, pp. 39–52.

Shirai, Taishirō, *Contemporary Industrial Relations in Japan* (Madison, Wisconsin: University of Wisconsin Press, 1983).

Shirai, Taishirō, 'Decision-making in Japanese Unions', in Vogel, Ezra, (ed.), *Japanese Modern Organization* (Berkeley and Los Angeles: University of California Press, 1975).

Shirai, Taishirō, and Shimada, Haruo, 'Japan', in Dunlop, J. T., and Galenson, Walter, (eds), *Labor in the Twentieth Century* (New York, San Francisco and London: Academic Press, 1978).

Sofer, Cyril, *Men in Mid-career: A Study of British Managers and Technical Specialists* (Cambridge: Cambridge University Press, 1970).

Sōrifu (Prime Minister's Office) *Shūgyō Kōzō Kihon Chōsa* (Employment Status Survey) (Tokyo: Nihon Tōkei Kyokai) every 3 years, 1956–.

Stieber, J., *The Steel Industry Wage Structure* (Cambridge, Mass.: Harvard University Press, 1959).

Susuki, Shinichi *et al.* (eds.) *Rōmūkanri* (Personnel Management) Tokyo: Kōbundō.

Taira, Kōji, *Economic Development and the Labor Market in Japan* (New York: Columbia University Press, 1970).

Takanashi, Akira, *Nihon Tekkōgyō no Rōshi Kankei* (Industrial Relations in the Japanese Steel Industry) (Tokyo: Tokyo University Press, 1967).

Tekkō Rōren (Japanese Federation of Steel Workers Union) *Tekkō Rōdō Handbook* (Steel Labour Handbook) (Tokyo: Tekkō Rōren) yearly.

Totsuka, Hideo, and Takahashi, Kō, 'Gōrika to Shokuba Chitsujo' (Rationalization and Job-ladders in a Workshop) in Meiji University (ed.) *Tekkōgyō no Gōrika to Rōdō* (Rationalization and Labour in the Steel Industry) (Tokyo: Hakutō Shōbō, 1961).

Tsuda, Masumi, *Rōdō Mondai to Rōmu Kanri* (Labour Problems and Personnel Management) (Kyoto: Mineruba, 1959).

Turner, Herbert Arthur (ed.), *Labour Relations in the Motor Industry, A Study of Industrial Unrest and an International Comparison* (London: Allen & Unwin, 1967).

Umemura, Mataji, 'Nenrei to Chingin' (Age and Wages), in Tōkei-Kenkyūkai (ed.) *Chingin Kōzō no Jittai Bunseki* (An Analysis of Wage Structure) (Tokyo: Tōkei-Kenkyūkai, 1956) (mimeo).

Umerura, Mataji, 'Nenrei-shotoku Profiles no Kokusai Hikaku' (An International Comparison of Age–Wage Profiles) *Keizai Kenkyū*, 22, 3, 1971, pp. 271–3.

Umetani, Shunichirō, *Vocational Training in Japan* (Hamburg: Institut für Asienkunde, 1980).

United States, Department of Commerce, Bureau of Census, *Census of*

Population, *1960, PC(2) 7B, Occupation by Earning and Education*, (Washington, D.C.).

United States, Department of Labor, Bureau of Labor Statistics, *Wage Chronology, US Steel Corporation*, Bulletin 1603 (Washington, D.C., 1968).

United States, Department of Labor, Bureau of Labor Statistics, *Trade Agreements, 1925*, Bulletin No. 419, 1926, 448, (1927).

United States, Department of Labor, Bureau of Labor Statistics (BLS), *Directory of National Unions and Employees Associations* (Washington, D. C., 1972).

United States, Department of Labor, Bureau of Labor Statistics, *Major Collective Bargaining Agreements*, Bulletin 1425–11, 1425–14 (Washington, D.C., 1970–2).

Walker, Charles Rumford, and Guest, Robert Henry, *The Man on the Assembly Line* (Cambridge, Mass.: Harvard University Press, 1952).

Whitehill, Arthur N. Jr, and Takezawa, Shinichi, *The Other Worker* (Honolulu: East–West Center, Hawaii University, 1968).

Woytinsky, Vladimir S., *Employment and Wages in the United States* (New York: Twentieth Century Fund, 1953).

Yasuba, Yasukichi, 'The Evolution of Dualistic Wage Structure', in Patrick, Hugh (ed.), *Japanese Industrialization and Its Social Consequences* (Berkeley: University of California Press, 1976).

Index

302